Outstanding Dissertations in Music from British Universities

Edited by
John Caldwell
Oxford University

A Garland Series

The Motet as a Formal Type in Northern Italy ca. 1500

Volume One

Jon Banks

Garland Publishing, Inc.
New York & London 1993

Library of Congress Cataloging-in-Publication Data

Banks, Jon.
    The motet as a formal type in northern Italy, ca. 1500 / by Jon
Banks.
            p.   cm.—(Outstanding dissertations in music from
British universities)
    Vol. 2 contains transcriptions.
    Includes bibliographical references and index.
    ISBN 0-8153-0950-3 (alk. paper)
    1. Motet—Italy, Northern—15th century. 2. Motet—Italy,
Northern—16th century. 3. Motets—Italy, Northern—15th
century. 4. Motets—Italy, Northern—16th century. I. Title.
II. Series.
ML2933.2.B3   1993
782.2'6'094509031—dc20   92–43439
                                                CIP
                                                MN

Designed by Valerie Mergentime

Printed on acid-free, 250-year-life paper.
Manufactured in the United States of America

For Rachel

CONTENTS

Volume 1

Volume 2

The Transcriptions:

Contents

PREFACE

The thesis that forms the basis of this book started life in 1983 at Exeter College, Oxford as a general dissertation on the motet in Italy in the Renaissance. It was finally submitted in late 1989 after a research period spent mainly in Oxford, but also in London and, most importantly, in Italy itself; the year 1985-6 was spent happily commuting by train from a small village in Tuscany to look at manuscripts in the Biblioteca Nazionale in Florence and the Civico Museo Bibliografico Musicale in Bologna.

The original purpose of the thesis was to examine the extraordinary diversity of the compositions that are generally classified as motets in writings on renaissance music. This investigation developed into the present book, which seeks to define specific sub-genres under the general heading of the term 'motet' and identify the various styles and formal procedures associated with them.

In order to take the widest possible sample of the motet repertory, three very different manuscripts have been chosen, which are, however, related by their common provenance from northern Italy around the first decade of the sixteenth century. In order to limit the scope of the study and to avoid duplication, attention is directed chiefly towards the compositions of the lesser-known and anonymous composers represented in these sources, rather than those of international reputation whose motets may be better understood in the context of their complete works.

Through analysis of this music I have attempted to distinguish a number of different motet types, some characterized by musical procedures based on abstract patterns that are entirely independent of the form of the text. The most important of these procedures appears to be derived from classical rhetoric, which was enjoying a revival in Italy at the end of the fifteenth century. It is also possible to detect common techniques for incorporating *cantus firmus* material or setting extremely long texts such as complete psalms; there is even a genuine spirit of emulation discernible in the way that different settings of certain texts are often so similar that they comprise a distinct genre of their own. These definitions in turn allow for the reclassification of a number of pieces as 'minor ritual works' or, in some cases, Latin *laude*, on account of their distinctive musical techniques. It also throws the stylistic peculiarities of the numerous incompletely-texted 'motets' into sharp relief, adding weight to the hypothesis that they were specifically composed as instrumental works.

In adapting the original thesis to its present published form, a certain amount of revision has been necessary, principally in the updating of the bibliography. The system of appendices, which aims to index and cross-refer the large number of individual compositions whose discussions make up a substantial part of the book, has been retained and perhaps requires a brief word of explanation. The first four appendices, A-D, index these pieces with reference to their sources; the fifth, E, is a critical commentary on them; and the remainder, F- J, list the pieces in the order in which they are discussed and hence provide a tabular summary of chapters 4-8.

This book has been a long time in the making, and having developed from a university thesis, is more than usually indebted to the help of others besides the author. Foremost among these is of course my supervisor, Dr. Bojan Bujic, who provided guidance and encouragement at every stage; I would also like to thank Dr. John Caldwell for his criticisms and improvements to the final version. I would further like to express my gratitude to the librarians at the Biblioteca Nazionale in Florence and the Civico Museo Bibliografico Musicale in Bologna, for their unfailing courtesy and cooperation both while I was there and also in the provision of microfilms and photocopies afterwards. Finally, my heartfelt thanks are due to all those who helped in the final stages of preparing the book, particularly Rachel Carter for proof reading and moral support, and Philip White for his endless patience and invaluable technical assistance.

The Motet as a Formal Type
in Northern Italy, ca. 1500

CHAPTER 1: INTRODUCTION

The sacred music emanating from Italy in the years around 1500 has been perhaps unjustly neglected by musicologists in the past. It is chiefly preserved in various anthologies from the first decade or so of the sixteenth century, many of which include works in the style of Busnois or Ockeghem side by side with the relatively *avant-garde* compositions of younger figures such as Cara and Tromboncino,[1] the originality of which latter has tended to overshadow any comparable changes in the more 'traditional' forms. Thus it is that while the development of the *frottola* into the madrigal with its new demands and consequent developments in compositional technique have been thoroughly chronicled, the same can not be said of the contemporaneous Latin sacred music even though many of the most acclaimed composers were active in both fields.[2] Other Italian forms like the *lauda* and *canto carnascialesco* have received their own monographs along with the *frottola* and early madrigal,[3] but the indigenous motet has yet to be treated in the same manner despite sharing a number of important characteristics with them. As well as re-emerging as a dominant form at about the same time, its apparently recreational as well as devotional use and stress on textual significance make it as much an expression of the new renaissance spirit in music as any of the more obviously Italian types of composition.[4]

Partly because of the way that religion penetrated into all aspects of daily life to an extent almost unimaginable today, any attempt to polarize music at this time into mutually exclusive sacred and secular components is liable to mislead. The Church was often the training ground for a young musician at this stage and a source of income for many an older one whose activities as a composer were seemingly confined to the secular field.[5] Besides, the private patronage of both types of music was in the hands of the same minority class of learned gentility, most of whom may be assumed to have had some direct connection with the Church anyway. Outside of the confines of ecclesiastical ritual, both the motet and the *frottola* fulfilled similar roles of aristocratic entertainment despite their disparity in style, and it is as narrow-minded to call the latter populist or anti-intellectual as it is to see the former as a last outpost of 'convoluted scholastic thought'.[6] They existed side by side and the changes in the motet form came about not from naïve emulation of a quaint local custom, but rather from the need to adapt to the new climate of humanist thought.

In deferring to a supposed hegemony of secular music, historians have tended to consign its sacred counterpart to a sort of stylistic limbo whereby the innovations manifest in Josquin's work, and particularly the technique of imitation, developed steadily but uneventfully until the stage of consummate mastery is reached in the works of Palestrina and Lassus. Such an approach overlooks some of the most fascinating aspects of the motet form, for the fundamental changes in outlook to which it was exposed resulted in an extremely flexible common technique and thus a wide variety of styles. That of Josquin was typically an expression of his supreme individuality: the popular conception of him as a kind of Janus figure looking back to the Middle Ages and forward to the Renaissance, while useful and appropriate to his stature as a composer, is apt to hide the fact that he was one among many contributors to an intricate complex of opposed currents of thought and technique at the end of the fifteenth century. The subsuming of these into the international language of the later sixteenth century was actually the end of the influence of genuinely renaissance thought on music rather than its high point.

Thus the field of the motet is particularly ripe for study, as in it can be assessed the full impact of humanist thought on the scholastic rigours of the traditional Franco-Flemish style. The motet is also the only form essayed by both indigenous Italians and *oltremontani* alike,[7] and it therefore serves as an ideal model in which to observe the mechanics of an interaction that was to prove of the greatest consequence for the subsequent history of music.

The earliest substantial records of a modification to the style of the Ockeghem generation are the choirbooks now known as the Gaffurius Codices, after the theorist and *maestro di cappella* who compiled them in the years between his arrival in Milan in 1484 and his death there in 1522. However, the works they contain, while being uniquely important to the overall evolution of the renaissance motet, belong more rightly to the history of Franco-Flemish rather than Italian music, the most important composers being foreigners like Compère, Weerbeke and Martini. Moreover, these codices serve the specific purpose of supplying the needs of the Cathedral choir with music for its unique Ambrosian liturgy, which was isolated from any other polyphonic practice in Italy. The brevity of the choir's halcyon days in the early 1470s is evidence that the music was written in haste and with a single-mindedness of purpose that shows up in the high degree of stylistic consistency exhibited by its composers. Any study taking as one of its themes the cornucopian variety of musical style at this time would be ill-advised to concentrate exclusively on such an introverted and functional repertory.

Because of this, the Gaffurius Codices are considered in chapter 2 of the present thesis only insofar as they provide the immediate musical background to three manuscript sources of a slightly later date, namely: Florence, Biblioteca Nazionale, MS Panciatichi 27 (= FP27), Bologna, Civico Museo Storico Bibliografico, MSS Q18 (= BQ18) and Q19 (= BQ19). Although all three seem to have been copied in the years between about 1500 and 1518, as will be demonstrated below, certain elements of their repertories can be traced back to the time of the Gaffurius Codices or even beyond, while others appear to have been composed at around the same time as the manuscripts themselves. In all but a few cases, the approximate date of a piece can only be deduced from its author's biography (where details are known) or its style and technique, with the result that it is not possible to establish any unambiguous chronology for the music. This wide and uncharted timespan should not be viewed as an insurmountable obstacle to the treatment of this music as a coherent repertory, however; it is essentially no different from that so often encountered with individual composers such as Josquin or Palestrina, within whose long careers few works are precisely dateable but whose *opera omnia* are customarily discussed as consistent and developing wholes.

It is particularly convenient to examine these manuscripts together, as not only are they the most important sources of motets originating in northern Italy in the years after the Gaffurius Codices, but they also include a high proportion of native Italian composers along with the omnipresent Netherlanders. The latter peculiarity, along with the partly retrospective nature of the manuscripts, means that the sheer variety of types they contain even under the general heading of the word 'motet' turns out to be quite astonishing and paints a richly diverse picture of musical life at the time. FP27 is a principally secular manuscript wherein the motet form is found alongside *frottole* and *laude* embodying 'Italianism' at its most extreme: BQ18, though ostensibly a truly international compendium of motets, chansons and pieces in Italian and even Spanish, preserves a peculiarly consistent repertory that seems in fact to have been specifically intended for instruments;[8] and BQ19 is almost exclusively a motet manuscript, but one that is unusual in its relatively high representation of lesser-known Italians along with the illustrious names of their northern contemporaries.

While all three manuscripts naturally preserve copious amounts of music by non-Italians, this has been discarded except in the most general terms for the purposes of this study, which is concerned with a peninsular style that arose partly in opposition to it. The foreigners were also for the greater part celebrities, whose plentiful works are most profitably approached as an *oeuvre* bearing the stamp of a particular personality and its formative biography, whereas the Italians are largely obscure musicians who each left a mere handful of pieces behind them at best. Through nothing more incriminating than the want of a famous name or biographical peg to hang their works on, these composers have been neglected regardless of their purely musical merits. This can be turned to advantage, however, as their combined output is a well-defined corpus of music particularly closely bound by place and time, so that they can be studied together as a group. The majority of Italian composers appear sporadically, either in one source only, or perhaps two or three from the same area, and their works are frequently *unica*. It seems reasonable to deduce from this that these figures would have had no international reputation comparable with that of Josquin or Obrecht, and more importantly that their pieces were written in the course of service to the institutions whose codices now preserve them. The vagaries of transmission afflicting the study of somebody like Mouton's motets, which are ubiquitous in sources over a wide geographical area and a long period of years, are thus of less consequence, and these Italian works may be seen to represent a wide cross-section of contemporary styles coordinated by their peculiarly local qualities.

This argument applies equally to those pieces lacking any attribution at all; being in the present case unanimously *unica*, there is a high likelihood of their having a local origin. There are very few instances in the manuscripts under consideration of a single motet by a relatively obscure northern composer who is thought never to have lived or worked in Italy (Hutinet's 'Peccantem me quotidie' and Divitis's 'Per lignum crucis' are the two notable exceptions),[9] so neatly do the categories of works by non-international figures and actual Italian origin overlap. Besides, a broad approach should take into account all those pieces that are not susceptible to investigation through the medium of a personal biography, especially as they are unlikely to receive any attention at all otherwise despite their jostling for inclusion in a manuscript with the more famous compositions of the day. This is not of course to say that a consideration of such personal data as may be available has no part to play in the analysis of their music, but rather that their characteristics are to be viewed in the 'horizontal' context of a repertory instead of the 'vertical' one of their individual careers. The compatibility of this approach with the aim of investigating the cornucopia of styles alluded to above should be readily evident.

An immediate problem besetting the study of a wide range of motets is that it has never been possible to take for granted a watertight definition of the form, even within a period as limited as the first two decades of the sixteenth century. Despite the fact that it is the most common compositional type at the time and the assurances in modern worklists that, for example, Costanzo Festa wrote 63 and Francesco de Layolle wrote 35,[10] its essential nature remains elusive and the borderlines between it and other types have yet to be adequately mapped out. The problem occurs less with the categorization of works by individual composers, within whose generally consistent production the odd 'special case' can be postulated, than with the inventories of manuscripts which can contain short and functional liturgical pieces along with more protracted Latin compositions, *laude*, instrumental and secular pieces. In these instances the scope of the designation 'motet' is expanded to the extent that it loses all meaning; the use of the same word to describe Josquin's monumental 'Miserere mei, Deus' on the one hand and the tiny anonymous 'Qui nos fecit' in FP27[11] is surely absurd. The catch-all status of the term is clearly recognized in the preface to *HammCC*, i, p.xix:

> The designation "motet" is used for all pieces in
> Latin which do not fit into any of the other
> categories [i.e. Psalm, Magnificat, Hymn etc.]. ...In
> some instances, either because of an oversight on
> our part, or because sufficiently precise information
> was unavailable, we may have counted as "motets"
> some pieces which should properly be included in
> one of our other categories, and vice-versa.

The 'motets' examined in this thesis include many that are incompatible with the form as associated wih Josquin, but it is intended that by taking criteria of musical style as well as textual form into consideration, some valid distinctions between types may be made. Grouping different 'motets' together on the basis of shared musical characteristics yields a surprisingly well-defined variety of sub-species that are generally concealed by the categorizations usually imposed on them by textual definitions and their accompanying liturgical functions.[12]

In order to make these distinctions, it is necessary to concentrate on the structural aspects of the music. The devices used to combine the voices into differing textures, and the way in which the resultant short sections are built up into the occasionally vast edifices typical of the period is as yet poorly understood. Such work as has been done on the music has concentrated on cataloguing, establishing biographies and publishing editions rather than examining its actual substance. An example of this might be Frank D'Accone's *Music of the Florentine Renaissance* anthology[13] which, although equipped with an invaluable introduction dealing with matters of biography, texts, and collation of sources, makes no attempt to analyse, criticize or place what it presents in its cultural context - even the appearance and origins of *cantus firmi* go unacknowledged. Whilst it may not be possible to ascribe to each note a function within the whole as has been done with the music of later ages, it seems blinkered to limit the conception of renaissance music to that of a series of imitative points with nothing in common save mode and textual idea. Analysis reveals a wealth of detail backed up by symmetries, proportions and repetition schemes that show overall structure to have been as much the concern of the renaissance composer as of any other; and this should hardly be surprising in an era left with the legacy of the formidable intellectual and formal achievements of Josquin and Obrecht. A style of rigorous through-imitation was of course in the process of evolution, but its eventual predominance in the later sixteenth century should not obscure the fact that it was initially only one of many parallel solutions to the problems posed by the renunciation of medieval part-hierarchy in favour of the simultaneous conception of voices that is one of the most essential features of the earlier period.[14]

Before proceeding to the main part of the thesis, one last digression is necessary in order to give a more detailed account of the sources than the frugal allusions afforded above. The precise origins and purpose of each manuscript have yet to be determined with absolute certainty, although the assumptions made above about approximate date and provenance are comfortably secure. The following discussion does not pretend to set a definitive seal on them or even contribute any substantially new information; rather it is intended as a *resumé* of what is already known, with a fresh look at them in the light of their various motet repertories.

Florence, Biblioteca Nazionale, MS Panciatichi 27

This manuscript has not yet really attracted the scholarly attention it deserves, in view of the number and diversity of its contents. Although uniformly copied in one hand (except for ff.207v.-209r.) the present book is actually a binding between modern covers of two smaller manuscripts, the first of which retains its original foliation of 1-120 and the second of which carries a modern foliation of 121-216. There are also 9 unnumbered folios at each end; the second of those at the beginning bears the inscription 'Cantilene sacre e profane'. The total of 185 pieces[15] are set out in choirbook format and the size of the pages (153 by 214mm), functional hand and lack of decoration betoken a compilation for practical use rather than as an ornament for display. A discussion including a more detailed physical description and a full critical bibliography is given in *JeppFR*, ii, pp.37-42,[16] where he notes that the book probably comes from the very beginning of the sixteenth century on the basis of handwriting and and concordances with *F-Pn* Rés. Vm^7 676 (which carries the date 1502) and the Petrucci prints of 1501-3 from which it seems partly to have been compiled. Since the pieces concordant with the latter's second book of *laude* (*RISM* 1508^3) are evidently not direct copies - there are notational discrepancies as well as a *contrafactum*[17] - and given the retrospective nature of this publication in general,[18] it seems probable that the manuscript predates this print. There is certainly nothing to contradict an origin from the very first years of the sixteenth century in either repertory or external circumstance.

It is from Jeppesen's emendations of the inventory by Becherini[19] that the contents list in *HammCC*, i, p.232 is derived, which shows that it transmits in roughly equal quantities Italian secular and Latin sacred music (mostly classified as 'motets') with a handful of chansons and a Flemish piece making up the total. Jeppesen is chiefly concerned with the secular repertory in his discussion but notes the following inaccuracies in Becherini's catalogue with regard to the sacred pieces:

1)   There are 5 'Benedicamus Domino' settings, 2 for four and 3 for three voices, on ff.18v.-19r. (Becherini just indicates the number by 'vari').

2)   There are 2 'O Domine Jesu Christe' settings (for which only the incipits of the text are given) on ff.86v.-88r., both for four voices (Becherini only counts one).

3)   There are 2 'Litanie' on ff.102v.-103r. (Becherini does not specify the number).

4)   There is an additional two-voiced 'Requiem' and 'Dies irae' on ff.210v.-211r. as well as the 'Kyrie eleison', 'Tremens factus sum' and 'Dies illa' indicated by Becherini.

5)   The 'Verbum caro' settings on ff.56v. and 109v. are identical.

Jeppesen's fourth and fifth observations still require some further qualification here. In the fourth, it should be noted that the

'Dies illa', 'Tremens factus sum' and 'Requiem' on ff.210v.-211r. are actually the three verses of the Responsary 'Libera me' (see *LU* p.1767); his counting of them as separate items contradicts his assessment of exactly the same music as only one item (called 'Dies illa' in both *BecherC* and *JeppFR*), when it appears on f.103v. In the fifth, his assertion is not exactly true; although they are almost identical, they are best considered as two examples of a large group of broadly similar 'Verbum caro' settings, which will be further discussed in chapter 7 of this thesis.

Such details aside, the only real dispute in all the available literature concerns the provenance of the book. Jeppesen takes the inclusion of a piece work by Renaldo (whom he identifies as the Don Renaldo Franciose who was *maestro di cappella* at the SS. Annunziata in Florence from 1482-3),[20] the Florentine Bernardo Pisano and Antonius Peragulfus Lucensis (i.e. from Lucca) as indications of a Florentine or Tuscan origin, whereas Allan Atlas views it as emanating from the court of Mantua, presumably on account of the shared repertory with *F-Pn* Rés. Vm^7 676 which also comes from there or neighbouring Ferrara,[21] and its inclusion of only one specifically Florentine *canto carnascialesco*,[22] which is itself described by Ghisi as '...una novità, da me rintracciata fra le numerose composizioni religiose e profane...'.[23] Further support is lent by the fact that the composer Domenicus is known to have served the Gonzaga family at the court of Mantua.[24] Neither proposition is conclusive, but the Mantuan argument seems to have the most evidence in favour of it; whatever the case may be, it is still undisputed that FP27 preserves music current in northern Italy in the first decade or so of the sixteenth century, which is sufficient for the purposes of this study.

Bologna, Civico Museo Storico Bibliografico, MS Q18

BQ18 shares the oblong choirbook format of FP27 and is of similar dimensions (168 by 240mm). The covers and foliation, running from 1-90, are original, though ff.10, 47 and 56 are missing and the manuscript is incomplete at the end. It was copied by three or four music scribes, one of whom has been identified as the famous theorist Giovanni Spataro.[25] As with FP27, the plainness of the paper pages and their binding indicates that this book was designed for use rather than decoration.[26] None of the 90 pieces that survive are fully texted and in fact the majority are identified by no more than incipits in a variety of languages again comparable to that found in the Florentine manuscript. There is a great deal of circumstantial evidence in addition to this to suggest that the book was compiled specifically with instrumental ensemble performance in mind, a matter that will be discussed more fully in chapter 8.

Published information concerning BQ18 was if anything even more scanty than that on FP27 until the publication of *WeissB* in 1988. Before then, the only traceable references (such as those given in the full bibliography in *HammCC*, i, p.72) were to passing mentions or concordance tables that merely acknowledged the manuscript's existence and assumed a provenance from around the first decade of the sixteenth century on the basis of handwriting and repertory. However, not only does Weiss's article collate and reassess what little specific information was previously available, but a further examination of the paper, watermark, scribes and historical context would seem to confirm that the book originated in Bologna in the years around 1500, as had been previously supposed.

Bologna, Civico Museo Storico Bibliografico, MS Q19

This manuscript, otherwise known as the Rusconi Codex after the Bolognese family through whom it came into the library's posession, differs from FP27 and BQ18 in its size and shape (293 by 212mm) as well as its repertory. It also carries eight illuminated initials, albeit pasted in from elsewhere, at the beginnings of eight pieces in addition to a montage, on f.2v., of a chained stag with the initials 'D. P.' The book survives with its original covers, index and foliation from 1-202;[27] its 98 compositions, nearly all of which are motets, were copied by one scribe throughout, apparently at the same time.

The origins of BQ19 have been the subject of some debate in recent years. Neither its compiler, provenance or original owner are safely established beyond the reach of conflicting opinion. The uniform scribal hand is traditionally supposed to be that of Sebastiano Festa on account of his name appearing, together with the date of '1518 adi 10. de zugno' at the head of the first page. However, as Lowinsky points out in the first lengthy discussion of the manuscript,[28] this attribution is only really applicable to the opening piece itself, the name being found in the standard position above the Cantus voice common to all the many other identifications in the book. The deduction from this that Festa was the scribe of the entire manuscript is hardly justifiable even if the relatively high proportion of his own motets invites suspicion that he had a hand in its compilation. Lowinsky proceeds, via a recognition of various similarities with the Medici Codex and inspection of the repertory and the bookplate at the beginning to propose a French origin for the manuscript as the property of Diane de Poitiers, mistress to Henry II, the son and successor to François I of France. However, this argument and all the buttresses needed to support it in the face of a plainly Italian scribe are based on a series of assumptions that are successfully challenged by Leeman Perkins, who argues in favour of an Italian provenance from around the ducal court of Ferrara on the basis of paper, watermark, hand and a more convincing interpretation of the repertory and circumstantial evidence;[29] the case would seem to rest fairly with him, especially as his speculation provides a more plausible reason for the subsequent ownership of the book by the Rusconi family, the circumstances and times of which are unfortunately not known.[30]

David Crawford's analysis of the physical construction of the book[31] reveals that both the montage of the chained stag at the beginning (seen as the personal emblem of Diane de Poitiers and thus proof of her ownership by Lowinsky but shown to be commonplace by Perkins) and the motet 'Angele Dei' which bears the date of 1518 were in fact inserted after the main body of the manuscript was written, though by the same scribe. However, this does not make matters very much clearer; while it undermines Lowinsky's thesis and Sebastiano's authorship still further it also calls into doubt what is otherwise the most precise information about the codex, its overall date of 1518. Crawford suggests that the date may refer to the composition of 'Angele Dei' (which implies that the rest of the pieces could be either earlier or later) or to a revision of the book and insertion of the extra folio (which implies that the rest had already been copied). In fact, given the rarity of dated autograph compositions in the Renaissance, the time must surely apply to the copying of the piece and hence revision of the manuscript, and besides it is far more likely that a new piece should be dated than an old; thus it seems most probable that the bulk of the codex was copied before 1518. Since its contents seem to have been copied all at one time and include Antoine Bruhier's 'Vivite felices', whose text celebrates the meeting of François I and Pope Leo X in Bologna in December 1515, the date of copying can reasonably be narrowed down to the two and a half years between then and the date above the opening piece.

The conflicting interpretations of the repertory by the two

scholars stem from a difference of approach; Lowinsky was principally concerned with the Medici Codex to which he saw BQ19 as an adjunct on the basis of a good deal of material in common. Perkins rightly points out that although French composers are well represented (Mouton by 12 pieces, Richafort by 3 among others), there is an equally and even more distinctively high proportion of musicians almost exclusively associated with Italy (11 works by Renaldo, 7 by Jacquet of Mantua, 3 by Jhan of Ferrara and 2 by Symon Ferrariensis among others) as well as those of obscure origin such as Lupus and de Silva, who seem to have been Italian by adoption if not by birth.   This then makes the manuscript a particularly interesting one for the study of indigenous peninsular music, and nearly all of the lesser-known names are those of Italians or persons known to have spent the best parts of their creative lives there rather than in France.

Of the 98 pieces in the codex, 77 are motets and 10 others are Mass or Magnificat sections, leaving 2 motet-chansons, 8 genuine chansons and a single canon bearing an undecipherably macaronic text.[32] This is a very different repertory from that in either FP27 or BQ18, principally because of the emphasis on Latin sacred music at the expense of Italian forms such as the *lauda* and *frottola*. While the book is clearly orientated towards religious music, the inclusion of ceremonial motets such as Bruhier's 'Vivite felices', Costanzo Festa's 'Quis dabit oculos meos', eight chansons (some of which may be instrumental) and what looks like another instrumental piece (the anonymous 'Hec dies' on f.5v.-6r., which will be discussed further in chapter 8), gives the impression that it had a parallel function as a recreational anthology, as does the omission of any of the hymns or minor liturgical works found, for example, in the first Gaffurius Codex. The absence of any music with Italian text therefore indicates nothing more than a bias of taste towards the learned and international Franco-Flemish style, so that the inclusion of the French chansons should not be seen in this light as a challenge to the Italian provenance of the codex. The style of Italian secular music was as yet antithetical to that of the Mass and motet, or so at least it might have been considered in certain conservative quarters; even if both were beginning to compete in their appeal to the same renaissance sensibilities, they were still radically different in both conception and execution. The compilers of this collection were presumably pandering to a taste rooted in the old Netherlandish tradition and would have discriminated accordingly against examples of its peninsular rival. The French chanson, on the other hand, was a part of that same tradition and therefore much more acceptable as a vehicle for expression compatible with the motet. It is only in the most catholic collections, as indeed are FP27 and BQ18, that the motet and *frottola* types are found together.

One last point in favour of an Italian origin for BQ19 is that the month in the date on the first folio is spelt as *zugno* as opposed to the more normal *giugno*. The replacement of the *gi-* orthography by *z-* is significant as it is a dialectical variant typical of the Veneto region.[33] This is of course not absolutely conclusive, but if it seems odd for a scribe preparing a codex for a foreign potentate to use his own language on the very first page (as Perkins points out), it is distinctly improbable that he should lapse into his own particular dialect. Such an objection would not arise had the book been compiled for a patron in nearby Ferrara, and all in all the evidence would seem to favour this interpretation as postulated by Perkins.

Whatever their differences of contents or purpose may be, these three manuscripts can still be seen to have a great deal in common in terms of the times and places of their respective compilations. BQ18 and FP27 would appear to be almost exactly contemporary and though there are very few concordances between them, they preserve similarly all-inclusive repertories. The bulk of BQ19 may be from as little as a decade later (and certainly not more than two), even if it is quite distinct in that its format, decoration and certain of its contents indicate that it was, in contrast to the other two manuscripts, intended as a treasury of a certain style rather than as an all-purpose anthology.

As far as geography is concerned, all three sources seem to have originated within about fifty miles of each other in the neighbouring and politically related cities of Mantua, Bologna, and Ferrara. Such close links make it all the more interesting that they should contain such a wide diversity of compositions in so many different styles and particularly that there should be such a rich variety even within the confines of the designation 'motet'.

Notes

[1]This is apparent not only within individual manuscripts, such as those to be considered in detail below, but also in the scope of the various publications issued in close succession by Ottaviano Petrucci at the very beginning of the sixteenth century.

[2]For example, Sebastiano Festa, Arcadelt and Tromboncino all left a body of sacred music behind them although they are today almost exclusively associated with the early madrigal.

[3]For the *lauda* see *JeppL*, and the relevant entry in *Grove*; for the *canto carnascialesco* see *GhisiCC*; for the *frottola* see *JeppFR*, which also contains a full bibliography.

[4]The argument that the motet is a form sacred in text but not necessarily function is a convincing one based on source studies, documentary testimonials and circumstantial evidence. *NobleF* contains a full exposition of the case, which although intended to apply to the motets of Josquin is equally valid for his contemporaries.

[5]For example, Marchetto Cara was *maestro di cappella* (both *da chiesa* and *da camera*) to Francesco and his son Federico Gonzaga, and Busnois had held benefices on account of his service to the Burgundian chapel in Dijon.

[6]The phrase is used in *PirrPM*, p.22, to suggest the impression

polyphony would make on a listener of humanistic inclinations.

[7]There are hardly any compositions for the Ordinary of the Mass by Italian composers in the first two decades of the sixteenth century, the two cycles by Renaldo in BQ19 being the most notable exceptions; and while there are extant *frottole* by Josquin and Isaac they are exact imitations of the style they found in Italy rather than attempts to synthesize them with their own precepts into a personal musical idiom.

[8]The 'instrumental' nature of these works is discussed fully in chapter 8.

[9]'Peccantem me quotidie' can be found among the transcriptions at the end of this thesis; for 'Per lignum crucis' see *LowMC*, iii, p.188 and iv, p.255.

[10]These figures are taken from the entries under the composers' names in *Grove*.

[11]This piece is discussed further in chapter 7 (see p. 206) and transcribed in vol. ii, p.158.

[12]The bearing of such groupings on matters of performing location and whether certain pieces with apparently liturgical texts may in fact have been intended for secular performance will be discussed in chapter 2.

[13]See *D'AccFR*.

[14]This proposition, originally made in *LowMH*, has recently been elaborated in *BlackCP*.

[15]This number is preferred to the accepted standard of 187 (given by Jeppesen and subsequently used in *HammCC*, i, p.232), due to a reconsideration of the pieces on ff. 210v.- 211r; see chapter 7 for further details.

[16]See also *JeppL*, p.lxiii.

[17]'Dolce regina' (FP27, f.29v.-30r., anon.) appears in print as 'Popule meus, quid feci tibi?' (*1508³*, f.31v.-32r., anon.; this version is transcribed and edited in *JeppL*, no.32).

[18]Certain of its contents are reprinted from the *Motetti B* of 1503, though adapted as *laude* through abbreviation, simplification and substitution of different words (details are given in chapter 7 of this thesis), and another piece, 'Sancta Maria, ora pro nobis', is a *contrafactum* of 'Me stesso incolpo' on f.19v. of the *Strambotti, Ode...libro quarto* of 1505.

[19]*BecherC*, pp.118-22.

[20]See chapter 4, p.104ff., for an extensive discussion of Renaldo's biography and compositions.

[21]Unfortunately Atlas's arguments have had to be deduced from the statement in *HammCC*, i, p.232, rather than stated directly and in their entirety, as they are rehearsed (presumably) in an unpublished Ph.D dissertation which has not been available for inspection.

[22]'Siamo tre donne romei', on f.110v.-111r.

[23]*GhisiCC*, p.55.

[24]See *JeppFR*, i, p.153.

[25]By Sergio Paganelli: see *WeissB*, p.68.

[26]See *WeissB*, pp.63-71, for an extended discussion of the physical characteristics and scribal composition of the manuscript.

[27]The latter has however been disturbed by the insertion of additional pages at the beginning; see *CrawCF*, pp.107-8.

[28]See *LowMC*, iii, p.59ff.

[29]See *PerkR*, p.266.

[30]Further support for the Ferrarese provenance of BQ19 is lent by the eight decorated initials, which 'appear to be in the style of the Ferrarese school of illumination' (*HammCC*, i, p.72) However, it has not proved possible to trace any further either the sources or justifications behind this observation.

[31]See *CrawCF*, pp.107-8.

[32]These figures correspond to those in *HammCC*, iv, p.277. For a transcription of the latter macaronic text, see *PerkR*, p.266.

[33]It appears consistently, for example, in the correspondence between Isabella d'Este and Lorenzo da Pavia; see *BrownIE*, *passim*.

CHAPTER 2: THE RE-EMERGENCE OF AN ITALIAN NATIONAL STYLE?

When Johannes Ciconia left his native Liège to take up a post as *magister* and canon at Padua cathedral, he unwittingly initiated a tradition that was to endure for nearly two centuries. He was employed as a foreigner in a country where the innovations of the Ars Nova had developed into a thrivingly independent musical art, which moreover exerted a considerable influence over his own compositions.[1] In his wake, however, followed a steady stream of his northern compatriots under the weight of whose personalities the peninsular strain of composed polyphony comparable in stature to that of the rest of Europe was completely ousted by the international Franco-Flemish style. For while Italians continued to sing, play and build musical instruments in every city, major institutions such as the Papal Chapel took on foreigners in growing numbers whose almost total dominance in the field of written composition is clear from the musical sources that survive from the middle and end of the fifteenth century.[2] Thus it was that by the time Galeazzo Maria Sforza came to found his capella at Milan in 1471, it was not simply as a matter of taste that he sent his emissaries to the North as much as to the surrounding provinces; the presence of 'oltremontani' was a political necessity in order to secure the prestige and credibility of his new musical establishment, competing as it was with others whose function as ambassadors and symbols of wealth and power was often a greater incentive to the munificence of prince or potentate than beauty of sound alone.[3]

As impressive an achievement as this may have been on the part of Franco-Flemish musicians, it is rather disconcerting to find such a lacuna in the otherwise continuous history of native Italian musical self-sufficiency. Even when it is acknowledged that the written sources that offer us our chief insight into the period give a one-sided account of it by their very documentary nature, the virtual absence of Italians among the composers venerated by the most cultured and affluent society of patrons remains a mystery that has yet to be satisfactorily explained.[4]

This is not to say, however, that Italians had simply bowed
their heads in humble submission to the inimitable musicality of the
North. An equation of fifteenth-century Italy with nineteenth-century
Britain as 'das Land ohne Musik' is out of the question, as there is
plentiful evidence that a good deal was going on besides the
specialized and restricted cultivation of mensural polyphony. Because
this alternative culture was apparently largely improvised and based
on oral traditions, it has tended to seem peripheral when viewed
through the distorting lens of the sources of notated music. However,
contemporaneous literary accounts and the circumstances of a society
that had grown to distrust scholasticism and its associated art-forms
suggest that it not only enjoyed widespread favour among the
populace at large, but also won a respect comparable to that awarded
to northern artifice among the nobility and intellegentsia, who appear
to have cultivated both types together.[5]

This Italian counter-culture is usually approached from the
viewpoint of its opposition to the style of the Franco-Flemish
contrapuntists, so that the shared characteristics of its various forms
tend to be made more of than their differences. The three main
categories into which it can be conveniently divided - the sacred
lauda, the later fifteenth-century Florentine *canto carnascialesco* and
the *frottola* - all have important features in common such as the use of
similar vernacular verse forms, principally the *strambotto* and
barzeletta, and their setting (where polyphony is employed) to simple,
chordal music. Nevertheless,an examination of their respective
histories reveals that each had its own function, social context, and
probably performance medium, so that they would have been
perceived as completely different entities despite the similar
appearance on the page of such examples as came to be written
down.[6] Therefore in order to assess their possible influences on the
motet, it is most prudent to look at each in turn.

The *lauda* is the form that would appear to have the longest
traceable history, its earliest origins going right back to the early

twelfth century. At this time it was a monophonic setting of a sacred vernacular text, the *ballata* being the preferred form, and in fact this type continued to flourish throughout the fifteenth and sixteenth centuries (and even into the nineteenth, for that matter[7]), adapting itself along the way to the acceptance of the *strambotto* and other textual types. The fourteenth century saw the introduction of polyphony, but even as late as the end of the fifteenth the surviving examples are generally for two or three voices rather than four.[8] This conservatism, together with an unpretentious simplicity, is natural in what remained an essentially popular and amateur form; the companies of *laudesi* that are known to have performed in the cities of northern Italy[9] were still well distinct from professional polyphonists, by comparison with whom they would have seemed 'woefully inadequate'.[10]

The four-voiced type seems virtually to have been pioneered by Petrucci, who brought out his *Libro primo* in 1508.[11] By this time he had already published eight anthologies of *frottole*, four of motets (as well as those included in the *Odhecaton* and *Canti B* and *C*) and two lute books, among many other editions of Masses and assorted sacred music. Such tardiness to venture into the publication of *laude* implies a certain insecurity on Petrucci's part as to their compatibility with the tastes of his public that he had evidently not felt with the *frottola*. This seems to be confirmed by the way that he insisted on the four-voiced medium as a standard (in the process disbarring many older pieces from publication and necessitating the commission of an entirely new book by the otherwise utterly unknown Innocentus Dammonis); he seems to have considered it a 'popular' form whose acceptance by his public depended on its being put on a level, at least in terms of performance ensemble and general sonority, with his other publications. The fact that he waited so long to publish *laude* and dropped them immediately afterwards[12] shows the enterprise not to have been a complete success, again possibly because of an inherent prejudice in his target market against a traditionally amateur form.

The relationship of the *lauda* to the motet would therefore seem to have been submissive rather than dominant, given these conditions. Motets betraying a strong 'Italian influence' can be securely dated to the early years of the 1470s, when composers like Weerbeke, Compère and Martini (among others) were in the service of the cathedral and court of the Sforza family in Milan.[13] At that time there is no evidence for the existence of a four-voiced *lauda* type, and those for two or three voices surviving in manuscript sources exhibit an improvised, ungainly rhythmic character and direct melodic style that is totally at odds with the smooth and controlled chordal writing characteristic of the motets.[14] Besides, in founding his *cappella*, Galeazzo Maria Sforza made quite explicit his intention of employing northerners to provide him with a jewel of music to outshine all others in Italy, to which end he expended a considerable amount of effort and money.[15] It is hardly likely that a company of musicians assembled with the express purpose of gilding the ducal chapel with music of international currency and prestige should have chosen to emulate an amateur local idiom.

The *canto carnascialesco* is even less likely to have exerted any direct musical influence over the motet. The earliest of the handful of polyphonic sources that survive[16] is *I-PEc* 431, from *ca.*1485,[17] which contains three-voiced pieces that are assumed to have been written in the 1480s. The other sources are all from the sixteenth century[18] and represent a later stage of development, with a four-voiced texture becoming the norm. As with the *lauda*, the efflorescence of the *canto carnascialesco* seems to postdate the 'Italian' motets of Weerbeke and his fellows altogether, certainly insofar as the four-voiced version that comes nearest to their style is concerned. Again like the *lauda*, the form was essentially popular, but in this case boisterous, outdoor and festive, making it an even less likely candidate for imitation by composers of sacred motets.

The term 'frottola' is generally associated with an unsophisticated prototype of later forms, a sort of crude form whence the higher fractions of the madrigal were later distilled. This does not quite do it justice, however, and the stress laid on its simplicity and its importance as a contrasting style to that of the northern composers has tended to mask the fact that it springs from an improvised tradition of some refinement. There is no suggestion in contemporary accounts that the recitation of verse to the lute was considered an inferior sort of musical expression, in fact quite the reverse; there is convincing evidence from diarists and commentators that personal interpretations of classical as well as more recent authors were held to be superior in humanistic circles to the fragmentation of texts in polyphony.[19]   The 'art of the Netherlands' and its theoretical apparatus embodied the idea of music as an avenue of numerical speculation, along with the other quadrivial subjects of arithmetic, geometry and astronomy.   Humanist thought, on the other hand, looked to a reversion to the classical idea of music as a 'natural extension of the process by which language becomes poetry'[20] so that the rejection of contrapuntal artifice was a conscious effort to move in the direction of greater subtlety and sophistication, not lesser.   The early *frottola* was therefore not necessarily a popular form like the *lauda* and *canto carnascialesco* but one whose fidelity to the text and emphasis on individualism and spontaneity was seized upon as an antidote to the scholastic disciplines of mensural polyphony.

The style of the frottolists was of course considered as fundamentally distinct from that of the 'oltremontani' in the fifteenth century. This is aptly illustrated by their respective attitudes towards their pasts. On the one hand, Tinctoris could say in the prologue to his *Liber de arte contrapuncti* of 1477 that 'there is no composition written over forty years ago which is thought by the learned as worthy of performance'.[21]   On the other, Petrucci was prepared to publish 'giustinianae' in his *Frottole libro sexto* of 1505, which are thought to date from no later than the 1440s.[22] Leonardo Giustiniani (*ca.* 1383-1446) had enjoyed a high reputation as a performer of his own poetry to the *lira di braccio*,[23] and similar fame accrued to his successors Serafino de'Ciminelli dell'Aquila (1466-1500) and Benedetto Gareth, also known as Il Chariteo (*ca.* 1450-1514) at the end of the fifteenth century. On account of its predominantly improvised nature their music has come down to us in a few instances only[24] but it must be remembered that it was their performances that were praised in contemporary accounts, not their compositions. The number of these documentary records is enormous and a systematic critical collection of them is well overdue; Pirrotta provides a fair sample of them[25] but there are still many more references to be wrested from contemporaneous literature.[26]

Besides those pieces thought to be by Giustiniani, there are others in Petrucci's *Libro primo* that are not exactly the paeans of lusty extroversion that *frottole* are often assumed to be. Michele Pesenti, for example, contributes a setting of Horace's Sapphic Ode 'Integer vitae scelerisque purus'[27] on f.44r., to music striking in its restrained simplicity. Certainly its relationship to the later *villanella*-type *frottola*, in terms of language, verse form and musical style, is tenuous to say the least. Although it is the only setting of a classical text in the book,[28] it may well be representative of a type, as its sobriety contrasts strongly with what is known of Pesenti's other work. The diarist Paulus Cortesius mentions that Il Chariteo was accustomed to sing Virgil's poems at the request of Ferdinand II at the court of Naples,[29] and Pirrotta postulates that Pesenti's piece is 'under the persisting influence of a stylistic convention'.[30]

Thus the *frottola* did have a capacity for seriousness and nobility of expression that puts it more on a level with the motet, despite their differences in technique, than its more obviously similar musical cousins, the *lauda* and *canto carnascialesco*. Its sudden ubiquity in manuscripts and prints at the beginning of the sixteenth century marks a shift in emphasis away from improvised performance by charismatic figures like Serafino or Il Chariteo towards a written codification for wide distribution. The potential market for these books of written music was of course well established but only extended to those musically literate enough to have any use for them;

exactly the same group of people, in fact, as would have paid for the Mass and motet volumes for recreational use. For the first time, the forms of Italian music and the imported Franco-Flemish tradition, which had coexisted peacefully and independently throughout the fifteenth century, came into direct competition. The extent to which this in itself directly influenced the style of the motet form is open to debate, as has been argued above, but the adoption of Franco-Flemish notation and four-voiced texture by the *frottole* in Petrucci's books is an undisputed fact, which may have substantially contributed to the subsequent demise of the *frottola* form. What had been an improvised oral tradition based on humanistic ideas of the relationship between words and music was squeezed into the confines of the old mensural notation, which was presumably as adequate to the task as our present system is for the representation of jazz or folk idioms. There is no reason to suppose that the ungainly rhythms of the notated *frottola* were really supposed to be performed exactly as written; rather they were a necessary but incidental adjunct to the pitches of the melody and chords, to be freely interpreted in accord with the new ideals of recitation. A solo performer had no need to apply the rules of mensuration with anything like the discipline necessary for ensemble performance. What is recorded is thus no more than the outline of the piece; but since the essence of charismatic performance lies in its unrepeatable elements, its subtleties of nuance and inflection and its sense of occasion, such a containment in a form suitable for mass distribution is anathema to it. Only the most popular types could have survived in this form, hence the care necessary in tracing the sources of Petrucci's *frottola* repertory, which are obscured by the very process he used to publicize them. Improvised performance must have continued into the sixteenth century, but there are no records of comparably great singers to the lute after Il Chariteo. The serious poetic stance of that style was subsumed into that of the madrigal, which achieved widespread popularity through being eminently suited to the medium of publication. However, the spirit of the improvisers seems to have lived on with the instrumentalists who impressed courts with their spontaneity, virtuosity and individuality throughout the sixteenth century.[31]

The motet itself had something of a chequered career in the fifteenth century, at least as far as can be ascertained from the surviving sources. In the hands of composers like Dufay it suffered a period of mild isorhythmic fossilization as a relic of *trecento* style and ceremonial.[32] The mid-century saw it thoroughly neglected, the Mass becoming the favoured sacred form and the chanson retaining its predominance for court entertainment. Again, the non-liturgical character of the motet meant that it was not essential in church, while its religious text would have rendered it inappropriate as a recreational form in the prevailing climate of hierarchical scholasticism; God still conferred with the Church and State, not with the bourgeois individual. Such motets as do come down to us from that time (by for example Busnois, Ockeghem and Regis) tend to be conservative in style and comparatively few in number, so that they can hardly be said to constitute a repertory comparable to that of the chansons or even the Masses of the time. However, towards the end of the fifteenth century the motet quite suddenly became the dominant vehicle of expression within the Franco-Flemish tradition, surpassing both the Mass and any secular form. Comparison of the worklists of the composers named above with those of Weerbeke, Compère and Josquin readily indicates how drastic a change it was and how quickly it took place. Thus it was not as if any outside influence could have come along and exerted its leverage on a stable 'motet tradition'; rather, the form re-established itself virtually *ex nihilo* at the end of the century fully equipped with its new style, to serve a very different function from its exemplars at the beginning.

The earliest substantial testament to the resurgence of interest in the motet is furnished by the four 'Gaffurius Codices'.[33] These books preserve a repertory that was specifically written for the choir of Milan cathedral, a good deal of which can be comfortably assigned not just to the years before 1490 (the completion date on the first book), but to the years 1472-6, during which time Galeazzo Maria

Sforza assembled a veritable galaxy of luminaries into one of the largest and most impressive (though also the shortest lived) musical establishments in the entire Renaissance.[34] The most original feature of these codices is their inclusion of what are now designated as '*motetti missales*', in other words cycles of up to eight motets designed to substitute for the elements of both the Ordinary and Proper of the Mass.   Such attention as has been turned to the Gaffurius Codices has concentrated mainly on these and the purpose and extent of the cyclical groupings, which are still not altogether clear despite the extremely valuable and thorough work that has been devoted to them in recent years.[35]   This has, however, tended to obscure the novelty of the fact that they are motets at all in a liturgical collection of this time; it could well be that the *motetti missales* repertory is directly responsible for the re-establishment of the motet as a formal type, as the majority of the motets written for Milan, including all the crucial works by Weerbeke and Compère exhibiting 'Italian traits', seem to belong to cycles of one sort or another.[36]

The reasoning behind the substitution of a cycle of motets for the formal elements of the Mass has not yet been explained to the extent that such a radical step would seem to require. Noblitt sees the *motetti missales* as an expression of 'humanistic subjectivism'[37] as well as an extension of the medieval idea of troping[38] and Halpern Ward does not advance any further in this direction beyond a general accord with Noblitt. A detailed discussion of the matter would be out of place here; but it is worth noting all the same that these substitution cycles, irrespective of any considerations of the more complex interaction of renaissance philosophical and musical thought, are actually highly expedient in the context of the Ambrosian rite for which they were written. This rite, a liturgical 'dialect' of the Roman, was confined in the late fifteenth century to the city of Milan and its immediate surrounds as far as Italy was concerned.[39] There does not seem to be any precedent in the setting of its texts or the use of its melodies in polyphony until these motets of the 1470s, so that their composers were in fact setting out to create an entirely original repertory, which they achieved, moreover, in a remarkably short time; the bulk of the music would have been written between when the choir reached its full strength in 1474 and its disbandment immediately after Galeazzo Maria's assassination in 1476.[40]

The ritual of the Ambrosian Mass differs from the Roman in that its Ordinary comprises only the 'Gloria', 'Credo' and 'Sanctus', the role of the Proper movements being proportionately greater to compensate.[41] Because of this, the usefulness of a cyclic setting as a provider of a substantial amount of polyphony suitable for a wide variety of feasts is severely limited; the splendour of the occasion would require more than three items in order to compete with the pomp of the Roman ceremony. By their very nature, the items of the Proper are bound to particular occasions, so the possibility of compiling a set valid for any service does not exist. In lieu of composing a complete cycle of Propers (and it should be remembered here that the music must have been brought into being in some haste to establish a full and wholly unprecedented repertory in the short lifespan of the choir), the idea of combining elements of the Ordinary and Proper into one unified and versatile structure is a very useful one. Substituting motets with non-specific texts for the parts of the Proper weakens any association with particular days and the extension of the principle to the Ordinary is a confirmation of their liturgical 'neutrality', the whole amounting to a coherent body of music applicable to any given feast. Radical as it may seem, this solution need not have upset even a conservative churchman, who could have perceived the occasional wholesale replacement of the elements of the traditional Mass on the occasional feast worthy of polyphony as less of a threat than an attempt to reorganize the ancient order of service itself. That order is adhered to rigidly by a motet cycle and the rubric 'loco' at the head of each substitution reassuring proof that it has no ambitions to permanently alter the liturgy.

An interpretation of the *motetti missales* repertory as a compromise to allow the application of a limited body of polyphony to a wide variety of liturgical occasions squares with some of its other peculiarities. The existence of partial cycles, for example, is simply an expression of the versatility of the form; according to the solemnity of the feast, a greater or smaller proportion of its constituent elements may have been replaced by polyphony. In some cases there are no 'loco' designations for the motets and no textual hints as to which part of the service they may have been intended to replace, so that the various polyphonic items may have been strategically deployed around the mass at will.[42] This apparently cavalier attitude does actually gain a little more credibility in the light of comments such as those of Burchardus, who in his *Diary* for 1496 reports a practice whereby singers performed

> part of the Introit, an "Et in terra", a "Patrem", a "Sanctus" and an "Agnus dei", without the celebrant's singing "Gloria in excelsis" or "Credo" or anything at all: at the same time as he was speaking or giving these incipits in a low voice, they sang - a practice which is strange to us, but customary at Duke Ludovico [Sforza]'s court.[43]

As Noble rightly points out,[44] he is necessarily referring to a Roman mass (in a Franciscan church), but the novelty of the practice to Burchardus is obvious, and the incident suggests the climate in which substitutions (perhaps with the correct liturgical text intoned *sotto voce* under the motet?) could have occurred. Again, while it should be noted that it is a ceremony at the Sforza court and not the Milanese cathedral that Burchardus is describing, the common use of the Ambrosian rite and the fact that the bulk of the cathedral repertory, including the *motetti missales*, was written by composers like Compère, Weerbeke and Martini who were in fact employed by the court, suggest that similar practices may have prevailed at both institutions.

The fact that the *motetti missales* are a purely polyphonic phenomenon (there is no evidence of any equivalent in the plainsong repertory) not only eases their burden as radical subvertors of the liturgy, (in view of the presumed infrequency of polyphonic as opposed to chanted performance), but actually focuses attention onto the composers and singers themselves. It was they, and not the Church, who must have initiated the form for their own convenience, the unusually high regard in which they were held sufficing to licence it for ecclesistical use.[45] Granted a certain amount of liturgical leeway, an approved form whereby as many as eight different texts could be chosen and set at will as a cycle with suchever degree of unity as seemed appropriate must have been a very attractive proposition to the ambitions of a composer.

The broader musical situation at Milan was indeed so unique that the evolution of a highly original form was almost inevitable. Not only was the largest body of musicians of the time assembled from scratch in the space of about two years or so, but it had the formidable task of providing a repertory for a liturgy that had never been subjected to polyphony before. That this was substantially achieved in the few years before the assassination of Galeazzo Maria Sforza in 1476 indicates an impressive expenditure of creative energy. Moreover, the weight of tradition can not have been felt to bear down quite so heavily as in other institutions; of the musicians for whom any biographical data are available, Josquin and Martini are the oldest, in their early thirties if their common birthdate of *ca.* 1440 is accepted. Others, including the 'vice-abbate' Weerbeke were still in their twenties. Since both the charter and composition of such a body was so radical and their task so unprecedented, it is hardly surprising that music of some originality should have come into being as a result.

The motet form seems to have been revived, then, in response to a particular liturgical situation, and any outside 'Italian' influence was restricted to the spirit rather than the letter of the *frottola*, in other words the new climate of humanistic thought. Nevertheless, it has been customary to link the *frottola* and motet in terms of direct technical influence, particularly regarding the increased use of chordal rather than contrapuntal textures in the works of Josquin and his contemporaries. Thus Reese fairly describes 'Amor che sospirar', one of the three surviving Italian songs of Alexander Agricola, as 'written in a simple Italian chordal style' but then uses it as an example that 'shows Northerners in the process of assimilating Italian traits and combining them with their own Franco-Netherlandish tradition'.[46] Elsewhere he remarks that 'the Italian influence was simplifying the texture of music in the direction of chordal writing',[47] refers to Weerbeke's motet 'Virgo Maria' as opening and closing 'in a chordal style reminiscent of the *lauda* and *frottola*' and claims on behalf of *frottole* that 'through them Italy influenced the art of the Northerners'.[48] In a study of Weerbeke's life and works, Croll writes that his 'four-voiced motets show strong Italian influences' and defines the Italian style as 'characterized by four voiced settings in strict homophony, by simplicity and lucidity of form and by a harmony which is sometimes pronouncedly functional'.[49]

The novel qualities of Weerbeke's motet writing as opposed to, for example, Ockeghem's are plain to see from the surviving examples; their designation as 'Italian' stems on the one hand from the geographical origins of the sources and on the other from their coincidence with the *frottola* and its related forms. The clear assumption is that 'Italianism' is made manifest in its most essential state in the simplicity and homophony of the vernacular forms and from there was taken over into the mainstream of the Franco-Flemish tradition. That assumption has been challenged above on grounds of chronology and style, and it now remains to suggest an alternative mechanism by means of which the changes in philosophical outlook may have surfaced in the music of the time.

As it happens, most of the elements of the new style are discernible in the northern tradition itself, though they are of course less widely applied. Homophony and rhythmic simplicity are not features generally associated with composers such as Dufay and

Ockeghem but nonetheless play a significant part in their work, manifesting themselves in two different techniques, both of which appear unchanged, though greatly expanded in scope, in the works of the Milanese composers.

The first of these is the setting of a slow, but rhythmic homophonic passage against a typically contrapuntal one to effect a contrast and hence achieve some kind of structural articulation. This kind of writing is particularly apparent in certain works of Ockeghem, a good example being the 'Gloria' of the 'Cujusvis Toni' Mass. The chordal setting of the portion of the text beginning 'Qui tollis...' could be said to have served as a model for the homophonic passages of Weerbeke and Compère quite as easily as any Italian secular form. Similar episodes occur throughout Ockeghem's *oeuvre*, for instance in the 'Credo' of his five-voiced 'Sine nomine' Mass (particularly from 'suscipe deprecationem'), in the final sections of the 'Gloria' and 'Osanna' from the 'Au travail suis' Mass and all over the Requiem, to point out only the most extended and obvious examples. Chordal writing, whether slow and solemn or quasi-declamatory (as in the 'Sine nomine' Mass) is thus a regular part of Ockeghem's musical vocabulary, and there is nothing to suggest that he was influenced in the above works by the new sounds filtering up from the south.[50]

The second aspect of fifteenth-century homophonic technique was the underlining of a particular phrase of the text by casting it in block chords (often notated with *fermata* signs), thereby severing any rhythmic connection with other musical material as well as providing a textural contrast. Ockeghem, interestingly enough, never opted for this style, but Dufay made consistent use of it to the exclusion of that favoured by his younger contemporary. Apart from using it for the brief 'Amen' settings at the end of the isorhythmic motets, Dufay also applies it to significant words in the middle of a section. Thus proper names are illuminated (as in the motets 'O Beate Sebastiane' and 'Proles Hispaniae') and likewise important penitential prayers such as the striking passage at the end of the motet 'Flos florum' or the final invocation of the 'Kyrie eleison' in the 'Ecce ancilla domini' Mass. Comparing the end of 'Flos florum' with that of Weerbeke's motet 'Ave regina caelorum' (from the 'Ave mundi Domina' cycle) shows the style to be much the same, the difference in length being one of degree rather than principle. If Weerbeke wanted to point up his words more under the influence of humanistic thought or for any other reason, he could hardly have chosen a more traditional way to go about it than to set them to smooth progressions of simple chords.

It seems, therefore, that it is inaccurate to view the changes in the Franco-Netherlandish style that define the new 'renaissance' motet as being a direct result of its encounter with indigenous Italian music. The composers deemed to be most 'Italianate', such as Weerbeke, produced the greater and more characteristic part of their work in the 1470s, probably before 1476, when the forms of the *frottola* and *lauda* were significantly different from the published examples of thirty or so years later. Such similarities as these latter may have to the motets of the time are in fact largely attributable to their succumbing to the style of the North, particularly in the adoption of its notational system and target market, rather than vice-versa. What little is known of the vernacular tradition before Petrucci's intervention indicates moreover that it was a very different affair in all respects and principally literary rather than musical, so that it could hardly have held much sway over foreigners imported with the express aim of bringing their own training with them to grace cathedral and court alike with internationally recognizable prestige.

Most of the novelties of style found in the motets of the Gaffurius Codices are in fact traceable back to the works of the previous generation, so that it is not even necessary to postulate the effect of an outside influence to explain the various technical features of the music. The case of homophony has been examined above; the use of a harmony corresponding more to a modern idea of tonality was something that had been developing throughout the fifteenth century to the extent that Tinctoris and Gaffurius could be quite openly disparaging about the value of modal theory in its application to polyphony. Other aspects, like the contrivance of well-articulated structures by the use of contrasting textures are again much more the province of the involved processes of the Franco-Netherlandish tradition, within which passages for reduced numbers of voices or involving imitation or ostinato were an established fact, than the small-scale and texturally bland *frottola*.

Nevertheless, the style of Weerbeke, Compère and ultimately Josquin is very different from that of their elders and as such represents one of the most significant milestones in the transition in music from the Middle Ages to the Renaissance. This originality can not, however, be understood in purely musical terms, as it involves a more fundamental change in outlook. The same basic array of techniques and contrapuntal laws was available to both the Ockeghem and Josquin generations, but it was their diverse applications that distinguished the two. The mathematically disposed *cantus firmus* was a supreme symbol of authoritarian scholastic discipline and thus it guided the medieval consciousness of early fifteenth-century musicians and continued to exert a strong influence well into the the sixteenth century, as many of the compositions of Josquin and Obrecht demonstrate. However, alongside such works these composers and others of their generation increasingly wrote music free of any such constraints. It is in these works that the ascendant influence of humanism can most clearly be seen to assert itself, in the adoption of a structural method based on aurally perceptible contrasts and varieties of texture designed to follow the meaning of the text, instead of one governed by an abstract numerical pattern. The tenets of humanism were exactly those that shaped the course of the *frottola* and its related forms, but this unique coincidence of time, place and intellectual climate does not necessarily mean that the Italian forms exerted any direct technical influence over the motet.

The last element of change is a formal one, namely the re-emergence of the motet itself as a distinct type.[51]   A new form naturally lends itself to experimentation, so that its introduction has stylistic ramifications far beyond the simple provision of another heading in a composer's worklist. However, the reasons for the revival of interest in an otherwise neglected genre seem to be inextricably bound up with the cultivation of the *motetti missales* repertory in Milan, whose nature and usage need to be known more precisely before any conclusions are drawn beyond speculation. What is certain, though, is that these pieces are the essential prototypes of the entire sixteenth-century motet tradition and are thus crucially important in the formation of the high renaissance style. This new way of writing music, forged in the heat of a time of profound and universal changes in human thought, proved to be extremely flexible, so that while the effect of humanism can be observed in its purest form in the *frottola*, its grafting on to the rich tradition of Franco-Netherlandish contrapuntal art is no less characteristic. Indeed, the variety of forms and idioms that arose from the interaction of the disciplines of polyphony with the liberating influence of humanism constitute an enormously impressive achievement, which will be examined more closely in the chapters to come.

Notes

[1]Ciconia's life has been the subject of some controversy, as can be seen by comparing the biography proposed in *ClerxC* and *ClerxAC* with that in *FallowC*; the most recent and definitive account, however, is that given in the introduction to *CiconO*.

[2]Reese holds up the example of Bartolomeo Brollo as the exception to prove the rule (see *ReeseMR*, p.153), but otherwise accepts the decline of Italian musical activity in the *quattrocento* as a fact.

[3]In this connection, it is worth recalling Einstein's observation that the courts noted for encouraging the the 'alternative' style of the *frottola* were the poorer, weaker and less politically motivated ones

such as those at Ferrara and Mantua, which could not afford to keep a well-stocked choir of trained singers from the North in competition with Rome, Milan or Florence (see *EinsM*, i, p.34).

[4]It has recently been fully analysed, however, by J. Haar in 'The Problem of the Quattrocento' (see *HaarIP*, pp.22-48).

[5]For an extended argument of this hypothesis, see *PirrPM*, p.21ff.

[6]It should be noted too that our sources for such pieces are mostly from the early sixteenth century, principally the prints issued by Petrucci, so that in many ways they probably do not represent the form exactly as it had flourished in the fifteenth.

[7]See *Grove*, 'Lauda' (x, p.538).

[8]The last important source before the Petrucci prints, *US-Wc* ML 171 J6, from about 1490, preserves pieces of this type.

[9]A full account of their activities, based on documentary and source evidence, can be found in *D'AccF* and *D'AccL*.

[10]The expression is taken from *D'AccF*, p.2; though he is perhaps being a little unfair in assuming mensural polyphony to be the standard against which any group of singers would be judged.

[11]Apart from a handful of pieces in FP27 (apparently predating Petrucci's book, as was argued in chapter 1), which are to be examined in chapter 7, the four-voiced *lauda* seems only to have existed in these later publications.

[12]After Petrucci's two publications of 1508 no further books of *laude* were issued until Serafino Razzi's *Libro primo delle laudi spirituali* and Giovanni Animuccia's *Il primo libro delle laudi*, both printed in 1563, in Venice (by Rampazetto) and Rome (by Dorico) respectively.

[13]The chronology and style of these Milanese works are discussed at

length in the latter part of the present chapter.

[14]Compare, for example, any of the *laude* published in *JeppL* with the motets 'ad elevationem' from the *motetti missales* cycles.

[15]An admirably full and detailed history of the early years of the Sforza *cappella* can be found in *BarbS* and also *SartM*, which publish a large range of facsimiles as well as transcriptions of the surviving documents.

[16]A complete list of these may be found in *GhisiCC*, p.45.

[17]See *AtlNP*, pp.56-8.

[18]*I-Fn* BR 62 is considered in *GhisiCC* as fifteenth-century, but *BecherC* and *JeppFR* both opt for a later date. The manuscript, in two fragments, only contains three pieces in any case.

[19]These ideas are given a much fuller treatment in the first chapter of *PirrPM* (especially p.22ff.), where he also cites contemporaneous accounts of improvising musicians and the esteem in which they were held.

[20]The phrase is taken from *PirrPM*, p.22.

[21]See the edited translation in *SeayT*, p.14.

[22]See *RubsJ*, p.175 and *passim*.

[23]For an account of his career, see *PirrCT*.

[24]Only one example of music with a definite attribution to either Serafino or Il Chariteo appears in any source, namely the latter's 'Amando e desiando io vivo' which came to be printed in Petrucci's *Frottole libro nono* of 1507, f.55v., and also arranged for lute by Bossinensis in the *Tenori e contrabassi intabulati libro secondo* issued by the same publisher in 1511, f.11v.(13v.)-12r. However, it is possible that the ostensibly anonymous settings of Serafino's verse,

for example in *F-Pn* Rés. Vm[7] 676 and *I-Mt* 55, may have been by
the poet himself. The poetry of these two important figures is
surprisingly inaccessible in modern prints; the only comprehensive
edition of Serafino after the *Opere* of 1510 is *MenghS* (published in
1894), although I am indebted to Dr. M. Thackeray of Exeter
College, Oxford, for informing me that the most generous source of
his verse since then is the commentary at the back of *WyattO*.
Similarly the edition of Il Chariteo's works in *PèrG* (published in
1892) has yet to be superseded by a more modern one.

[25]See *PirrPM*, p.21ff.

[26]A broad impression can be gleaned from *HarasI* (based on the
diaries of Cortese from 1510), *BarbS*, *PirrCT*, *PirrPM*, *PirrMC*,
BollinLM or *Grove*, 'Cara' (iii, p.764), 'Frottola' (vi, p.867) or
'Gareth' (= Il Chariteo) (vii, 166).

[27]The text is from the *Carmina*, I:22, and is translated and edited in
HoraceO, pp.64-5. Pesenti's setting is published in *SchwarP*, no. 47
(p.34) and is also included in *DiserFB*, p.393.

[28]'In hospites per alpes' (f.43v.), though in Latin, is in fact a
medieval song (see *SchwarP*, p.xix) and Josquin's 'In te domine'
(ff.49v.-50r.) uses Latin only in the refrain that gives it its title, the
rest being in Italian.

[29]See *Grove*, 'Gareth' (vii, 166).

[30]See *PirrPM*, p.31.

[31]See *ReeseMR*, chapter 10 for an extensive account of the
instrumental traditions of the sixteenth century.

[32]The survival of the isorhythmic motet as an archaic form has been
compared to that of the fugue in the nineteenth century: see *FallowD*,
p.123.

[33]*I-Md* 1-4. The first three are in good condition but the fourth was almost completely destroyed by fire in 1906. Nevertheless, it has been possible to reconstruct the bulk of the repertory it contained (see *HalpMM*) and a facsimile edition exists of the charred remains (published as *AMMM* xvi).

[34]There is a general consensus that a good deal of the music from books 1, 2 and 4 originated in those years, with book 3 representing a slightly later choice of pieces (see *HalpMM* for an analysis of the repertory of book 4).   There is in books 1 and 2 a clear scribal demarcation between those works by composers active under Galeazzo Maria Sforza before 1476 - Compère, Weerbeke and Martini - and those whose music was included after the re-establishment of the cathedral choir with the appointment of Gaffurius as *maestro di cappella* in 1484 - principally Gaffurius himself (see *JeppG* for a scribal description of books 1-3).   It is natural to conclude from this that the compilation of the codices was a composite and partly retrospective affair (as is claimed for book 4 in *HalpMM*, p.496), different scribes drawing on material from either before 1476 or after 1484.   The intervening years seem to have been something of a fallow patch.   Compère definitely left for France in January 1477 along with several other lesser figures (see *LowAS*, p.41) and while Josquin and Weerbeke are not mentioned in these lists cited by Lowinsky as proof of the dissolution of the ducal chapel, there is no concrete evidence to prove that they stayed in Milan; certainly they were employed elsewhere by 1479 and 1480 respectively.   Anomalies in the scribal pattern such as the copying of three motets of Weerbeke's ('Christi mater ave', 'Mater digna dei' and 'Ave stella mattutina') by scribe I of book 1 (Jeppesen's designation) might be explicable through Weerbeke's later visits to Milan, for instance when he contributed to the   wedding celebrations of Giangaleazzo Sforza and Isabella d'Aragona in 1488 (see *AMMM*, xi, p.i for a list of such visits).

---

[35]*NoblitMM* provides the first definitive study of the *motetti missales* repertory, to which *HalpMM* has added a discussion of the fourth Gaffurius codex and greatly expanded the scope of Noblitt's original ideas.

[36]It is suggested in *HalpMM*, p.523, that incomplete cycles may have been common and that the accepted cycles in the Gaffurius codices represent only a fraction of the original repertory.

[37]*NoblitMM*, p.77.

[38]*Idem*, p.102.

[39]The history of the Ambrosian rite is a long and tortuous one, being inextricably bound up with the fortunes of the Milanese state. It had been much more widespread in the earlier Middle Ages, and vestigial pockets of the practice still remained in northern countries such as Bohemia at the end of the fifteenth century; however, since there was no equivalent polyphonic tradition in these places, they can be reasonably ignored for the purposes of this discussion.

[40]See *BarbS*, *SartM* and *LowAS* for full details.

[41]See *NoblitMM*, p.95, for a comparative table of the main items of the two rites.

[42]This is, however, by no means true in all cases; see *HalpMM*, p.519ff., for a review of the various liturgical links of the texts of motets in cycles with specific parts of the Mass.

[43]This translation is taken from *NobleF*, p.17, where the passage is discussed further in some detail and Noble hypothesizes that the words of a low Mass could have been spoken under the performance of music to a different text of its own. For the original text, see *BurchD*.

[44]*Idem*, p.18.

[45]The circumstances in Milan, where a vast body of musicians had been assembled in a short space of time in direct competition with other establishments such as Ferrara and Rome, would have conferred upon musicians an especially high degree of prestige, as is argued in *BarbS*.

[46]See *ReeseMR*, p.208.

[47]*Idem*, p.211.

[48]*Idem*, p.218.

[49]See *CrollGW*, p.67.

[50]The only source for the 'Sine nomine' and 'Requiem' Masses, *I-Rvat* Chigi C.VIII. 234, is known to be of Netherlands origin.

[51]Though the vagaries of transmission may have played a part in the apparently dramatic increase in the popularity of the motet, it should be noted that the difference is not just one of numbers, nor even of style, though this too is evidence of a profound change. The very sources that preserve the works of Weerbeke, Compère, Josquin *et al.* such as the Gaffurius codices or BQ19 belong to an entirely new genre, that of the motet collection, once again indicating a markedly different conception and use of the form.

CHAPTER 3: THE CONCEPTUALIZATION OF STRUCTURE

In a recent publication, Claude Palisca analyses the effect of humanism on what he calls 'musical thought'.[1] As a preliminary for this he undertakes a detailed survey of the premises and goals of humanism, examines the general nature of the intellectual climate of the Renaissance and puts them in the context of the social and historical changes that took place during the fourteenth and fifteenth centuries. By taking into account the peculiarly important role that oral and improvised traditions had to play in the musical life of the time, he arrives at a foundation for his subsequent discussions that can be best expressed by quoting one of his own sentences:

> Renaissance music is not a set of compositional techniques but a complex of social conditions, intellectual states of mind, attitudes, aspirations, habits of performers, artistic support systems, intra-cultural communication, and many other such ingredients, which add up to a thriving matrix of musical energy.[2]

From this point he proceeds to apply his definitions of what the terms 'renaissance' and 'humanism' actually embody to the subject of 'musical thought', in other words the corpus of theoretical, didactic and critical literature concerning music that stretched back in an unbroken line to the early Middle Ages.

The present thesis aims to start from the same fundamental viewpoint as Palisca's book but proceed in a different direction, looking for the effects of humanism in the music itself rather than in the literature surrounding it. Of course, notes on their own can have no 'meaning' in the sense that a verbal text does; however, their arrangement into anything more than the most basic configurations and their large-scale disposition through time is a craft that necessarily draws on concepts external to the purely musical criteria of proportion and contrapuntal propriety, and it is here that relationships to other arts and ideas are to be found. Indeed, it is precisely in this respect

that the renaissance musician was so original compared to his
medieval predecessors; his notions of structure are conditioned by a
response to the rhetoric of a verbal text rather than to any mechanical
cantus prius factus.   All of his innovations of technique serve to
emulate the ebb and flow of semantic logic, involving as they do
distinctions of texture to match the various changes of verbal register
and style.

          Palisca,   essentially   following   the   example   of   Jacob
Burckhardt,[3] isolates   a   number   of   traits   that   he   considers
characteristic of the Renaissance, the most fundamental of which is the
emancipation of the individual, a symptom of the devolution of a
feudal agrarian economy into the hands of a wealthy urban
bourgeoisie.   From this phenonemon others such as the reaction
against   ecclesiastical   dogma   with   its   concomitant   general
secularization, and the development of distinct and competitive forms
of patronage can be seen as derivative.   The other crucial feature of
the period is of course the revival of classical learning, which
extended well beyond an informed antiquarianism to a profound re-
evaluation of the nature of ancient authority due as much to the re-
interpretation of texts already known as to the discovery of new ones.
The purpose of Palisca's chapter is to trace the origins of these traits
and establish a boundary for the term 'renaissance', a matter that is
surely less relevant here (as only the most radical definition would
exclude the first two decades of the sixteenth century) than the
analysis of their manifestation in music and the extent to which the
'audible surface'[4] of renaissance style belies its deeper essence.

          The   technical   innovations   associated   with   the   Josquin
generation are generally accepted as marking the final turning point
from the great tradition of the Middle Ages to the more 'modern' style
of the Renaissance.[5]   As stated above, the most important common
denominator between them is that they are all, apart from the
increased emphasis on text declamation, concerned with the working
of different contrapuntal textures out of the voices that make up the

musical fabric. While the essential rules of consonance and dissonance, modality and cadence formation remained the same, the entire armoury of techniques that were to serve music until the introduction of the *stile recitativo* can be found as a conspicious feature of motets from the turn of the fifteenth century, whereas they were only discernible as traces in the works of the previous generation.[6] True, examples of imitation, duets and particularly homophony can be found in compositions by Ockeghem and Dufay, as was seen in chapter 2, and there is no doubt that the new style grew directly out of these. However, it is the frequency and concentration with which they are used that is so striking. A change in the number of voices might be used to characterize a whole section in a Mass by Ockeghem, but can be found in almost every other phrase in a motet by Weerbeke or Compère, and the homophony originally reserved for only the most vital parts of the text has become a commonplace. This emphasis on diversity instead of homogeneity is particularly significant at a time when traditional structural devices such as cantus firmus and canon were falling into abeyance, as it provides a pool of musical resources whose potential for contrast could be exploited to yield audibly articulated structures. Whereas organic polyphony used to provide a kind of musical substance, which was then cast into blocks defined by broad changes in the number of participating voices or mensuration, this substance came to be eliminated so that only the means of articulation remained.[7] By expansion and elaboration, this skeleton then became the music itself, so that each part assumed a function in relation to the whole, without any of the passive neutrality typical of even the most energetic passages of the older masters. The increase in the preferred total number of voices to four and expansion of the range that took place during the fifteenth century made possible a number of variations on the basic theme of textural contrast. The idea of duet writing gave rise to antiphonal voice-pairing in varying registers; plain homophony spawned a number of heterophonic techniques; and occasional imitation was developed into genuinely motivic work by which a longer passage could be imbued with a sense of identity capable of contrast with another. The progressive logic by

which the music then sustains itself is analogous to that of a verbal
text and a far cry from the static disposition of notes in an essentially
speculative system that was still a characteristic of musical thought in
the late fifteenth century. This change of approach has been widely
interpreted as being symptomatic of the erosion of scholastic teaching
by the burgeoning humanistic ideals that were spreading throughout
Italy at the time,[8] and it is of note that it is a primarily conceptual
change which in turn engendered a new set of musical procedures.

It is perhaps for this reason that contemporaneous theorists like
Tinctoris and Ramos are so unforthcoming about the new style, even
though some actually composed in it: these developments took place
without violating any of the conventions of Quadrivial music theory
or practical counterpoint. Although both writers (Ramos especially)
are themselves quite original in their rejection of Boethian and other
authorities and the trimming off of some of the centuries' worth of
accumulated speculative surplus that they now considered as
redundant, they are original as theorists within the accepted confines
of their discipline, whereas the new concern for structural methods in
practical music begged an equally novel branch of music theory that
did not begin to be supplied until the later sixteenth century.

Modern criticism of early renaissance music has also tended to
ignore its structural aspects, or at least those to do with the ordered
progression from one idea to the next. There are examples of
numerical or speculative analyses to be sure (those in the notorious
Obrecht editions of van Crevel are a case in point[9]), generally of the
more abstract forms like the Mass, but few 'humanistic' examinations
of either these or the smaller-scale forms. Jeppesen's pioneering work
in codifying the 'Palestrina style' has contributed to its consecration as
a model of refined imitative technique to whose heights the
'transitory' forms of the earlier sixteenth century have come to be
seen as vain aspirants, an attitude reinforced by the teaching of this
style as that of 'the Renaissance' as a formative part of school and
university curricula. By venerating the sixteenth century as 'an

angelically faceless golden age of polyphony',[10] its music has been denied the scope for individuality that was one of its most vital features. For all its virtues, the music of the 'Palestrina school' cannot fairly be said to represent the entire Renaissance, and indeed its classical mastery can sometimes appear almost sterile compared to the vigorous profusion of ideas found with Josquin and his contemporaries.

Nevertheless, as an example of both his personal style and that of the motet in his time generally, *Grove* chooses to cite Josquin's 'Ave Maria...virgo serena' in two separate articles,[11] both of which single out the long chain of imitative entries at the start as pointing to the style of Gombert and ultimately Palestrina. While the piece is indeed representative of its type in many ways, it needs to be said that the scale and sheer simplicity of this particular imitative opening is exceptional not only in Josquin's work but also in the entire repertory of motets from that time (as far as I know); such a prominent use of imitation surely has to be understood differently from imitative passages from later in the century, when the technique was standard practice.

The beginning of this famous motet is so simple that a modern score of it almost reads as its own graphic analysis, and in fact a close formal examination has been carried out in recent years by Cristle Collins Judd.[12] Although her opening paragraph makes it clear that 'Historical description and analysis when taken separately may provide an unbalanced perspective of the music...',[13] her reconciliation of the two is confined to a consideration of 'mode, counterpoint, cadence and imitation',[14] seen in terms of contemporaneous theorists. The limited relevance of the latter has been argued above, but what is more interesting is that the work is taken in the context of theory rather than other motets; it is never even made clear why this particular example was chosen out of so large and varied a repertory. Thus the uniqueness of the opening is again passed over, accepted as an example of 'imitation' (i.e. definitive normality) and no more. Moreover, while the relationship of the first theme (and indeed the whole motet) to the original sequence melody is taken into account, the fact that it appears in exactly the same melodic and rhythmic form and is even briefly imitated along similar lines in a setting of the same text by Johannes Regis[15] is not. Although the only source of the latter is Petrucci's *Motetti a cinque libro primo* of 1508,[16] the death of its composer around 1485 and the inclusion of others of his works in the Chigi Codex[17] indicate that it was in all probability written before Josquin's setting and may have exerted a direct influence over it.[18]

The opening of 'Ave Maria...virgo serena' is sufficiently distinctive to hint at some kind of external influence or motivation. In the absence of any clear documentary testimony it is impossible to draw any definitive conclusions, but a suggestion might be made along the following lines. The imitation that opens the work and continues right up to b.32 is wholly regular, occuring solely at the octave (or unison), at identical time intervals and repeatedly tracing the same linear descent through the voices from top to bottom. The effect is analogous to the reduplication of an object at identical distances, the only change being in its height (i.e. the pitch level); in other words it is an aural perspective effect like that of a series of columns receding into a vanishing point. The music sets the words of the Annunciation, one of the most venerated moments in the story of Mary. Contemporaneous paintings of this scene are particularly blessed with similar perspective effects[19] and although such backgrounds were not so rare at the time, there may well have been a more tangible connection.

Direct lines of sight and the ability to see unimpeded into infinity were equated with an elevated spirituality in several religious treatises influential in Italy during Josquin's time.[20] It has further been proposed that the renaissance eye may have interpreted a painted perspective effect not merely as an artistic *tour de force*, but as '...a type of visual metaphor... suggestive of, say, the Virgin's spiritual condition in the last stages of the Annunciation', '... an analogical emblem of moral certainty...', or '... an eschatological glimpse of beatitude'.[21] Recognizing Josquin's extraordinary passage as an attempt to translate the intense symbolic power of a pictorial device into music thus has implications far deeper than mere conceit and provides moreover a convincing explanation of why he should have set that particular text in such a distinctive way.   Such an interpretation depends on an acknowledgement of the unique qualities of the music itself, which can only be gained from its consideration in the context of its associated repertory as well as that of theoretical writing.

*   *   *

It has already been said that there are no hints in the treatises of Tinctoris, Gaffurius, or even Zarlino to guide the study of either the subtleties of implicit symbolism or simply the more general aspects of formal design. If this is so, then attention must of necessity be directed elsewhere. Remarks about music in purely literary sources are as rare as they are prodigiously imprecise and ambiguous as to what sort of music they refer to,[22] and though often fascinating are of little help.[23] General treatises on the arts do not appear until right at the end of the sixteenth century and are even then particularly unsatisfactory with regard to music. For example, the relevant chapter in Michele Monaldi's *Della Bellezza*, published in 1599,[24] limits itself to Platonic platitudes and a discussion of numbers and harmonic proportions that only escapes being a total anachronism by addressing itself to the late cinquecento dilettante rather than the professional of a hundred years before.   The ancient Roman manuals on rhetoric, originating as they did from the first century B.C., are hardly the most obvious places to look out for comments pertinent to the music of a millenium and a half later. Even so, the resurgence of interest in them at the end of the fifteenth century and their status as representatives of the only practically codified classical performance art are of considerable importance. The lack of any

actual ancient music to serve as a model for imitation and the
confusion surrounding such writings on the subject as were available
in the fifteenth century barred to it the paths that were leading to such
rich pastures in the realm of the literary and plastic arts, and even the
momentous innovations of the Florentine Camerata of nearly a
hundred years later hardly claimed to be an accurate recreation of the
glories of antiquity. Yet in these rhetorical treatises lie models of
constructive technique that bear a striking resemblance to the
procedures followed by early sixteenth- century motet composers,
whose susceptibility to classical influences can hardly have been less
than that of their fellow artists in other fields, and who would in all
probability have come across the art of rhetoric in the course of their
general education.

The evolution of the art of rhetoric is a fascinating subject in
itself, and has been investigated with increasing thoroughness in
recent years.[25] It is sufficient for the purposes of this chapter to state
that after its origins in the Athenian law courts of the fifth century
B.C. and a period of lively and creative formulation and competition
between schools, it became institutionalized into a set of broadly
agreed conventions. It was in this form that it was inherited by the
Romans, for whom it was a basic curriculum subject to train
professional lawyers in the more practical aspects of speaking in
court, as well as in public places generally. Originally Greek tutors
had been imported into Rome to pass on this art like so many others,
but its popularity and prestige gave rise, in the first century B.C., to a
set of manuals in Latin that set out an abstracted and concise form of
Hellenistic doctrine. The most important author is of course Cicero,
of whose output two works in particular are of interest to the student
of renaissance music. His *Rhetorica Vetus* and *Rhetorica Nova*, now
known as the *Rhetorica ad Herrenium* (which is today accepted as not
being by Cicero at all, though contemporary with his work), and the
De Inventione respectively, had remained popular throughout the
Middle Ages, to the extent that over one hundred manuscript copies of
the former survive from the fifteenth century.[26] Both books were

first printed in Venice in 1470 and the *Rhetorica ad Herrenium* was published in at least 28 different editions before the end of the century;[27] Cicero's authority was such at this time that his virtues of style were set up as absolutes by litterati such as Pietro Bembo in the early 1500s. Bembo evidently came across these works in the course of studying at the university of Padua, and there is plentiful evidence to suggest that they were taught also at Bologna and Pisa,[28] so that it is unlikely that any educated man with humanistic interests could have been unaware of their contents.[29]

Another work on rhetoric that is often cited is Quintilian's *Institutio Oratoria*, which was circulated in manuscript after the first complete copy was rediscovered in 1416 and then printed in Rome in 1470. However it never seemed to gain the popularity of the Ciceronian works until well into the sixteenth century, to judge from the number of reprints, perhaps on account of its contents: it is a comparatively long work whose style falls well short of the then fashionable Ciceronian ideals, and whose greater bulk is taken up with rather depressingly pragmatic details of legal minutiae. Beside this quantity of relatively tedious case history the sections on the abstract conceptualization of the art appear somewhat withered and derive straight from Cicero anyway, as Quintilian readily admits, so that his writings in this area - which is that most relevant to the music in hand - are of little originality. Therefore the following discussion will concentrate exclusively on the structural principles in the Ciceronian works, which are not contradicted by anything Quintilian has to say.

There are no direct references to music that could warrant direct 'imitation' of any sort, but the remarks on the ordering of the parts of a speech would not have been lost on musicians forging a new style based on clear structural articulation. Both the *Rhetorica ad Herrenium* and the *De Inventione* agree to a great extent on these matters, suggesting that their authors had sources in common,[30] and divide the speech (which is conceived as a legal address to a court) into six parts, thus:

1) *Exordium*:   introduction.

2) *Narratio*:   statement of the facts of the case.

3) *Divisio (Partitio)*:   statement of what is agreed, and
                                  what contested.

4) *Confirmatio*:   production of the arguments and
                                  documents in favour of the client.

5) *Confutatio (Reprehensio)*:   dismissal of the opponents' case.

6) *Conclusio*:   conclusion.

(The nomenclature preferred is that of the *Rhetorica ad Herrenium*, that of the *De Inventione* being appended in brackets where it differs)[31]

In both treatises these six headings are then discussed in greater depth as to their purpose and form. It is of particular interest that the discussions can be divided into two types, namely those concerned with structure, as applied to 1, 2, and 6 above, and those concerned with purely semantic matters, as in 3, 4 and 5, where the niceties of argument and examples of purely verbal logic are dealt with. These latter are considered structurally to be a summing up or climax of the *narratio* (a point made even more explicitly by Quintilian), so that in terms of abstract form the important elements are the *exordium*, *narratio*, and *conclusio*.

The two books agree again on the nature and function of these sections. The *exordium* may be of two kinds, the direct 'prooimion' ('principium') or subtle 'ephodos' ('insinuatio'), but the purpose of both is to make the listener well disposed, attentive and receptive.[32] The distinction between them arises solely out of legal expediency and the same criteria of quality apply to both: they should achieve the ends enumerated above by brevity and plainness of language to the point of

feigning improvisation.[33] Both writers insist too that it should be at
once distinctive to command attention and of such aptness as to be
only applicable to the speech in question, to which it should be
'closely knit, as a limb to a body', as Cicero puts it.[34]

   The virtues sought in the *narratio* are those of brevity, clarity
and plausibility. Brevity being self-explanatory and plausibility a
purely verbal matter, clarity is the only goal whose attainment by
structural means is outlined; the *Rhetorica ad Herrenium* warns
against undue repetition and the *De Inventione* advises the observation
of a strict chronological order. As for the *conclusio*, the former book
fails to elaborate on it through inflation of its section on the legal
technicalities of *confirmatio* and *refutatio*, but the latter suggests that
it should run over previous material and be an emotional plea to
invoke a spirit of gentleness and mercy[35] although stylistic details of
how this might be done are not included.

   The abstracted form thus consists of the following elements:

   Exordium: a relatively short introduction relying on simplicity
and emotional appeal for effect. Two kinds are possible, the direct or
subtle; in either case they should be distinctive and uniquely
appropriate to the speech in hand.

   Narratio: the most substantial part of the speech, which should
present things clearly and in their proper order.

   Conclusio: this should act as a summary by repeating previous
material and prey on the emotions in the same way as the exordium.

   The claim that analogous principles are at work in early
sixteenth-century motets is not meant to be a mere facetious play on
the obvious fact that they all have a beginning, middle and end. The
above elements were exactly those isolated by Gallus Dressler in his
Praecepta musicae poeticae of 1563,[36] even if he used the terms

'medium' and 'finis' instead of 'narratio' and 'conclusio': although based on a different repertory from that under consideration, his treatise shows that such ideas were not entirely foreign to the renaissance mind.[37]   More importantly, the motets that follow putatively 'rhetorical' procedures appear in sources like the Rusconi Codex that come from the same region and time as the renewed interest in and printing of the classical rhetoric manuals. While it may be methodologically unsound to assert any direct influence categorically, a composer's familiarity with at least the terminology of rhetoric can be assumed with a reasonable degree of certainty,[38] and besides such correspondences as do exist provide a useful analytical tool even if they were not consciously intended.

Examination of the pieces from FP27 and BQ19 that seem to follow some kind of structural pattern reveals that the opening, middle and closing sections are made distinct not only by virtue of their positions, but also by the ranges of techniques used in their respective constructions. This occurs consistently and in such a specific way that the rhetorical terms seem peculiarly apposite for their description, as follows:

Exordium: an introductory passage characterized by simplicity and the use of either plain undeclamatory chordal homophony (often structured by a modal melodic arch in the Cantus) or regular imitation for all voices at equal time intervals and on a limited number of pitches. In either case the section is usually clearly marked off by a full and obvious cadence on the modal tonic, at times emphasized by a corona sign.

Narratio: the longest and most flexible portion, varying widely from piece to piece, but usually starting with a duet to contrast with the *exordium*. It consists of the whole gamut of voice-pairing, binary repeats, ostinato, long-range imitation , variation, and declamatory or decorated homophony. As most of these involve some kind of answering phrase structure or rely on verbal rhythm, the music tends to have a logical discursive quality; conspicuous by their absence therefore are the two techniques mentioned above as typifying the *exordium*.

Conclusio: typically based on a repeated last line of music or text, usually more substantial and exact than any local repeats in the *narratio*. Occasionally a final character is imparted merely by the sequential use of harmony or melody in a single line, but the 'summing-up' by repetition or variation of previous material is unmistakeable. There is often of course a 'pedal coda' after the last cadence in certain modes, which while being part of the *conclusio* is hardly ever all of it, as it usually follows some kind of preparation of the kind described.

The close similarity between these definitions and those given in the rhetorical treatises is at once apparent. The chordal and imitative types of musical *exordium* correspond to the 'direct' and 'subtle' strategies respectively[39] and in either case the textures are strongly profiled and distinct from the *narratio* material. The quasi-improvisatory quality recommended in the manuals can be found in the plain chordal openings, whose austerity is entirely compatible with the notion of dignity and seriousness; while the imitative starts are more contrived, their basic logic and simplicity of idea do not contradict these latter prerequisites. Moreover, the musical *exordia* are often closely linked to the main body of the motet in all manner of ways, as will be seen presently in the discussion of individual pieces. The discursive answering style of the musical *narratio* likewise conforms with the principles of clarity and progressive orderliness, while the repetitions in the *conclusio* provide an apt musical summary with the frequent recourse to chordal textures recalling the direct appeal of the *exordium* and Cicero's advice to plead for gentleness and mercy.

A rhetorical approach to the setting of a text in the early sixteenth century should be hardly surprising as increased attention to verbal detail is an undisputed element in the music of the time. Moreover, motet texts were often associated with traditional plainchant melodies, where the frequent use of a discrete intonation provides a perfect prototype for the rhetorical *exordium* and the stereotyped ending formulae can be compared to the *conclusio*. Even the antiphonal psalms were rationalized into *intonation*, *medium* and variable *termination*, and it must be remembered that ancient as all these melodies may have been even in renaissance times they still formed the kernel of any musician's experience and would have had a fundamental effect on his intuitions.

It would be a mistake to view this conformity with past models as a conservative anomaly in a basically progressive medium like the motet. Respect for the ancients and the revival of the art of rhetoric was a cornerstone of the new humanistic culture[40] and the very concern for a more accurate representation of the word through music looks forward to the rest of the century rather than back to the last. There is indeed no contradiction between this relationship of words and music and that which was taken to such heights of sophistication later in the century in the madrigal. The differences between the two approaches are partly explicable in terms of external phenomena anyway; the ancient Latin prose of the liturgy was constructed along different lines from the Italian verse of Petrarch or his emulators and it is natural that each should find its own expression in music.[41]

*   *   *

In order to demonstrate more precisely the relationship of certain types of musical form to Ciceronian structural prescriptions, the motet 'Ave sanctissima Maria', attributed to 'Renaldo' in BQ19 (and edited as 'Ave sanctissima Maria II' in vol. ii, p.37) may be taken as an illustration. This piece contains the essence of its composer's highly distinctive style, which will be discussed more fully in chapter 4; it has been isolated as an example on account of the clarity of its form and the sophistication with which its contrasting textures are handled.

The piece is built on a series of full cadences which give rise, after the *exordium*, to a *narratio* composed of two contrasting formal elements, through composed homophony and answering passages for paired voices. These elements are made to overlap as the work progresses and eventually combine to yield the repeated homophonic music that makes up the *conclusio*. The scheme is as follows, where H = through composed homophony, AVP = answering voice pairing and AH = answering homophony:

bar 1:	*Exordium*			(12bb: plain chordal homphony)
13:	*Narratio*		AVP	(9bb.)
22:		H		(14bb.)
35:			AVP	(6bb.)
41:		H		(14bb.)
55:			AH	(5bb.)
60:			AVP^{42}	(7bb.)
67:	*Conclusio*		AH	(7 + 7bb. + 3bb. coda)

The conformity of this outline to that of the proposed rhetorical scheme both in the order of the sections and the techniques that make them up is immediately apparent in the broad homophony of the *exordium*, progressive alternation of the *narratio* and a *conclusio* that consists of a repeat of both words and music varied only by the recasting of the second statement into triple time. Examination in more detail reveals that the *exordium* is indeed bound as tightly to the rest of the motet as Cicero could have wished for, as its material is manipulated to form the basis of the other two homophonic passages in the *narratio*.

Although the symmetrical rise and fall of the Tenor in bb.1-12 begs to be considered as the foundation of the opening passage it is in fact the Cantus that carries the structural weight, falling as it does into three parts whose peculiar characteristics can be summed up as:

a)   the melodic *G-F-G-A* (bb.1-5)

b)   the ascent to high *B-flat* (b.8)

c)   the fall back to *G* (bb.10-12)

It is this that the two subsequent homophonic passages vary, the elements appearing in the same order thus:

a)   bb.   22-26 then bb.   43-49

b)   27-30   49-51

c)   31-35   51-54

The lower voices proceed independently of this, but it is worth noting the almost identical cadences coming between a) and b) of the first and second passages (bb.7 and 26), the like of which appear nowhere else in the piece. It is also important that the first passage (bb.1-12) moves predominantly in *breves*, the second (bb.22-34) in *semibreves* and the third (bb.41-55) in *semibreves* with a rhythmically diminished ending. This overall acceleration is typical, and moreover prepares the ground for the answering homophony that is to come.

Such careful melodic control is not simply a response to the demands of rhetorical form, but is discernible in the finer details of the piece as well. For example, the varied 'theme' of the homophonic sections also provides, almost exactly, the material of the first duet (bb.13-16). The answer to this duet uniquely does not repeat it but takes the element of a rising fourth and develops it sequentially as a way of avoiding the further duplication of the idea, especially as it leads into another statement of it in the next homophonic passage at b.22. The other duets are not so sophisticated, being really just reiterated cadence formulae: however the last phrases of the second and third (bb.39-40 and 63-67) treat their duet material *à4* in a manner that presages the imminent answering homophony. In this way the voice pairing idea is drawn into the progression towards this texture along with the homophony.

The declamatory homophony makes its definitive intrusion into the piece at b.55, as an interpolation into the previous alternation scheme that neatly prepares its fuller development later on. This significant event is related to another before it that also stands outside the alternating structure: the two chords used are the same as those used for 'Jesum' (bb.41-42) whose corona marks the first complete caesura in the motet. Thus integrated, the new texture proceeds by local repeats to the end, where the 'Amen' formally corresponds to the addition of 'Jesum' to the end of the first section of the motet.

Proportionally it is interesting that the first section ends (at b.42) exactly halfway through, and that the early homophonic and duet passages maintain their relative lengths to a reasonable degree. Tonally the piece stays firmly in the Dorian mode on *G*, although the homophony at the end allows for a little more harmonic freedom, of which advantage is taken to recapitulate the *B-flat* colouring of b.30 at b.70 and its repeat at b.79.

This work is remarkable not for any contrapuntal intricacies or proportional symbolism, but for the care and grace with which its formal contours are handled and dovetailed into an ending that combines elements of all the previous material. This is done independently of the text (which actually suffers repeats for the sake of the musical scheme, although on a smaller scale the rhythms are made to fit the words) and with hardly any recourse to the technique of imitation. The basic division into the rhetorical parts is plain to see in spite of the more obviously musical constructive devices, and in fact it is this sort of formula that provides the common ground on which a great many motets from this time can be compared and appreciated.

The proposition of compositional models not even mentioned in the writings of contemporaneous theorists or writers on music may seem a little alarming at first. However, the manuals of counterpoint have been scoured before for hints on matters of purely local structural significance, with little success,[43] and other more esoteric sources have been found to be just as distressingly vague, giving no help in determining how works were formally planned by their composers. Such a dearth of information actually corresponding to the music itself necessarily requires the net to be cast wider in the search for an explanation of its intricacies and eccentricities, which are hardly likely to have developed in isolation at a time like the early sixteenth century.[44]

This discrepancy is entirely natural, though, if the fact that the theory of music was geared to its written rather than its sounding form along with a review of the strengths and weaknesses of the notational system itself is considered. The latter, while strong on abstract intellectual elements, especially rhythm (the immense complexities of the proportional system were still very much part of the early sixteenth century musical consciousness even if their demise was imminent), is notoriously deficient in the realm of practical performance: tempo, dynamics, absolute pitch, musica ficta, performing forces and text underlay are matters left wide open to speculation, whose interpretation today is the subject of continuing debate. The emphasis of even the most practical books on the numerical aspects of the art, be they the temporal proportions of rhythm or the harmonic relationships of intervals, is the point at which they interlock with the theories originating in Hellenistic antiquity and filtered down in whatever distorted form through generations of writers in the Middle Ages. The relative neglect of the sounding aspects listed above in the notational system is directly analogous to the lack of advice from theorists on ordering large scale compositions or even the appropriate succession of one idea by the next; a blind eye was turned to the entire vocabulary of constructive techniques because its characteristic humanism defied rationalization within the old philosophical framework.

The genuinely critical commentaries by Lodovico Zacconi[45] or Gallus Dressler are the first attempts to rectify the situation by introducing justifications in terms of non-numerical and occasionally extra-musical ideas, and their novelty at the time is one of the reasons for their apparently elliptical style, working as they did outside the authority of the centuries-old traditions or even an accepted vocabulary of meaningful terms, all of which needed to be invented as time went by. This new branch of theoretical investigation was prompted by the innovations that took place in Josquin's time, and eventually reached its apotheosis in the deliberations of the Florentine Camerata at the end of the sixteenth century. The novelties of technique sanctioned by their conclusions are less fundamentally significant than their prescription for a new understanding and critical reception of music, a shift in attitudes without which the new innovations would have had no master to serve. Such a change would have been unthinkable in the stable world of Tinctoris and Gaffurius; however it is the work of their generation and successors that initiated the fundamental review of musical ideology on which the new style was based.

Notes

[1]Claude Palisca: Humanism in Italian Renaissance Musical Thought (New Haven, 1985).

[2]*Idem*, p.5.

[3]He quotes extensively from Burckhardt's *Die Kultur der Renaissance* (Basel, 1860) throughout his opening chapter.

[4]The metaphor is taken from Palisca's book, pp.4-5.

[5]For an extended discussion of this topic, see E. Lowinsky: 'Music in the Culture of the Renaissance', *Journal of the History of Ideas*, xv (1954), p.509 (see bibliography for further information).

[6]The article on Josquin in *Grove* (ix, 726), stresses this, saying (of the 'Pange lingua' Mass) that it represents 'a new synthesis that was in essence to remain valid for the whole of the sixteenth century'.

[7]It is tempting here to use the transition from the weighty Romanesque to the traceried Gothic styles in architecture as an analogy, though it would be nonsense to try to push the comparison any further.

[8]See *LowCR*.

[9]*ObrO*; see also *EldersG*, *GamerB*, *PowellF*, or *VelleO*, for example.

[10]The expression is taken from *HaarMC*, p.209.

[11]*Grove*, 'Josquin Desprez' (ix, 719), and 'Motet', (xii, 633).

[12]See *JuddAM*.

[13]*Idem*, p.201.

[14]*Idem*, p.202.

[15]Modern edition in *RegisO*, p.42. It should be noted that Regis's imitation occurs in an opening section for reduced texture and continues for only four bars before dissolving into the denser and more rhythmically complex writing characteristic of his work; thus although he anticipates Josquin's theme, the cumulative effect of successive regular entries that is the most original aspect of Josquin's

setting is wholly absent.

[16] *1508¹*, no.16.

[17] This manuscript has been dated to within the decade before 1503; see *KellC*, p.17.

[18] If Petrucci knew of it, then it was presumably circulated around northern Italy, so that there is a reasonable probability that Josquin was familiar with the work, which surely predates his own (see the entry under 'Josquin des Prez' in *Grove*, ix, p.719).

[19] See M. Baxandall: *Painting and Experience in Fifteenth-Century Italy* (Oxford, 1972), p.108, for a verification of this.

[20] See for example Petrus Lacepiera's *Libro del occhio morale et spirituale* (Venice, 1496), Bartholomeus Rimbertinus's *De deliciis sensibilibus paradisi* (Venice, 1498) and Celsus Maffeus's *De sensibilibus deliciis paradisi* (Verona, 1504).

[21] *BaxPE* p.208; for a more detailed discussion of the topic, see *Idem*, pp.103-108.

[22] This applies not only to poetic works like Poliziano's *Orfeo* but also to the various theoretical treatises on the art of writing such as those gathered together and published in *WeinT*. Though most of these date from the latter part of the sixteenth century, the first volume contains several from the early decades, all of which originated in northern Italy. Though music is occasionally mentioned, the references are to its purpose and moral effects rather than to any more technical matters; otherwise the books are highly specific to the intricacies of verbal manipulation and steer well clear of any more open speculation.

[23] One exception is the discussion of the qualities of music by Lodovico Zacconi, which is given a detailed commentary in *HaarMC*.

---

[24]As yet unavailable in any modern publication, though copies of the original edition can be found in the Bodleian and British Libraries.

[25]For the best general introduction to a subject that has only recently come to receive the attention it deserves, see G. Kennedy: *Classical Rhetoric and its Christian and Secular Traditions* (University of N. Carolina Press, 1980).

[26]See Cicero: *Rhetorica ad Herrenium*, ed. H. Caplan (London, 1954), p.xxxv.

[27]See J. C. Orelli's *Onomasticon Tullianum* in the Orelli-Baiter edition of Cicero's works (Zurich, 1836), vol.6, pp.197, 215, 218 and 233.

[28]See KennCR, pp.195, 198 and 200, also A. Grafton and L. Jardine: *From Humanism to the Humanities: Education and the Liberal Arts in Fifteenth- and Sixteenth-Century Europe* (London, 1987).

[29]That Tinctoris was familiar with the *Rhetorica ad Herrenium* is made clear by his quoting from it in his *Liber de arte contrapuncti* of 1477, albeit only in the most general way:

> ...as Cicero says in his Ad Herrenium, in every
> discipline the teaching of art is weak without the
> highest constant effort of practice...

(see *SeayT*, p.140). There is also clear evidence for the influence of classical rhetoric on contemporaneous literary thought in northern Italy, in the direct citation of certain key phrases. For example, the Ciceronian expression 'benivolus, docilis et attentus' can be recognized in various guises in Celio Calcagnini's *Super Imitatione Commentio* of 1532 (see *WeinT*, vol. i, p.210), Bernadino Daniello's *Della Poetica* of 1536 (*Idem*, p.258), Bartolomeo Ricci's *De Imitatione Liber Primus* of 1541 (*Idem*, p.420) and Francesco

Sansovino's *La Retorica* of 1543 (*Idem*, p.455), which is actually a fully fledged rhetoric treatise drawing heavily on ancient models throughout its length.

[30]For the precise relationship between them, see *CiceroRH*, pp.xxv-xxviii.

[31]Cicero feels obliged to mention a *digressio* between his *reprehensio* and *conclusio* on account of the authority of Hermagoras. However, his explanation of it is confused and he quite baldly states his own belief in its irrelevance.

[32]The same phrase, 'benivolus, docilis et attentus' is used in both books; compare *De Inventione* I, xv:23 and *Ad Herrenium* I, iv:6. It also finds its way, translated as 'benevolezza, attenzione et insegnamento', into Francesco Sansovino's 'La Retorica' of 1543: see *WeinT*, i, p.455.

[33]See *De Inventione* I, xv:23 and *Ad Herrenium* I, vii:11.

[34]'... sicut aliquod membrum annexum...', *De Inventione* I, xviii:26.

[35]*De Inventione* I, lv:106.

[36]A modern edition by B. Engelke can be found in the *Geschichtsblätter für Stadt und Land Magdeburg*, xlix-l (1914- 15), pp.213-50.

[37]The whole subject of rhetoric became much more important for critics of the later sixteenth and early eventeenth centuries. After Dressler's apparently original introduction of the idea into music theory others were quick to elaborate on it, although the correspondence was seen mainly in terms of local *affect* rather than overall structure. Thus both Dressler and particularly Joachim Burmeister after him (in the *Musica Poetica* of 1606) were keen to catalogue long lists of diverse musical *topoi* as analogous to the

figures of speech defined by the ancient rhetoricians and grammaticians, while paying only passing attention to matters of formal unity. For an analysis of their approach, see *Grove*, 'Rhetoric and Music' (xv, p.794ff., with a list of treatises on pp.794-5), and *PalUM*.

[38]It is interesting to note in this respect that rhetorical terms would also have been familiar from their use in Italian literature, as for example in the 'Proemio' of Boccaccio's *Decameron*.

[39]For a similar conclusion reached, however, by consideration of a completely different repertory, see *KirkCA*. Moreover Gallus Dressler, in his *Praecepta musica poetica* of 1563, makes the same distinction between the full ('plenum') *exordium* where the voices begin together ('uno tempore ictu') and the bare ('nudum'), where they come in one after another: see *Grove*, 'Dressler' (xii, 404).

[40]This point is argued more fully in *WeinT*, i, pp.546- 8.

[41]See *MacePB* for a further discussion of this topic.

[42]Although this passage is ostensibly a duet followed by a full section, the identical Cantus and Tenor lines in both reveal it to be constructed essentially as a repeated voice pair, with the answering statement modified by the decorative addition of the other two voices; a similar technique can be observed in bb.35-40.

[43]See for example *ReynCP* or *BrownTI*, both of which emphasize the incomplete nature of renaissance writings on music.

[44]Further arguments for the adoption of critical approaches beyond the scope of contemporaneous theory are to be found in *LeechM*, p.9ff.

[45]See *HaarMC* for a full discussion of Zacconi's *Prattica di Musica Seconda Parte* of 1622.

CHAPTER 4: THE SINGLE-MOVEMENT FREE MOTETS

While there is no strict uniformity of style even within a relatively consistent 'motet manuscript' like BQ19, there is little to warrant disqualification of any of its pieces from classification as motets. The same is not true, however, of FP27 and BQ18, whose contents are more diverse and whose original crediting with 76 and 26 motets respectively[1] is largely a matter of the 'default' status of the form under the categorization system in *HammCC*.

In fact, fewer than half of the 'motets' in FP27 are realistically comparable to those in BQ19, the others being either Latin *laude*[2] or 'minor ritual works'. The latter can be recognized by their brevity, strictly liturgical function and lack of compositional sophistication. This description, though based on apparently arbitrary criteria, neatly defines a subgroup of pieces written with the simplest of notation, little or no independence of voice parts (frequently limited to two or three) and a high proportion of 'errors', such as consecutive perfect intervals.[3] By eliminating these pieces, the remainder can be assured of a reasonable length, competence (or ambition, at least) and general parity with the 'classic' motet style of BQ19.

Even given such a distinction, other divisions are possible and indeed necessary. A minority of works from both FP27 and BQ19 are based on pre-composed material - *cantus firmus* or chant paraphrase - and are thus constructed along profoundly different lines from the 'free' pieces. In BQ19, there are some very long bipartite settings of entire psalms which although comparable in technique to their shorter brethren involve different organizational problems and are better understood as a separate group: to this can also be added the long bipartite settings of *Canticum canticorum* texts and the one secular motet, likewise in two *partes*. Lastly, there are pieces, such as all those from BQ18 and a handful from FP27, that exhibit positive signs of an instrumental style, on account of which they too need to be segregated and herded together. All these sub-categories will be considered in detail in their own chapters: the present one is concerned only with the 'genuine' single-movement free motets as defined above.

The formal archetype detailed in the preceding chapter is, needless to say, not the only way of exploiting the possibilities inherent in a musical fabric made up of contrasting textures. It is, then, a remarkable fact that a great many of the free motets in FP27 and BQ19 by the composers under consideration do conform to that arrangement, even in the face of contrary structures dictated by the text, such as refrains, repeats, changes in sense or argument and so forth. There are all the same an approximately equal number of these motets that function independently of any such formulae, taking their cues from either the local whims of the text or some other musical device.

A division of the free motets on this basis into 'rhetorical' and 'non-rhetorical' groups is therefore possible, but it is not necessarily the best way of reviewing the various styles of the time. Such designations do approximately correspond to what can be inferred of the relative chronology of the pieces, in that the those in BQ19 (whose composers are of a younger generation) have a more strictly defined 'rhetoric' than those in FP27. However, works can be found in FP27 that would not look out of place in BQ19 (the sources have the composers Brumel, Josquin and Renaldo in common anyway) and conversely the latter manuscript contains the occasional archaic piece ('Beata Appolonia', for example) as well as others that go against the rhetorical grain in a thoroughly forward-looking manner. Thus consideration of the two sources separately would be detrimental to the understanding of the many stylistic cross- references between them: besides, such anomalies occur even among the works of individual composers, so that no hard and fast distinctions can safely be made on these grounds.

An analysis by composer is still the most revealing approach to this large corpus of music. While those 'lesser' figures who are credited with a multiplicity of works are happily varied in their technical and formal procedures, they each display a certain consistency that endows the diverse motets within their *oeuvres* with a strong sense of common personality. If the wide range of styles current in the two manuscripts is to be described in any meaningful way, such personalities furnish a much stronger basis for comparison and contrast than any abstracted elements of technique or chronology. It is of course necessary to resort to these means in order to make sense of the numerous anonymous pieces, but it is intended in the present chapter to proceed principally in terms of the composer as an individual with his own distinct style.

Gaspar van Weerbeke

Although Weerbeke is a relatively major composer and as such technically excluded from this study, his seven motets from FP27 deserve attention here for a number of reasons. Firstly, four of these have yet to be published in any modern edition[4] and are thus as obscure as any of the anonymous works. Secondly, Weerbeke is generally reckoned to be the most 'Italianate' of the composers born around the 1440s and his work is crucial in the establishment of the new motet style; and lastly this particular composer provides an excellent example of the sort of distinct musical personality referred to above.

The circumstances of his life have been fairly well established from surviving documentary evidence and the source distribution of his works;[5] he appears to have had no connection with Mantua or Florence and it seems most likely that his motets found their way into FP27 via Petrucci's *Motetti A* of 1502.[6] None of them are from the *motetti missales* cycles in the Gaffurius Codices, and the three that do also appear in Librone 1 are precisely those that were copied by a scribe (possibly Gaffurius himself[7]) associated with a later repertory from after 1484.[8] It seems most likely therefore that these pieces are from the corresponding period in Weerbeke's life, when he was still connected with the Milanese court though not apparently directly employed there. Certainly they are more extended and elaborate than the occasionally pedestrian components of his cycles and constitute a contribution to a different species of motet, one not directly tied to any ecclesiastical function as can be seen from the preponderance of non-liturgical verse and *Canticum canticorum* texts.

Five of these pieces, namely 'Christi mater ave', 'Ibo mihi', 'Mater digna Dei', 'O pulcherrima mulierum' and 'Virgo Maria', are imbued with a particularly formidable unity of style, largely due to their common length, clefs and mode, which latter is used by Weerbeke in a highly distinctive way. He has his own peculiar formula for cadential patterns, consisting of octave and fifth movements in the bass, often combined with homophonic syncopations in all voices, which lend them a very 'modern', and above all tonal feel (see, for example, bb.12-14 or 20-21 of 'Mater digna Dei'). The given mode being the plagal Phrygian, *E*, *A* and *C* are the standard cadence points and because of the common clefs and Weerbeke's rigid apportioning of formal cadential progressions to the Cantus and Tenor only, each assumes its own pitch level and has a similar impact from piece to piece. Those on *A* are in the middle of the range and hence final sounding, those on *E* low and sombre and those on *C* high and climactic. It is clear from Weerbeke's distribution of these, particularly those on *C*, that he was aware of these implications and deliberately exploited their structural and expressive possibilities.

Nevertheless, each motet is lent its own individuality of form by its response to the structural exigencies of the given text. Individual lines of verse or short clauses of prose are set to their own contrasted sections of music according to their sense, an even-handed approach that tends to mask any overall shape and rules out 'rhetorical' features like repeated sections at the end. Hovever, care is taken to ensure continuity and the recurrence of semantic ideas is exploited to the full; a functional threefold form is actually still visible in all these motets, as will be seen when they are discussed individually.

There are, as well as the cadences, more distinctive techniques shared by several of these pieces. Weerbeke observes, oddly for an otherwise forward-looking composer, a strict part-hierarchy. The Cantus and Tenor carry all the melodic substance, frequently imitating it between them, and form all the cadences. The Altus and Bassus, on the other hand, are used simply to provide support and decoration of this framework. Paradoxically, it is the use of this most conservative procedure that most distinguishes Weerbeke's work from that of the previous generation, in that his 'free' voices quite clearly function as a genuine accompaniment, subordinate to the main melody and designed to set it off rather than bury it in elaborate traceries. Though there may not be motivic material common to all the voices in a section, the apparent diversity of ideas is to some extent an illusion; a single melody usually lies at the heart of the texture while the remainder focuses rather than distracts attention. This sort of writing can be found in all these motets ('Ibo mihi' is a particularly good example, as will be seen below) and is as convincing a demonstration of the ascendancy of melodic over contrapuntal principles as any amount of regular through imitation. Some of the music does indeed look forward to the 'vocal orchestration' of the later madrigal (again, 'Ibo mihi' is a good example) and though the origins of such a melodic supremacy may lie in a debasement of the *cantus firmus* principle, it is equally characteristic of the contemporaneous Italian secular forms. Weerbeke's work thus reconciles both medieval and humanistic elements into a musical synthesis that makes him one of the most distinctive composers of his time, and not merely an imitator of southern chordal simplicity as is sometimes supposed.

More specifically, 'Ibo mihi', 'O pulcherrima' and 'Virgo Maria' all use exactly the same idea in exactly the same place (a bass pedal *C* supporting plain triadic imitation in the upper three voices towards the beginning of the *narratio*; see their bb. 14-15, 14-17 and 19-22 respectively) and there are other striking instances of material in common (compare, for example, the Cantus-Tenor imitation in bb. 50-54 of 'Mater digna Dei' with that in bb.34-8 of 'O pulcherrima'). All this, along with an affinity of language in general, imposes an immediately recognizable character on these motets and might even prompt an accusation against Weerbeke of paucity of invention. This would however be unfair as each piece still maintains its individuality and is moreover extremely effective, so that it is easy to understand their evident popularity in the early 1500s.

The longest of these five motets, 'Mater digna Dei' (edited in vol. ii, p.115) shows Weerbeke at his most flexible and inventive, while maintaining a strict dependency on the text for its overall structure. The words themselves are in a quasi-sequence form, proceeding by unmetrical and irregular rhymed couplets and triplets;[9] each of these groups is set as a self-contained unit so that the music falls neatly into discrete sections.

The opening direct invocation and the 'miserere' passages at the middle and end receive like settings to simple block chords, a procedure that not only complements their tone of direct supplication but also endows the music with a symmetrical closed structure. The intervening body of the motet therefore falls into two episodes which are also similar in form and function, the first phrase of each (bb.7 and 39) matching the melody and harmony of the preceding homophony to create a recognizable *exordial* effect at the beginning and a sense of continuity and renewed momentum the second time. A similar instance can be found at the end, where the final phrase of the homophonic section (at b.73) is decorated so that its Cantus condenses the melodic motion of the previous ones. The repeated device of plain homophony followed by a melodically related passage thus serves to define the *exordium*, propel the *narratio* and provide a summing-up for the *conclusio*, at the same time as giving the whole motet a symmetrical foundation.

As well as this, both the second and third homophonic sections are preceded by passages for reduced texture (at bb.26-32 and 55-63) that although different have a common function as a foil, to make the coming chords stand out to a more impressive and monumental effect. The previous part of the second episode is also notable for the only really continuous music of the piece, where phrases overlap without cadences into a relatively extended section (bb.43-54). This too is due to scrupulous adherence to the structure of the text, though; it is elicited by a short rhymed tercet ('digna coli/ regina poli/ me linquere noli') whose constituents are too slight to receive sections to themselves. Weerbeke takes full advantage of the opportunity to generate a cumulative climax on the plea 'me linquere noli', the most emotive line of the entire poem. By contrast, the quiet simplicity of the succeeding duet acquires a uniquely personal flavour, a consciously dramatic technique that can be found also at the climax of the same composer's 'Tenebrae' setting.[10]

Thus a matching of words and music is achieved without any recourse to the later devices of 'expression', word-painting or dramatic declamation. While the text is followed to a profound degree, the music is rescued from being no more than an open progression by symmetrically recurring elements and parallelisms in the choices of the successive textures in its two main sections. Thus a structural solution is found to the problem of appropriate text setting, which is entirely compatible with Ciceronian rhetorical ideals, and shows a lively and intelligent use of the possibilities offered by the new techniques of musical articulation.

A curious feature of 'Ibo mihi' (edited in vol. ii, p.90) is its notation in the obsolescent *tempus perfectum* despite the music's consistent tendency to slip into a duple metre, this being especially notable in the first four phrases (up to b.6). It is one of the very few of Weerbeke's surviving motets to be so written,[11] the only other example being 'Tota pulchra es'/ 'Iam enim hiems' from the 'Quam pulchra es' cycle.[12] In both the latter cases the metre goes hand in hand with a full homogenous texture quite distinct from the

composer's other writing (including the 'Ave caelorum regina' Mass;
see note 11) and it may be that its use is as much a symbolic homage
to the older Netherlands masters as a matter of notational practicality.

Having said this, the piece has much in common with 'Mater
digna Dei'. The open and rather languorous text is similarly rallied
into a closed musical form by repeated material, bb.10-14 reappearing
at bb.22-27. Although neither words nor music are exactly the same,
the basic idea is highly distinctive in its originality and is developed in
similar ways. The use of an organic approach to the climax of the
work the second time is also reminiscent of the equivalent passage in
'Mater digna Dei'.

As mentioned above, the sense of purely melodic direction in
this piece is particularly strong. Structural imitation between the
Cantus and Tenor supports the entire motet, though in some cases (for
instance bb.28-30) the 'imitation' is limited to a shared ambitus,
direction and cadence. Moreover, the very last phrase is based solely
on the sequential logic of the Cantus line and thus represents a further
instance of the structural advance of melody over counterpoint. These
foundations are supported not so much by distinct counterpoints as by
simultaneously conceived accompaniments enhancing and reinforcing
their effect. Thus the same principle of Cantus-Tenor imitation is at
work in bb.1-10 as in bb.10-13, but the first is superficially
polyphonic and the second chordal, on account of the varied natures
of the supporting voices. Comparable effects occur all the way
through this motet and are one of its strongest features; with a firm
sense of direction supplied by the Cantus and Tenor, Weerbeke can
allow himself complete freedom in the establishment of differing
textures. The mercurial imagination with which these are hinted at
and then eddy away mark 'Ibo mihi' out as one of its composer's most
successful and interesting works.

So similar is the style of 'O pulcherrima mulierum' (edited in
vol. ii, p.145) that there is little that needs to be said about it in

addition to the comments above. Indeed, since the passage at bb.14-17 is almost identical to bb.14-15 of 'Ibo mihi', while bb.34-8 rework the same idea as bb.50-54 of 'Mater digna Dei' among other correspondences (compare, for example, bb.30-31 with bb.13-14 Of 'Ibo mihi') the piece seems like something of a compendium. It is in fact probable that the other two derive their material from this one rather than vice-versa, since the lack of any attempt to impose a comparable closed musical order together with clumsier writing (see the textures around bb.21-23 for example) and generally blander material imply that 'O pulcherrima' is a less mature work than its counterparts. Taken apart from them, it is still an attractive and effective piece, but it pales somewhat in the face of more strongly characterized executions of similar basic ideas.

'Virgo Maria, non est tibi similis' (edited in vol. ii, p.210) was selected by Ambros for publication in his *Geschichte der Musik* of 1862-8[13] as a representative sample of Weerbeke's work, since when it has been cited by Reese as an illustration of the influence of the *frottola*.[14] Within the context of the composer's other mature motets it assumes a slightly different aspect, however. It is certainly characteristic, to the extent of sharing material with 'Ibo mihi' and 'O pulcherrima' (see above), but asserts its individuality through a greater sense of structural purpose. It is in fact the most 'rhetorical' of these motets, a fact that derives partly from its text, which can be neatly divided into an *exordium* (salutation to the Virgin), a *narratio* (list of her qualities) and *conclusio* (prayer for intercession).

A corresponding musical *exordium* can be distinguished in bb.1-15, its boundary marked by the first cadence onto the tonic A (in b.16), and hence fulfilment of the harmonic direction implied by the opening on E. This is not just a chordal matter; the more obviously perceptible surface of the music is the gradual exploration by the Cantus of the dominant degrees of the mode, which is likewise closed by a return to the tonic in b.16. A duet follows to mark the transition to the *narratio*, giving way at bb.19-22 to the static chordal idea shared with 'Ibo mihi' and 'O pulcherrima' and more duet writing. The *conclusio* (starting at b.37) reverts to the style of the opening, lending a sense of symmetry (it is about the same length) as well as rhetorical completion. Although it does not make any use of any repeated material, it does include the only example in Weerbeke's mature motets of the long pedal coda so typical of later composers. Thus the novelty of rhetorical form makes itself felt in the music's local as well as overall features and distinguishes 'Virgo Maria' from its fellows in spite of its many similarities.

'Christi mater ave' (edited in vol. ii, p.56) is wrought from the barest minimum of material and shows Weerbeke at his most succinct and rigid in his imposition of a musical structure on the text. As in 'Virgo Maria', there are elements of rhetorical form but here they are simplified and less subtly incorporated; the clarity of outline is due to lesser rather than greater sophistication.

The regular imitation leading up to the cadence in b.8 comprises a classic *exordium*, firmly establishing the mode. The *narratio* then proceeds by reduced textures and local repeats until the more extended reiteration of material in the *conclusio* from b.39 onwards. This lucidity of form is stressed by the extraordinary way in which the motet is virtually monothematic. Apart from the opening, every melodic idea is a variation of that at b.19, itself an inversion of that at b.10, and each is worked into a binary (or as in bb.19-28, ternary) repetition, the second statement being slightly varied, often by transposition up or down by a third. The form can hence be schematized, as follows:

b.1:	*Exordium*		(8bb.)
9:	*Narratio:*	AA_1	(4+4bb.)
19:		BB_1B_2	(4+4+4bb., overlapping)
29:		CC_1	(5+5bb., C_1 up a third)

39: *Conclusio:* DD_1 (D_1 down a third, with added cadence)

46: D_2D_3 (D_2 = D down two thirds; D_3 = D_1 down a third)

where the same motivic pattern runs through A, B, C and D.

The regularity is made even more prominent by the consistent use of four bar phrases in the *exordium* and *narratio*, those of C and C_1 only being lengthened to five bars by the addition of a 'codetta'. The functions of the rhetorical sections are also enhanced by the transpositions, rising to a climax at the end of the *narratio* and steadily sinking in the *conclusio*, appropriately enough for a peroration.

The motet is still recognisably close to Weerbeke's others in style, particularly 'Mater digna Dei', with which it shares textual features; both are Marian and include the line 'me linquere noli', though it is set differently each time.[15] Although its neat arrangement and balance are gained at the expense of the subtle responsiveness to the text and imaginative variation of for example 'Ibo mihi', the cumulative effect of the repeated material and the transpositions makes for an impressive climax, which was presumably the composer's intention, and so the piece should not be underestimated.

More genuinely mechanical in its form is 'Ave stella matutina' (edited in vol. ii, p.40), whose slavish adherence to the words makes it a very different proposition to the above in spite of being in the same mode. The five tercet verses of the sequence are set so that the first two lines of each are taken by identical duets and the last one by full chordal wrtiting (vv.1-3) or, repeated, to two identical duets again (vv.4 and 5).[16] The rest of the text is a short prose plea that is set to similar alternating duets, and is thus integrated with the previous verses. Moreover, the setting of its twenty bars in *tempus imperfectum* balance the twenty-five of the first two verses, forming a

symmetrical and proportionally apt surround to the forty-nine bars in
triple time in the middle. This organization, careful as it may be,
hardly compensates for the facility of the musical substance whose
automatic adoption of the forms and basic rhythms of the verse show
this piece to be markedly less ambitious and sophisticated than its
composer's others in FP27.

Finally, 'Adonai' (edited in vol. ii, p.3) is also unique, but for
different reasons. Not only is the mode Dorian, as opposed to the
Phrygian of the six motets already discussed, but the entire fabric of
the music is differently composed. The piece is an object lesson in
rhetorical form, even more so than 'Christi mater ave', with a full,
imitative *exordium* establishing the mode in bb.1-14, a *narratio* of
chiefly duet textures from bb.15-51 and a *conclusio* based on a
sequential extension of material at the end. A concern for balance is
also apparent in that both the *exordium* and *conclusio* end in free
homophonic writing and are about the same length, while the *narratio*
is almost entirely symmetrical, as can be seen from the following
scheme:

b.1:	*Exordium*	(14bb.)
14:	*Narratio:*	Duet (13bb.)
27:		Full (8bb.)
36:		Duet (10bb.)
46:		Answering duets (3+3bb.)
52:	*Conclusio*	(14bb.)

The duets at bb.14 and 36 are for the two lower and upper
voices respectively and are variations of the same material, which also
provides the structural Cantus part in the intervening full section. The
only assymmetrical element in the scheme is the short answering duet
passage at b.46, but this is necessary to return the tonality to *G* and it
also serves to condense the movement of the entire *narratio* into a

brief reprise to round it off.

The scribe of FP27 omitted to copy the text (except for the first word) of this one particular motet, even though it is clearly included in Petrucci's *Motetti A*, which was surely one of his sources (see note 4). This apparently deliberate omission would seem to indicate that he intended it for use as an instrumental piece like some of the other textless 'motets' in the manuscript, the adaption presumably inspired by stylistic peculiarities such as the sequence at the end. However, since the supposedly earlier source provides a text that fits perfectly, its authority must be accepted as representing the composer's original intentions. Indeed, the passage in question, whose purely musical regularity and quick movement would be major obstacles in the underlaying of any text, is actually a melismatic setting of the word 'canentium' in the *Motetti A* version, thus making it an unusually early example of explicit word painting.

In his structural use of melody, attention to the text and concern for easily apprehensible and occasionally dramatic forms, Weerbeke reveals himself to be very much a renaissance composer. The traditional image of him as a simplifier and compromiser with popular forms deserves revision if the subtlety and effect of his work is to be properly understood. Certainly he was among the first northern composers to leave traces of the influence of humanism in their music, and he did so in a way far more profound than the mere adoption of an indigenous local style.

RENALDO

A composer with a similar consistency of approach to Weerbeke's, although in a rather different style, is the figure known from his attributions in FP27 and BQ19 simply as 'Renaldo'.[17] In the context of the latter source he is a much more important figure than might be expected from the unfamiliarity of his name, as his legacy there of seven motets, two settings of the Magnificat and two

of the entire Mass Ordinary nearly doubles that of any other composer
except Mouton (who contributes twelve motets). In addition to these
a Renaldo is credited with a further motet in FP27 ('Tristitia',
ff.71v.-72r.). All these are unica with the sole exception of 'Paradisi
portas aperuit' which appears in one other source, bearing a probably
spurious attribution to Lupus.[18] Thus a total of twelve works survive
in early sixteenth-century sources under the name 'Renaldo'.

Published transcriptions of the two Magnificats and five of the
motets are to be found in *MaldTM*,[19] clearly taken from BQ19 though
as usual the source is not mentioned. Maldeghem ascribes them to
'Renaldus van Melle', an expansion of the name given in the sources
that is both inaccurate and misleading. Inaccurate, because the name
'van Melle' is not given in any of the clear manuscript attributions of
the music, and misleading because it implies a historically impossible
identification. Renaldus van Melle was a Flemish composer born in
ca. 1554, whose creative activity began in the 1580s; he is completely
irreconcilable with a source firmly dated around 36 years before his
birth.[20]

There are on the other hand several documentary references to
musicians called Renaldo or something recognizably similar around
the end of the fifteenth and beginning of the sixteenth centuries.
Though these have been partly gathered together[21] and connections
occasionally made between some appearances of the name, no
systematic discussion of the biography (or biographies) they imply has
yet emerged even to the extent of a dictionary article.[22] A complete
list of the references to a Renaldo around the turn of the fifteenth
century in chronological order runs as follows:

Apr. 1471 - Jun. 1472:   a *Rinaldo* mentioned in the archives of
                         the Duomo in Rieti.[23]

1473:   a *Raynaldino* among the *cantori da
                         camera* in the service of the Sforza
                         family in Milan.[24]

15 July 1474:   a *Raynaldino* among the *cantori da
                         cappella* again in the service of the
                         Sforza in Milan.[25]

1474-6:   a *Rainaldetto Cambrai* among the
                         singers listed in three Ferrarese
                         documents from 1474, 1475 and
                         1476.[26]

1477-88:   a *presbiter Raynaldus Odenoch de
                         Flandra cantor stipendiatus* among the
                         singers listed in the registers of
                         Treviso cathedral.[27]

Nov. 22 1482 - Mar. 21   a *Don Rinaldo Francioso, maestro di
1483:   canto e cantori* in the paylists of the
                         SS. Annunziata in Florence.[28]

1489-90:   a *presbyter Raynaldus francigena
                         magister cantus* mentioned in the
                         salary lists of Padua cathedral.[29]

Apr. - Jun. 1491:   a *Raynaldus* among the members of the
                         papal chapel.[30]

1492-3:   a *Ray de Odena* (also referred to as
                         Ray de Honderic) among the members
                         of the papal chapel.[31]

ca. 1505-1508:   a *Renaldo* credited with a motet in
                         FP27.[32]

| *ca.* 1518: | a *Renaldo* credited with eleven compositions in the Rusconi Codex; referred to in the index twice as *Renaldino* and once as *Renaldus*. |
| Oct. 1529: | a *Renaldo francigene* mentioned in the records of the Chiesa della Staccata in Parma as a singer who died at that time.[33] |

The question remains as to how many personages are represented in these documents. The two Milanese references around 1474 are surely to the same man, likewise those from the papal chapel in 1491-3 to a Ray de Odena or Honderic, with whom the Treviso Raynaldus can be identified by the specification Odenoch. There are stylistic reasons for supposing that the composer in FP27 is the same as that in BQ19 (to be discussed below) and it would be logical to link the Florentine composition with the *maestro di cappella* at the SS. Annunziata.[34] Even so, it might still be presumed from the forms of the names that there were two or three singers, from France generally (francigene), or specific parts of Flanders (Honderic/Odena or Cambrai), any or none of which could have been the composer. Such a plural interpretation is favoured by the way that a Raynaldus de Flandria and a Rinaldo Francioso were employed in Treviso and Florence respectively at the same time, during the years 1482-3.

There are, however, several objections to this diversity. If the soubriquet 'Odena' or its variants refers to a place, the most likely identification (in lieu of any others) would be Oudenaarde (the birthplace also of Weerbeke), which is within fifty miles of Cambrai anyway so that the possibility of a birth in the former and training in the latter cannot be ruled out. This area was just on the Flemish side of the border with France and part of the Duchy of Burgundy; as an educated man, French may well have been his first language despite his ostensibly Flemish provenance, so that the appellations 'de Flandra' and 'francigena' are not necessarily mutually exclusive.

Ambiguity could easily have arisen in the designation of what was still an ill-defined foreign territory and there are in fact other instances of the two terms being used interchangeably.[35]

As for the simultaneous careers in Florence and Treviso, he appears to have stayed in the former city for no more than four months, the ample records of that time making no other mention of him.[36] Such a short leave is of the sort often encountered in the lives of musicians for visits and journeys and would not necessarily have affected his appearance in the yearly roster at Treviso. Unfortunately it has not been possible to inspect the original records for any hints of absence,[37] but until hard evidence is provided to the contrary it is not necessary to make too much of such a short and isolated break in a long period of service.

On the basis that the Parma Renaldo had a son,[38] Jeppesen has negated any identification with the priest ('Don') mentioned elsewhere. However, the assumption that he was married is completely unfounded[39] and indeed his paternity is only inferred from the fact that the 'son' was sometimes given the name 'de rainaldino'. He is also called 'musicus gallus hannonensis' (i.e. from Hainaut) and is known to have been a choirboy at Cambrai in 1520. Since the 'father' seems to have originated around Cambrai and is moreover untraceable in the first decade or so of the sixteenth century, it is not unreasonable to suggest that he returned there in those years and brought the boy back with him to Parma. The relationship between the two need not have been as direct as has been suggested (though this would not be the first case of a priest fathering a child); the nickname could have equally arisen through a more distant family connection or even adoption as a protégé.

Therefore the varying forms of the name found in the surviving documentation do not preclude the possibility that they all refer to the same man, and in fact this hypothesis has much else to support it. The spread of dates, from 1471 to a death in 1529 are entirely consistent with the life of a single figure, who would have been almost exactly contemporary with Josquin. With the exception of his stay in Florence they do not overlap but rather fall into a neat succession to give a complete and plausible account of a musician's career around the courts of northern Italy.[40] Moreover the title 'Presbyter' or 'Don' is found consistently in references to him after his appointment at Treviso, suggesting that he took orders around the year 1477. The omission of any title from the papal documents need not be taken too literally as it applies also to many other figures who are known to have taken orders (Josquin, for example) and membership of the clergy was stipulated for admission to the staff of the chapel anyway. The fact that no clerical rank is mentioned in the three documents prior to 1477 is more significant both for reasons of consistency and because the Milanese paylist of 1474 was scrupulous in specifying the status of singers as priests when appropriate.

It is thus possible to propose a tentative biographical outline for the musician Renaldo. His first archival appearance in 1471, taking orders around 1477 and death in 1527 are all compatible with a birthdate of *ca.* 1450. He was a northerner with some connection, either of birth or (more probably) training, with Cambrai, who in his youth moved down to Italy and remained there for the rest of his career. The list of references given above may be read as a chronicle of his progress there that leaves only one important gap, the end of his life after 1493, when he left the papal chapel. However, the disproportionately high number of his compositions in BQ19 raise the suspicion that he may have been personally involved in its compilation. If this were indeed the case, it implies that he was an established composer working in the Romagna in the years around 1518, which accords well with his known geographical orbit and his presumed age and maturity at the time.

*   *   *

One of Renaldo's motets, 'Ave sanctissima Maria', has already been held up as an example of rhetorical form in chapter 3. The remaining seven are for the most part very similar to it in style, with the exception of 'Regina caeli', which on account of its unique foundation on pre-composed material will be considered along with the other motets of that type in chapter 5. Even so, it does not disturb the consistency of its composer's motet output to any significant extent, as apart from its structural peculiarity it still has much in common with the others in terms of musical personality.

This personality can be distinguished by three main features. The first of these is harmonic; like Weerbeke, Renaldo seems to have had a favourite mode, in his case not the Phrygian but a very 'tonal' form of the Lydian that he uses in six out of his eight surviving motets and which anticipates the manner of Palestrina.[41] The second, the smoothness and balance of the melodic writing, is similarly forward looking (again, to Palestrina in particular) and in fact related to the first. Lastly, there is the high degree of overall formal definition which has already been observed in the case of 'Ave sanctissima Maria'. While arising partly out of Renaldo's harmonic and cadential style, the absence of imitative writing and the stronger emphasis on contrast make it quite different from the practice of the later sixteenth-century. Equally distinct is the attention paid to matters of overall form; in the motets of no other composer can the principles of rhetorical construction be so clearly observed.

All of these features are apparent in 'Illuminavit eum' (edited in vol. ii, p.92). Here, however, the music is made to accommodate the exigencies of a composite text that consists of a short (and unidentifiable) introductory passage, the command 'Oremus', and then a prayer for the feast of St. James;[42] these are set in bb.1-27, 28-31 and 31-91 respectively. Although this clearly rules out the rhetorical *exordium - narratio - conclusio* form observed in 'Ave sanctissima Maria', many of its elements are retained so that the kinship of this motet to Renaldo's others is immediately recognizable.

The regular imitation in all voices leading to the full cadence in b.9, for example, is unique in the piece and is clearly recognizable as an *exordium*. The way that this is followed (in bb.9-12) by a duet texture is characteristic of the change from *exordium* to *narratio*, even if it soon gives way to more consistently four-voiced writing. After the chordal 'Oremus' in bb.28-31, there is a short introductory imitative passage in bb.31-6, again rather like an *exordium* but less substantial or self-contained, before the music adopts the answering duet and homophonic techniques associated with the *narratio* through to b.69. The exact repetition of the ensuing bb.69-74 at bb.75-80 are typical of a *conclusio*, after which preparation an unrepetitive passage in triple time actually finishes off the work. In this way it is possible to discern the principles of a rhetorical form in operation even though the overall structure of the music was predetermined externally, by the divisions and proportions of the text.

The second part of the motet, from bb.31 to the *conclusio* beginning in b.69, is not merely a succession of varying textures but is carefully apportioned into three related sections. The first goes from bb.31-42, where the decorated homophony at b.37 expands the material of the previous imitation into a long arch. A similar development occurs in the second, which is made up of two duets (bb.43-54) with the one expanding the middle of the other, though maintaining the same length through the omission of the beginning. Likewise in the third, bb.62-69 are a free variation on bb.54-61, both in the succession of textures and the material itself. Thus in their nearly equal lengths and similar binary divisions all three sections are related though superficially independent; the careful attention to detail recalls that in the same composer's 'Ave sanctissima Maria'.

'Paradisi portas aperuit' (edited in vol. ii, p.150), though attributed to Renaldo in BQ19, bears the name of Lupus in *VEcap 760*. As the manuscripts are of roughly the same date it is not possible to assert any kind of chronological authority of one over the other, but Renaldo's putative personal involvement with the compilation of BQ19 implied by the quantity of his music found within it argues in favour of his authorship over Lupus's. The hypothesis is amply backed by the musical style of the work, which fits perfectly into the almost entirely consistent approach taken by Renaldo to composition while being wholly dissimilar to those works by Lupus preserved in the same source.

In fact it is a fairly typical example of Renaldo's style, though without the superb precision of 'Ave sanctissima Maria' or 'Illuminavit eum'. After the usual regularly imitative *exordium*, the music settles down to the *narratio*, a discursive alternation of duet (starting at bb.11, 27, 41 and 52) and homophonic textures (at bb.21, 31, 47 and 58) whose lengths depend on the words they set and which do not build up into larger subsections. There is a tendency to set the more important parts of the sentence homophonically, with duet treatment given to subordinate phrases; these duets are imitative (except at b.27) and that at b.41 is very Renaldo-like in its use of sequence, which compensates for its being the only one not to use answering repeats of music and text. The homophonic passages are either strictly declamatory (at bb. 21, 34 and 47) or freer (at b.37), the two styles being juxtaposed to provide variety in the flow of the music. Certain of the freer passages act as harmonically conceived preparations for full cadences (at bb.8, 24, 37 and 56): this is typical of Renaldo and indicates the course on which music was set for the later sixteenth century.

Despite the variegated material described above this is not a motet of strong contrasts. The *exordium* has a codetta at b.8 that provides the required link with the subsequent homophonic sections. This in turn is related to the repeats of the duets at bb.11, 27 and 52 which are masked by the addition of the other two voices to create a decorated homophonic texture.

It is interesting to note that the textual repeat at the end is not acted upon at all musically speaking, and in fact there is no obvious *conclusio*. Any possible abruptness at the end is averted, however, by the falling sequence of bb.52-57 which has something of a final character about it in its regularity, harmonic stability and placing after a full cadence; unusually it also presents an imitative texture in more than two voices, however irregularly, and in this way balances the opening *exordium*.

Tonally the piece is similar to 'Illuminavit eum' in its steady dependence on the Lydian mode, although it differs in the inclusion of a short section (bb.24-30) that contains three cadences onto *D*. These provide a harmonic darkening mirrored by the cadence onto *A* in b.46; the principle, as with the textures, is one of gentle and carefully balanced alternation.

The two miniatures 'O Domine Jesu Christe' and 'O Jesu Christe' are remarkably similar. The former (edited as 'O Domine Jesu Christe II' in vol. ii, p.141) is the less pretentious of the two and its plain chordal manner throughout is a far cry from the complex polyphony usually associated with the Netherlands school or for that matter Renaldo's other motets. Its relationship to the *lauda* is nonetheless one of spirit rather than letter, the style deriving more from contemporaneous extra-musical ideals of piety and reform than from the latter's actual musical technique.[43] Unlike most *laude*, the writing is smooth and contrapuntally assured without awkwardnesses, infelicities or 'errors', while the overall form is considered and not just dependent on the line- structure of the text. Its inclusion in a manuscript containing otherwise solely technically complex pieces shows that it was considered worthy of the same band of presumably highly competent singers and its 'advanced' harmonic technique makes it fully compatible with Renaldo's other pieces.

Being purely chordal, the motet lacks the means to articulate a proper rhetorical structure and instead falls into two parts, the second beginning at b.26. The opening phrase (up to b.7) of the first, however, does have some of the quality of an *exordium* in its Cantus arch and closed harmonic structure. The music then proceeds by answering phrases forming an *F-C-F* harmonic symmetry with a codetta at b.23 leading to the striking cadence onto *D*. This coincides with the climax of the text, which is thus highlighted harmonically in addition to a melodic emphasis by a climax onto the high Cantus *B-flat* and a repetition of the words that serves to underline them by stressing their functional position at the end of a section: a similar repetition occurs at the very end. The lack of a *fermata* sign over this cadence need not be overestimated as those that do appear simply acknowledge the punctuation (more specifically the colons) of the text. The remainder of the motet is another local repeat, the Cantus returning from its zenith to the original *F* again, before a short pedal coda matches that at b.23, balancing the *exordium*. Thus while the overall structure is different from those described further above, the principle of a self- sufficient chordal *exordium* followed by answering phrases is still adhered to.

The top line carries all the structural weight in a chordal piece like this, and the way in which its opening contour stands as a germinal cornerstone of the overall arch, while the whole form reflects that of the text exactly, is a tremendous feat of grace and economy. When the limitation of the Cantus to basically three notes (*F-G-A*, with extensions of a note up or down only occasionally), the consistent repeat form, the harmonic control and the balancing of *exordium* and *conclusio* are taken into account, it is hard to escape the conclusion that the standard of craftsmanship is equal to that of any of the longer and more contrapuntally involved motets.

The same applies in general to 'O Jesu Christe' (edited in vol. ii, p.142), which is so similar in text, form and substance. The texture is again chiefly homophonic, with cadences falling alternately on *F* and *C*, as in 'O Domine', and a similar *exordium* quality can be distinguished in the plainness of the block chords in the first four bars. However, the latter part of the motet breaks with the pattern of 'O Domine' by its incorporation of a short duet, the repetition of a

verbal phrase, 'tu es spes mea', and the musical recapitulation of a
texturally distinctive passage (the change from three to four voices in
bb.22-6) with different words at the end (bb.29-33). Thus despite
their similarities, the style of 'O Jesu Christe' is in some ways closer
to that of its composer's longer motets than the melodic ingenuity of
'O Domine'.

        Renaldo's setting of the joyful 'Haec dies' text (edited as 'Haec
dies II' in vol. ii, p.83) to low pitched dense polyphony in the
Phrygian mode serves as a prim reminder that renaissance ideas of
musical 'mood' could be very different to those of today.[44] The
work has other peculiarities besides its tonality, foremost among
which is the passage at 'exultemus' (bb.22-24), whose distinctive
ostinato syncopations under a pedal *E* appear in exactly the same form
in another motet from the Rusconi Codex, Sebastiano Festa's 'Haec
est illa'.[45] The possibility of a coincidence can not be eliminated
completely, but it would be surprising if the two composers, both of
whom are largely represented in this source,[46] were oblivious of the
selection of pieces or ignorant of each other's work. In fact, while the
passage in 'Haec dies' is an integral part of the work, in which
ostinato techniques predominate throughout, it appears as something
of an interpolated curiosity in 'Haec est illa', sounding unlike the rest
of the motet or indeed anything else in what little of Sebastiano's
output survives. The temptation therefore to ascribe the latter's use of
the passage in question to a desire to pay homage to or emulate
Renaldo is very strong, but as ever such internal evidence is not of the
kind that could ever constitute real proof.

        As usual the technique of imitation is only used right at the
beginning, but here its regularity is concealed by its use as a duet
only, whose repeat in the other two voices is masked by free
counterpoints in the originals (bb.6-11). The resultant *exordium*,
though functionally recognizable, has nothing like such a bold outline
as in Renaldo's other pieces, and in fact all the divisions of the music,
usually so crucial to this composer, are rigorously blurred so that one

short section runs into the next in a most atypical fashion. An example of the effort that has gone into this is the local repeat scheme of bb.12-18; while the Bassus line is repeated intact and b.13 = b.17 in all voices, the Cantus has been contrived to accompany the Bassus in parallel tenths for the first few notes, then lag behind (on the *G* in b.13) so as to imitate it in bb.13-14, after which it enters, varied, ahead of the regular Bassus repeat so that the latter seems like an imitation instead of the structural voice. Moreover the Tenor entries of bb.13 and 17 are prefigured by the Altus entry in b.10, linking them to the previous section, and at bb.19-20 the expected repeat of the cadence is interrupted and a neutral link passage inserted to lead into the next section, above which the climactic Cantus entry on the highest note of the piece steals all the attention.

Self-contained as the ensuing 'exultemus' may look, it grows out of the link passage (see the Altus, b.20) and overlaps into the next section (see b.26) where the upper voices play freely over a threefold ostinato in the Tenor and Bassus until the long pedal cadence whose peroration balances the opening. Thus the diverse sections are all subtly linked and varied to give the impression of continuous organic flow. The dependence of even the ostinato 'exultemus' section on what comes before and after is one of the reasons for the supposition earlier that if there were a connection between this and the identical music in Sebastiano Festa's 'Haec est illa', this would be the original rather than the latter, where the passage is interpolated *en bloc* into a work in a clearly sectional style.

Lastly, mention should be made of the melodic nature of the top voice, which describes a succession of rising arches whose extremes are governed by the important notes of the mode, *E*, *A* and *C*, with very few intervallic leaps (an important exception is the climactic gesture in b.20). This is in contrast to the other voices, which display more obviously thematic or harmonic qualities, imitation/ostinato and wide intervals being very common; it might in fact be appropriate to consider this motet as being in a treble dominated song style brought up to date by the handling of the lower voices.

The peculiar technique of this piece has undergone considerable scrutiny because it is so different from that of Renaldo's others in this medium. Even so, there are similarities in certain ways; the use of local repeat forms is reminiscent of 'O Domine' and the control of cumulative melodic arches like both this and the homophonic parts of 'Ave sanctissima Maria'. Renaldo stands as the most perfect exemplar of the new structural clarity and regularity, whose emphasis on proportion and balance invites comparison with the architecture of Brunelleschi as well as the classicism implicit in the following of rhetorical models. In 'Haec dies', while he may have been experimenting with techniques outside of what would seem to be his normal and highly original vocabulary, his competence and care are sufficiently in evidence to allay any suspicion that the work may be misattributed on stylistic grounds.

Rather different too is the motet 'Tristitia vestra' attributed to a Renaldo in FP27 (and edited in vol. ii, p.192), though again there is good reason to suppose it is indeed by the same composer. It is in fact in a very similar style to his first Mass in BQ19[47] in terms of material and handling of texture, to the extent that bb.47-56 work out the same idea as bb.105-113 of the 'Gloria'. A comparison of the melodic shapes, harmonic direction and cadence types with those of the 'Kyrie eleison' also reveals a great deal in common, so that it seems reasonable to assume the same author at work, given the identical attribution in two sources so close in time and geographical origin. All the same, the piece shows Renaldo at his most insecure and old-fashioned (see for example the contrapuntal sham at the beginning), and it may be that the earlier date of FP27 is significant in that it preserves a less mature work. It might even be conjectured that it came from 1482-3, when Renaldo was *maestro di cappella* in the SS. Annunziata in Florence, but it is of course impossible to confirm this without further evidence.

Traces of the style of the BQ19 motets are discernible here, but to nothing like the same extent. The opening motif is strikingly different, but the unusual use of undiminished time indicates an intention of spaciousness rather than liveliness. The ensuing section is recognizable as an *exordium*, but it actually inverts the usual harmonic procedure. Instead of letting the successive imitative entries drift towards another centre and then correcting them by means of a cadential passage to round off the section and establish the mode, he checks the harmony by a full tonic cadence (in b.9) before the fourth voice has even entered; this final entry is then used to move to a cadence on *D* in b.14. The formal cadence in the middle is thus glossed over by the use of the same material, regular two-bar phrase structure and steady increase in the number of voices, and a weaker 'ouvert' cadence is reached at the end. The *narratio* is more orthodox; the fleeting imitative passage at b.31 is unusual but its brevity and stretto style clearly distinguish it from the more spacious imitation typical of *exordium* sections.

The *conclusio* sets the final 'alleluia' and is defined musically by the sequence in the Bassus starting at b.56. That this sequence should be camouflaged by continual variation of the upper voices is typical of the structural oddity that characterizes the *exordium* as well; nevertheless the same principles are at work here, if in a less mature way, as in the motets from BQ19 alongside which 'Tristitia vestra' is an interesting addition to the canon of Renaldo's works.

Finally, mention should be made of one more piece in FP27, the anonymous 'O admirabile comertium' [sic] on f.8v.-9r. (edited in vol. ii, p.137), which shares many of the features of the motets examined above. Points of similarity are the smooth and clearly tonal harmony, unusual in this source (see the cadences in bb.5-6, 10-11, 14-16, 33-35 and at the end), the purposeful sectionalization of the music and the style and placing of the duet pair (see b.23ff.). More specifically, the opening is almost identical to that of his 'O Domine Jesu Christe' (see vol. ii, p.141, bb.1-7); the falling scale idea at the start of the *conclusio* is similar to the equivalent passage in 'Illuminavit eum' (at b.69ff.), as are the extended ending and almost identical last chords; bb.33-4 are unusual and notably similiar again to 'Illuminavit eum' (bb.39-40); and bb.19-23 are reminiscent of bb.18-21 of the 'Sanctus' of the Mass mentioned above. Unequivocal establishment of authorship is a historical, not a stylistic matter, but the inclusion of the firmly attributed 'Tristitia vestra' in the same manuscript at least raises the possibility that 'O admirabile comertium' may be Renaldo's.

*   *   *

There are two other pieces from BQ19 that are written in a comparable general style, though without the specific correspondances of detail manifest in 'O admirabile comertium'. Though their authorship is uncertain - one bears a deliberately oblique ascription (to be discussed below) while the other is anonymous - there are no grounds, stylistic or otherwise, for proposing Renaldo as the composer. Nevertheless, they are best taken together with his work as similar qualities of clear tonality and form distinguish them from the other motets in these sources.

The most obvious example of this is the 'Circumdederunt me' (edited in vol. ii, p.58) by a composer conventionally referred to as 'Remi'. This name is latent in a rebus attribution in BQ19 taking the form of the two notes *re-mi*,[48] which is unique and unidentifiable with any known figure. It may well not represent an exact name in the correct orthography anyway and so is of little assistance in establishing even the nationality of the composer it is meant to represent; therefore to all intents and purposes the work it graces remains anonymous and has to be considered as such.[49]

The overall strucure is governed by the layout of the text, which consists of the first four verses of Psalm 94 with a refrain at either end and in the middle, between verses two and three. This pattern suggests an association with the form of Invitatory, in which an Antiphon is reiterated between the successive verses of Psalm 94.[50] However, since only the first four verses are used and the refrain is an Introit rather than an Antiphon, it would appear that the present text is not a liturgically genuine Invitatory, although it may have used the form as a model and served a similar introductory function.

Not only are there no direct liturgical connections between the text of the refrain and the psalm verse, but the morbid gloom of the former could hardly stand in greater contrast to the exultation of the 'Venite'. The somewhat mannered effect resulting from their juxtaposition is something of which the mysterious composer was surely aware, as his setting not only takes advantage of the disparate elements but also succeeds in reconciling them into a musical whole.

The refrain is musically distinguished from the remainder by a predominantly homophonic texture. Its three statements become progressively shorter (16bb. through 11bb. to 7bb.) and are related additionally by tonality (each contains a structurally important cadence on D, in bb.6, 54 and 91; such cadences are found nowhere else in the piece), the literal repeat of a final phrase (bb.85-91 = bb.49-54) and other common material (the Cantus in bb.44-49 paraphrases its own bb.1-11). The quotation of a previous passage right at the end is typical of a *conclusio*, much as the distinct opening chordal section is a typical *exordium*. Moreover the striking final cadence onto D, after a motet solidly in F, is made less unexpected by repetition and is also anticipated by the harmonies of the opening phrase, which in effect contains in microcosm the tonal movement of the entire piece. The eccentricity of the ending on D, reflecting the peculiar duality of the text, is thus firmly integrated into the main body of the motet.

The two enclosed episodes are very different from the surrounding refrain. The first (bb.19-43) is the more straightforward, consisting of antiphonal voice-pairing with three bars of homophony in bb.32-4 to break up the texture. Before this point (bb.19-31), a pleasing polarity is set up in the way that the lower duets are non-imitative and the upper ones canonic; after it, the previous canonic melody is spun into an overlapping, but basically twin duet texture. The same developmental principle can be seen at work in the evolution of this idea from bb.27-29.

Development plays an even greater part in the curious second episode. With no textual cue, bb.60-61 are repeated as bb.65-66 and extended and from there onwards there is a notable lack of the clear cadences that grace the rest of the piece. The coordinating effect of the two exceptionally on A (bb.76 and 82) is minimized by the harmonization of the first with an F in the bass, while another cadence on F is likewise less conspicuous by harmonization by a low D, and all are concealed under overlapping upper voices. The texture is non-imitative and depends on flashes of sequence or linked voices for its continuity, along with the Cantus paraphrase of bb.74- 9 in bb.80-85, with free lower voices.

The very opening of this episode (bb.55-9) is of particular interest. The structural voice is clearly the Tenor, around whose monotone C the others are merely decorative. The unusual rising triad to this note (bb.55-6, emphasized by imitation in the Cantus) identifies the passage as a reference to the fifth psalm tone, whose intonation it is. The reason for this quotation, which is completely isolated (unless the fall of a minor third to the *finalis* in the tone is considered the inspiration behind the overall tonal movement from F to D in the motet), is not clear. The fifth tone matches the mode of the 'Circumdederunt me' Introit melody,[51] but there are no other references to chant material in the motet. It is notable all the same that the monotone C was prepared in the first duet section (Tenor bb.19-20 and again bb.26-7), just as the final D cadence was in the first two refrains.

While the bright tonality and and textural alternation are

reminiscent of Renaldo, 'Circumdederunt me' stands out by its peculiarly strong sense of organic development and unity. Quite how the composer came to adopt such a violently contrasting textual pastiche and why he chose to incorporate an isolated and unsolicited reference to a psalm tone into his setting of it are impossible to determine at present. However his binding together of this diversity and acknowledgement of it in his strange tonal movement are a fascinating reflection of the new preoccupation with the relationship of words and music in the early 1500s.

The genuinely anonymous composer of 'Hodie completi sunt' (edited in vol. ii, p.87) displays a similar concern for overall structure even though his approach is less sophisticated. He sets the Antiphon text as a series of well articulated sections that fall into the broad shape of *exordium - narratio - conclusio*, into which the 'alleluia' refrains are interpolated as discussed earlier. Although these 'alleluia' passages use similar material and mirror the original plainsong there are no other references to the Antiphon structure or to the melody itself. The main peculiarity of the work is the text setting which is subject to drastic variations of speed whereby the duet of bb.21-27 get through more words than the entire preceding part of the motet in a few bars of hectic syllabic writing. In fact, in bb.21-47 the fragmentation of the text and its matching to the succession of musical textures does seem a little clumsy and lacking in the facility evident in the other motets in this style: it might be expected that bb.21-27 be divided up, and the tiny duet at bb.44-47 seems gratuitous. It is inconceivable that the given text is not the original in view of the details of declamation and the 'alleluia' refrain, so that the incongruity must be put down to inexperience on the part of the composer.

The sectional structure is very clear and founded on the text, albeit erratically, and there are no traces of any attempts to balance out the lengths of the longer formal units. Each section ends on a full cadence, all with one exception on *G*: without any ambitions to emulate the tonal variety occasionally found elsewhere in BQ19 all

distinctions are made texturally. The *exordium* (bb.1-13) is typically
homophonic and based on a modal Cantus arch, its only odd feature
being the arpeggiated chord on 'completi sunt', reminiscent of the
beginning of the anonymous 'Benedicta mater matris' (see below)
though probably not related.   The succession of contrasts in the
narratio has already received comment but it is worth stressing the
free use of imitation here as a generator of duets rarely at perfect
intervals, and at bb.35-7 in a full texture with four different entries on
four different pitches. A similar approach can be seen too in bb.30-
32, where only the rhythm is imitated in the Altus; the idea is itself
derived from the previous duet.   This passage also shows an
interesting concern for balancing pitches around the *finalis*, as the
octave leap in the Cantus (b.31) is totally uncalled for by any other
consideration. Contrapuntally, g'-f' on '-tum' would be just as good
and stricter imitation to boot but it is renounced in favour of the high
d'', presumably for the sake of a stronger fall onto the cadence in
b.35, whose Cantus g' is thus circumscribed equally above and below.

The *conclusio* balances the *exordium* in its homophony and its
relapse into decorative cadential figuration at the end is cleverly
ordered by a motivic repeat in the Cantus. The very last part of the
motet is of course the 'alleluia' which builds on and varies the
imitation between the Altus and Cantus in bb.14-17 by altering the
accompaniments and adding a new cadential section instead of
extending the first idea as an ostinato (see the Tenor, b.18).   The
notable thing here is the reiteration of something that had already been
emphasized by inclusion as part of a previous repetition scheme, a
device used also in Hutinet's 'Peccantem' (see below). Another odd
feature is the strange clef disposition, which leaves the Cantus high
above the evenly ranged lower voices. This is also a feature of other
motets (e.g. Sebastiano Festa's 'Haec est illa', or Bruhier's 'Ave
caelorum regina' in BQ20) and seems of peripheral importance
anyway; certainly there are no grounds for associating this rather
insecure piece with either of the above composers.

Hutinet

Indications that Hutinet (more commonly known as Barra) may have spent some time in Italy in the early sixteenth century come from the source distribution of his works, even though all archival information concerning him links him with the Sainte-Chappelle in Paris.[52] Rifkin characterizes his style as 'built predominantly on short, frequently imitative duets, often overlapped to produce a full voiced texture',[53] which serves as an exact description of the opening of 'Peccantem me quotidie' (edited in vol. ii, p.152) and typifies one aspect of the structure of the piece. In terms of overall construction it is interesting to note that this duet technique occupies the first half of the motet only (up to b.36) at which point a cadence on the as yet uncharted tonal area of *G* opens up a new section based wholly on local repeats, where the text is set much more quickly and with fewer repetitions.

The two halves thus demarcated are not connected merely by their mutual dependence on binary repeats, (either à4 or as alternating duets), but also by the fact that their final passages are based on the same material, as a comparison of bb.49-51 with bb.31-33 makes clear. This structurally important passage is 'underlined' on its first appearance by insistent treatment of its Cantus melody over the preceding 10 bars, starting in the Bassus at b.21 and followed by a repeat in the Altus in b.25, a technique similar to that used in 'Hodie completi sunt'.

The extreme regularity of structure, the frequent melodic repetitions in the upper sounding voice (see for example the derivation of bb.11-13 from bb.9-11) and the alternation of homophonic or imitative duet textures are indicative of a simplistically musical approach usually considered to be typically French.[54] Certainly the style is at odds with the more subtle integration of words and music characteristic of Renaldo, who although apparently a northerner by birth seems to have spent all his creative life in Italy. The lack of any formal opening section is also striking, and together with the emphasis on closed form and musically stressed repeats as shown above is symptomatic of a marked difference of formal procedure discernible in other French pieces such as Bruhier's 'Vivite felices'.[55]

Pinarol

Although unique, the ascription of a piece in FP27 to one 'Jo. de Pinarol' does not relegate it to the same effective anonymity as Remi's 'Circumdederunt me'. The composer can be identified with Johannes de Pinarol (1467-*ca.*1536), known from archival records to have been organist in Brescia cathedral in 1507 and 1514-15.[56] In addition, the piece also appears in Petrucci's *Motetti A* of 1502[57] (from where it was probably copied into FP27), so that an activity in northern Italy in the decades around 1500 can be reasonably assumed.

'Surge propera' (edited in vol. ii, p.186) is a setting of a *Canticum canticorum* text and thus immediately invites comparison with those by Weerbeke in the same source. In fact, though highly individual, Pinarol's style is closest to that of the Fleming in its sectional structure, Cantus-Tenor part-hierarchy (see for instance bb.33-43) and exploitation of melody for its own sake rather than as a generator of counterpoint. It differs, however, in the use of the Mixolydian mode in a brazenly tonal way and in its extraordinarily flamboyant sense of drama, which alone makes it one of the outstanding pieces of its time.

Though the overall form is not strictly rhetorical, the elements are plain to see; an imitative *exordium* in bb.1-14 (which does not, however, establish the mode), a *narratio* of alternating duet and full textures, and a *conclusio* recalling previous material (though in some ways it is one of the most original parts of the piece).

The opening expresses the idea of 'Surge' by a rising fourth which itself proceeds by ascending repetitions in each voice, the hugely impressive dramatic effect being comparable to that of Vittoria's famous 'O quam gloriosum' opening of nearly a century later. The duets of the ensuing *narratio* all share a clarity of outline and phrasing that imbues each with a pronounced and individual character. This directness has its parallel in the functional harmonies of the full sections; the playful postponement of the cadence in b.30 (echoed at the end of the motet) and the shift to *D* in bb.44-7 are examples of purely harmonic manipulation quite novel in the context of fifteenth-century music. The most striking passage comes near the end, where the chords at b.89 even have a decidedly eighteenth-century tonic-dominant flavour to them.

It is regrettable that more of Pinarol's work has not come down to us, in view of the originality and invention of this one piece. Even more than Weerbeke, he seems to embody all that was new in the motet of his time in his formal clarity and drama. The way that he also manages to capture the extroversion of contemporaneous Italian secular music as well as its emphasis on melody and functional harmony results in a curious synthesis that, like Weerbeke's 'Ibo mihi', was to have less effect on subsequent motet-writing than on the early madrigal.

Sebastiano Festa

The biography of Sebastiano Festa is problematical, not because such meagre documentation as exists is contradictory - on the contrary it is all neatly consistent - but because the few sketches of his life written to date are dogged by unsubstantiated evidence and unfamiliarity with his music. Thus Alexander Main gives the date of his birth as *ca.*1495 and that of his death as 31 July 1524 without leaving any clues as to where he got the dates from;[58] the items listed in his bibliography claim at best that the only document pertaining to Sebastiano is a letter from the eight year old Giulia Gonzaga to her cousin, the Duke of Mantua, of 13 October 1520.[59] The year of death is also cited by Prizer in a publication conspicuous by its absence from Main's bibliography[60] but not the exact date so that Main cannot have been merely quoting him; a document must exist somewhere but has so far proved untraceable. Even if this is taken for granted the date of birth must still be a guess, as both writers qualify their dates with a *ca.*, and Prizer opts for one in 1485, ten years before Main. In view of Sebastiano's probable involvement with the compilation of BQ19, given his high representation there, the earlier date seems preferable as it is unlikely that a young man barely turned twenty years old would have been granted such influence over the contents of a manuscript. The theory proposed by Lowinsky,[61] that Costanzo Festa was the compiler and included his namesake through nepotism is also hard to credit as it assumes that the two were actually related (which is yet to be proven) and is closely linked with the idea that the codex originated in France (roundly refuted by Perkins[62]).

His high representation in the codex is relative, being limited to three motets, out of only four that he is known to have composed. 'Angele Dei' is unique to BQ19, while 'Haec est illa' can be found in one other source with no attribution (*ModE L.11.8*) and 'In illo tempore' appears in an Antico print (*1521[5]*) under Sebastiano's name, as well as twice in a single manuscript partbook (BudOS 23) of about 1550, attributed first to Costanzo Festa (no.4) and then to Sebastiano (no.109).[63] The fourth motet, 'Virgo gloriosa' is found in in another Bolognese source, *I-Bc* Q20, reinforcing the case for Sebastiano's activity in northern Italy. Although the date of *ca.*1530 proposed for this manuscript is after his death and the style is somewhat different, certain details indicate the same mind at work and there is nothing to point to Costanzo Festa instead, who would be the prime candidate if the piece were misattributed.

The letter of Giulia Gonzaga is important because, as Lowinsky points out, it shows that Sebastiano was connected with the circle around Pope Leo X in Rome via Ottoboni Fieschi, whose official title as Bishop of Mondovi from 1519-22 disguises the fact that he never set foot in the place but resided instead in the capital as Pronotarius, then assistant to the Pope. Prominent in this entourage was the secretary, later cardinal, Pietro Bembo, whose enormous influence on literary thought is well known[64] and whose enthusiasm for Petrarch and the Tuscan language was one of the distinguishing features of the court. It is no accident then that five of Sebastiano's eleven secular pieces are Petrarch settings, and the originality and influence of these even beyond their composer's short lifetime is now an acknowledged fact.[65] This connection does not argue against his activity in northern Italy however, as Ottoboni was the brother of Francesca Fieschi, Giulia's mother, and so a thorough acquaintance with the house of Gonzaga is one of the points upon which Lowinsky, Perkins and other writers are for once in full accord.

All this has little bearing on Sebastiano's putative compilation of BQ19. Rubsamen's theory that he copied it out himself in Rome[66] has its basis in the same assertions of Lowinsky that were so convincingly undermined by Perkins and later Crawford. The point is that recognition of his position as a member of a pro-Italian avant-garde is crucial to an understanding of his motets, which are otherwise quite extraordinary pieces of work. 'Haec est illa' and 'In illo tempore' are strikingly alike in compositional technique and equally different from anything in BQ19 or possibly the entire early sixteenth century motet repertory, not because they are in any direct way connected with the *lauda* as might be expected (and as Jeppesen suggests for 'Angele Dei'[67]), but on account of various contrapuntal peculiarities and an approach to melody that represents a genuine experiment in the reconciliation of Italian monody with the rigours expected of the motet.[68]

'In illo tempore' (edited in vol. ii, p.102) is a showcase for one of the more unusual aspects of the composer's style, that of his aversion to normal cadential progressions. This peculiarity, while manifest in some more spectacular eccentricities in 'Haec est illa' in fact reaches its apotheosis here, as there turn out to be no cadences whatsoever in the strict sense,[69] closes being arranged by progressions of chords rather than melodies. The bizarre interrupted close at b.41, repeated eight bars later at the end as part of a classic *conclusio* scheme, seems to cock a snook at the very idea of a cadence, although there is a certain modal logic to it which will be discussed in due course.

The first two thirds of the motet are composed entirely of regular imitation, and the last of simple chordal homophony which in its repetitive nature comprises the *conclusio*; the unusually generous length, the detachment and style are exactly as in 'Haec est illa', and also like this piece it has a clearly defined *exordium* marked off by a *fermata* sign, though this is almost inevitable due to the introductory nature of the 'In illo tempore' textual rubric. Nevertheless it is unified with the following *narratio* in an astonishingly comprehensive way. With a few exceptions of detail the voices are in fact strictly canonically derived from the Cantus throughout until the entries in b.26, providing a framework of great regularity as even the same order of entries is maintained until just before the end. This is modestly disguised by a few rhythmic variations and in particular the Cantus line at b.20 which is purely decorative and superfluous to the structure other than covering over a link between two distinct ideas in the canon. Far from seeming selfconsciously learned this canonic procedure generates an exceptionally light, tripping texture devoid of any real contrapuntal intrigue, which is handled with consummate grace. It should be noted too that each successive idea is a variation on the last (see the entries at bb.1, 9, 15 and even, though less directly, 21), so that the resulting unity quite compensates for the formal detachment of the *exordium*.

The homophony at b.30 is made up of a simply harmonized melodic arch in the first phrase, matched by a falling fifth in the second that is repeated in the third, the whole being a natural closed progression based on a single melodic line in four- and six-bar phrases.[70] The peculiar *B-flat* closes at bb.41 and 49, while apparently (and presumably consciously) flouting the expected progressions, are in fact the logical outcome of the modality of the piece as a whole: they match the opening entries and the close in b.8, where a *B-flat* tonality is unequivocally established before the gradual transition to *F* that takes place in the *narratio*.

All in all this is a most original motet, in its use of melody (which completely governs the homophonic section and is treated *per se* rather than as a generator of a contrapuntal texture in the opening quasi-canons, being shown off to best advantage by the arrangement of lines into pairs with only partial overlaps) and rhythm (as in 'Haec est illa' a wide range of values is employed, and the setting of 'circumcideretur' at bb.15-17 is particularly striking). None of these features is apparent even in Sebastiano's secular works, and so must be considered his exclusive contribution to the motet form.

'Haec est illa' (edited in vol. ii, p.85) shares some of the oddities of 'In illo tempore' but not its internal consistency of style, and there is even a temptation to charge the less orthodox passages with incompetence. However they all work satisfactorily enough and betray none of the shortwindedness often found in less inspired writing, seeming instead symptomatic of a new approach to the craft of setting a text.

The music falls into a regular pattern of sectional lengths, dividing into units of 15, 15, 12, 12, 15 and 6 bars successively. The exactitude of these figures indicate that the resultant balanced structure is due to contrivance as much as chance or a subconscious feeling for proportional propriety, and coincides with the fact that this is the only setting of metrical verse among these motets from BQ19. The relationship between these two phenomena is curiously indirect, and best demonstrated schematically as follows:

Haec est illa dulcis rosa,		15bb.
Pulchra, nimis, et formosa,	(7.5bb.)	
Qui transitis inclinate.	(7.5bb.)	15bb.
Haec est vera gratiosa,	(6bb.)	
Super omnis speciosa,	(6bb.)	12bb.
(" " ")	(6bb.)	
(" " ")	(6bb.)	12bb.
Illa ergo salutate.	(7.5bb.)	
(" " ")	(7.5bb.)	15bb.
(" " ")		6bb.

The verbal repeats are of course Festa's and not part of the unidentified Marian eulogy[71] that furnishes the poetry, and their arrangement is of some interest. If they are discounted, it becomes clear that the first and last lines are set to fifteen bar sections and the intervening ones to equal halves of fifteen or twelve bar sections. This has an obvious symmetry, where the change from fifteen to twelve bar sections is calculated to coincide with the start of the new stanza, and can be associated with the common technique of accelerating the music as it proceeds, noted also in Renaldo's 'Ave sanctissima Maria'. Disturbing this symmetry by repeating line five has a twofold purpose. The first is to take advantage of the words 'Super omnis speciosa', which provide the greatest scope for expressive musical setting, and the second concerns the reconciliation of the closed verse form with the open rhetorical progression. The *exordium* is clearly marked off as the first fifteen bars by the *fermata* sign over its last chord, and the *conclusio* is equally clear as the homophonic treatment of the last line (starting at b.54). However the length of this latter, similar to the end of 'In illo tempore', makes it almost a separate item, so that the repeat of line five is actually a *conclusio* section to the main body of the piece before this discrete epilogue. The lack of any comparable passage in 'In illo tempore' is easily explicable as the main part is so relatively small and also highly unified (see above). The combination of this *narratio* function with the expressive qualities of the line in question is a good example of a composer's response to the formal possibilities of a text.

As in 'In illo tempore' the rhythm is unusually flexible, fusae appearing in spite of a prevailing motion in *breves*, with many longer notes coming as a matter of course in each voice. Harmonically, there is only one *bona fide* cadence in the whole piece (at b.42), and one of the alternatives in particular merits special attention. The close in bb.14-15 is contrapuntally outrageous, a travesty of the traditional format, and given Sebastiano's previously noted aversion to cadences and alignment with an Italian avant-garde may well be a wry send-up of the theoretical rules handed down from generation to generation of *oltremontani*. It is certainly difficult to take it wholly seriously in spite of a certain charm in the Altus line, but the charge of incompetence is not in the least valid: an incompetent may have set down dull imitations of received ideas, but such originality as this surely stems from a deliberate desire to experiment.

The scarcity of cadences in the sense approved by Tinctoris does not mean that this is seamless music, merely that the means of arriving at a given resting place are not those usually prescribed, and those at bb.15, 30, 54 and 74 make their points very clearly. However the cultivation of an alternative cadential style also leads to a complete break with the modal unity found elsewhere in BQ19 ('In illo tempore' being one of the least representative in this respect). It is well nigh impossible to assign this piece a mode, though the beginning and end do roughly conform to the Mixolydian, as it proceeds rather as a controlled succession of different tonalities.

The relationship of bb.31-34 to bb.21-24 of Renaldo's 'Haec

dies' has already been observed and it should be further noted that advantage is taken here of the distinctive texture to underscore the first line of the second stanza, which it sets. There is no textual rationale behind this correspondance, although the two phrases ('Haec est vera gratiosa' and 'exultemus') are not contradictory in mood. The contention that Sebastiano may have stolen the passage from Renaldo is supported by the selfconscious and even witty spirit of this work, within which a quotation would be entirely appropriate. In terms of integration, the ostinato device spills over into the next section, the Tenor and Bassus making a powerful entry below the Cantus and Altus in b.36 so that for a time the texture is polarized between the two ideas, an event rare and remarkable in this repertory. Novel too is the way that the long range imitation of the Tenor and Cantus in bb.42-52 is harmonized in strongly differentiated ways, giving the local repeat a sense of progression without masking its identity (as Renaldo does in 'Haec dies', bb.12-18).

The assertive originality of this and 'In illo tempore' stand in contrast to the same composer's 'Angele Dei' (edited in *JeppIS*, ii, p.184). It is ironic that both *MGG*[72] and *LowMC*[73] should reproduce facsimiles of it and that Jeppesen edited it from BQ19 in his *Italia Sacra Musica* series,[74] as it was neither the original opening of the codex (see chapter 1), by virtue of which supposition it gained all the attention, nor is it the most interesting example of Sebastiano's style; it is presumably the work upon which the generally held idea that he was primarily a composer of light secular music was founded. In the absence of the originality of its companions its chief attraction lies in the cheery tunefulness that it still shares with them and if any of the three were to be selected as frontispieces to a collection (even though this was not the original intention) it would have to be this one; solid workmanship, however innocuous, is a safer bet at such a point than experiment and an individuality that must have raised a few eyebrows at the time.

The mode is the old-fashioned Dorian, which only becomes

evident in the latter part, as the opening is firmly in *A*. The use of one of the old modes is characteristic of Sebastiano (see 'In illo tempore') and quite unlike the harmonic practice of, say, Renaldo. The ambiguity is also typical, being evident in both the other pieces, but here is toned down after the beginning so that nearly all the cadences (formed for once in the usual manner) in fact fall on *D* except for the ends of the homophonic phrases.

Overall the motet is composed of two polyphonic sections of nearly exactly equal length (bb.1-21 and 36-55), alternating with two barely decorated chordal sections, the first (bb.22-35) about half the length of the second (b.55-end), though none of these proportions are contrived exactly. The opening has the rigorous character of an *exordium*, the ten bar duet in the lower voices being repeated exactly in the upper with the join veiled by a decorative prolongation of the lower pair that also serves to maintain the harmonic ambiguity, returning the music to *A* after a cadence in *D* (bb.11-12). Similar duet *exordia* can be found in Renaldo's 'Haec dies', Hutinet's 'Peccantem' and Lupus's 'In convertendo'. Of interest is the way that the long melodies are sustained by varied internal repetition, visible in the paraphrase in bb.6-10 of the Bassus's own bb.3-6, a technique not uncommon elsewhere. Even more subtle is the second polyphonic section, which is (most unusually) predominantly for three voices at a time. The rather run-of-the-mill Tenor line at bb.35-38 is taken up and varied in the Altus (bb.39-44) and the latter part of this again in the Tenor (bb.44-47). Meanwhile the entire arch of the counterpoint to it (first heard in the Bassus in bb.42-7) becomes the subject of long-range imitation (see the Altus b.45 and Cantus b.49), this overlapping being very reminiscent of the work of Symon Ferrariensis (see chapter 6). The section also features the only actual cadence on *A* in the piece, thus matching the tonality of the beginning and reinforcing the the textural alternation with a tonal one as well.

In contrast to the spacious text-setting of the polyphony, the homophony is chordal and syllabic with little decoration, though

Sebastiano is careful to arrange a brief codetta (bb.77-80) before the long final pedal coda to stress the new function of the passage as the *conclusio*. These deviancies from the norm are still well within the bounds of convention and the work seems generally pedestrian compared to the extraordinary qualities of its stablemates.

Although Sebastiano's other surviving motet, 'Virgo gloriosa' (edited in vol. ii, p.204) is not included in BQ19[75] it is worth comparing it to the three that are, as it is in many ways a retraction of the extreme position taken in 'In illo tempore' and 'Haec est illa'. It is a typical example of the more expansive sixteenth-century motet represented in BQ20 (and not at all short and simple as implied by Rubsamen[76]), featuring alternating duet and tutti sections, normal cadential procedures, consistent imitation and a triple time section at the end. It would be easy to pass it off as the work of another composer, notwithstanding the firm attribution, were it not for a few details with an oddly familiar ring to them. Not only are the duet sections consistently melodic and in their way representative of the compromise between melody and counterpoint mentioned above, but there are other subtle features like the tripping rhythms of 'preciosissima' (Tenor and Bassus, bb.40-41) or 'Deus qui beatam' (Cantus and Altus, bb.119-21) which recall the 'circumcideretur' of 'In illo tempore' (bb.16-20), or the fussy cadence formations in bb.11, 39-40 and 102 which are likewise reminiscent of, for example, b.48 of 'Haec est illa'. These features are rare enough to be distinctive and it is odd to note such correspondances between two works so obviously diverse in conception.

Lupus

The case of the composer Lupus is altogether different from that of Sebastiano Festa. While he has been successfully unravelled from the tangled threads of his near namesakes it is in the biographically negative sense that 'his identity has been clearly established on the basis of works ascribed to him in prints or manuscripts of the first half of the sixteenth century, but as yet we have not discovered any archival documents concerning him'.[77] The most hopeful avenue suggested is an identity with the Venetian singer Pietro Lupato, which not only has the testimony of a ceremonial motet to support it but also fits in with the distribution of his works in North Italian sources: unfortunately it can not be proved.

In *Grove*, it is proposed that 'the earliest source of his works, the so-called Medici Codex of 1518 and his style suggest that he may have been a northerner'.[78] Considering that BQ19 is contemporary with the Medici Codex, if not earlier, and contains five attributions to Lupus as opposed to one, the first part of the argument loses its force, especially as the northern provenance of the Medici Codex is open to dispute anyway. The point about style is harder to challenge, as a conservative Netherlandish vein runs through all five of his motets included in BQ19. Of these, two are single movements and three are more extended settings, which will be considered separately in chapter 6.

'Miserere...infirmus' (edited in vol. ii, p.118) is exceptional as the only essay for six voices among these lesser-known pieces from BQ19, although such works are to be found elsewhere in the manuscript by more established composers such as Mouton.[79] In Lupus's case, the anticipation of the textures of the later part of the sixteenth century is offset by the thickness of the writing, the low register and above all the recourse to the by now outmoded *tempus perfectum*, which all seem to nod back to the times of Ockeghem and Tinctoris. Nevertheless in most other respects the music is in the style of Lupus's own generation despite the distorting anachronisms. The low range is also a direct response to the intense penitential character of the text, the second verse of the first Penitential Psalm. In his efforts to express it adequately Lupus has excelled himself to produce something of a lugubrious Gothic monstrosity, though the music is not without charm as the gloomy originality of its conception is tempered by a certain lightness of touch, as will be shown below.

This is not the composer's only work for six voices, but is presumably among the earliest if the accepted dates of his activity are taken for granted. All the same it bears no trace of the weaknesses criticized in other early works[80] and the crowded texture is well handled within the self-imposed restraints of the low range, though most of the peculiarities of the piece are traceable to the decision to use six voices and the problems this entails. As is typical in this period the use of *tempus perfectum* goes hand in hand with a stately metrical lilt quite different from the complexity of the rhythms used by the generation of composers who used to write predominantly in this metre (see also Symon Ferrarensis's 'Maria ergo' on p.211ff. in chapter 6, or Coppini's 'Hodie nobis'[81] for like examples). It is the resultant regularity of phrase and structure that is responsible for a good measure of the clarity mentioned above and the relief of the dense texture.

The piece is in fact entirely fashioned as a series of regularly spaced ostinati, a procedure evident right from the start where the two-bar opening idea enters in every bar up to b.8. At b.9 a new two bar ostinato takes over, first heard in the Altus. Its accompaniments in the Cantus I and II parts (bb.9 and 10 respectively) reappear on each statement, strengthening the sense of regular repeat; the first of these does not even require transposition when the main idea is transposed to *E*. In fact, bb.13-14, 17-18 and 19-20 are virtually identical with the voices exchanged, an intensity of repetition unusual in music of this type but perhaps brought on by Lupus's inexperience in handling so many voices. He does break up the monotony by the omission, in bb.15-16, of the main idea and the accompaniment from the Cantus I at b.10, maintaining continuity by the retention of the two bar phrase unit and the admirably wily introduction of another past element (from the Cantus II at b.9, displaced by a *minima*) in the Cantus I, unsettling the rhythmic rigidity. A new ostinato is continued through bb.21-24 and from bb.25-30 the technique is taken to its extreme as the two Cantus parts and the Bassus I are in fact strictly canonic, this idea being carried through, buried in the Tenor and Bassus II under four free voices after b.31, until the ostinato principle is summed up in a one bar exchange between the Bassus parts (bb.34-35) as a fitting conclusion to the work.

The use of these two bar ostinati building up into sections of simple proportional length (8, 12, 4, 6, 4 and 2bb. successively) is not merely a way of cheating on the task of composing fresh material in a difficult and complex medium. It also does much to compensate for the dense texture, although this is additionally alleviated by a goodly amount of four voiced writing, especially in the middle, and contributes greatly to the effect of the piece.

The few words of the text are strung out comfortably over this abstract musical frame, whose finer details of rhythm have been devised especially for it, and in this sense the work is quite progressive. However it is interesting to note that in the triple ostinato section (bb.9-20) it is impossible to fit the same words to the same fragment of the ostinato when it comes round (and there is certainly no attempt to do this in the source underlay) so that music and words pursue their own independent logics in a way that is surprisingly medieval considering the expressive leanings of the piece. The opening theme is of course reminiscent of Josquin's famous setting of the same words (though as part of a different text). Since the latter seems to have originated in Ferrara in 1502-3,[82] it is more than likely that Lupus would have known it and used the idea as a conscious reference.[83]

'Miserere...tribulor' (edited in vol. ii, p.122) is also for more than four voices and has a similar textual mood to its counterpart. The oppressive tone is reflected in the choice of the Phrygian mode although the clefs are those of the standard four voice ensemble with an added Altus, so that there is no comparable expressive use of range. The mensuration is the more modern *tempus imperfectum diminutum* throughout, even if the overlapping style and consistently full texture are more typical of the generation of Ockeghem than that of Josquin.

In terms of overall construction, a rhetorical procedure is apparent but only in outline. The regular opening imitation in bb.1-11 is characteristic of an *exordium* and occurs nowhere else in the piece, but it is not marked off by any cadence and simply merges into the subsequent music, to which it is linked in a most unusual way. The next 22bb. are all founded on a free canon led by the Bassus, which is followed at a distance by close entries in the Altus and Contra, this dissolving only in the last three bars before the cadence in b.36. This rigidity is softened by free melodic writing in the other two voices, and particularly noteworthy is the way the Cantus masks the break out of the threefold local repeat in all five voices (bb.11-26) by developing its already florid writing into a spectacular melismatic sequence above the new ostinato idea (bb.26-32).

The cadence in b.36 is the first of the entire piece, and its conclusive nature is emphasized by a long pedal note in the Cantus (bb.36-9); this kind of writing is often found at the end of a compostion, but rarely in the middle. It divides the motet into two approximately equal halves, the second being formally distinct from the first, consisting of a homophonic section (the only one in the piece) built on variation and repetition, leading into a long ostinato preparation for the final pedal cadence, which incorporates the ostinato motif as well as the preceding Bassus line, in typical *conclusio* style.

This type of structure, comprising two halves distinct in texture and constructive technique, is rare in BQ19. Unusual too are the merging of sections with so few cadences and the reliance on local repeat and ostinato, but all these bear comparison to Lupus's own 'Miserere' for six voices. The canons of the opening are quite old-fashioned in their florid decorations and extensive melismae, while some of the craftsmanship involved in dovetailing consecutive sections (e.g. the subtle repeat of the free Cantus line from b.62 at b.67 to cover a gap in the ostinato) is Netherlandish indeed: despite Lupus's apparent connections with Italy it is hard to disagree with Blackburn that from his style 'he may have been a Northerner' (see above), at least on the basis of these two motets.

*   *   *

Two of the anonymous works from BQ19 are comparable to Lupus's work in their relatively extensive use of imitation. The first of these, 'Benedicta mater matris' (edited in vol. ii, p.49) is unique in the manuscript for other more striking reasons though, principally through the use of the same clef and hence range for each of the four voices. This has an obvious precedent in the music of the early fifteenth century, when voices were deliberately distinguished by rhythm and functional hierarchy; since the need to integrate rather than differentiate the various lines arose concomitantly with the increase in overall range pioneered by the Ockeghem generation, it is historically ironic that this motet should combine a narrow range with the most modern integrative techniques, such as pervading imitation throughout.

Not only are the ranges equal in all voices, but they are also artificially small, remaining mostly within a single octave except for the very occasional foray of a note above or below. There do not appear to be any textual grounds for this constriction and the hypothesis that it was due to the requirements of a particular band of singers is unlikely as 'normal' voice ranges encompass a twelfth or more, and it is certainly not a piece written for amateurs. Therefore it seems that the limit was self-imposed, a challenge to the ingenuity of the working out of a given tonal area. That the lowest voice sinks exceptionally to its low C in the last few bars shows that the lower range was available but deliberately ignored except here where the plagal cadence required by the mode is impossible to effect without it.

This tonal constraint, and the insistence on a full texture

throughout have far-reaching musical consequences. The peculiar harmonic stasis, reminiscent of a *cantus firmus* composition, and the frequent 'interruption' of a cadence by the third below the *finalis* appearing in the lowest voice (see bb.16, 27, 30 and 34), are all the results of the severe contrapuntal limitations set by working in four voices within a single octave. It is this that gives the piece a notably different character from any of the others in BQ19, governing as it does not only the structure but also the directions of individual lines and hence giving rise to some interesting melodic curiosities.

Although the opening regular imitation characterizes the first 9bb. as an *exordium*, the simple triadic homophony is distinctive and the crossovers serve to emphasize the narrow compass of the voices. The remainder of the motet can not be said to follow any rhetorical pattern, however, as the music is a homogenous blend of freely imitating polyphony and decorated homophony, the boundaries between them blurred by the development of ideas from one section to the next, the absence of any decisive full cadences, and the consistent recurrence of the same motivic idea (a falling scalar fifth). The imitative technique itself is rather old-fashioned as can be seen by its irregularity and propensity to variation (as in for example the expansion of the normal falling fifth to an octave in the Tenor at b.41, Bassus at b.45 and Altus at b.47). This is more like the paraphrase method of the previous century than contemporary motivic working, and is due as much to the dour precompositional strictures of limited range and full texture throughout than any particular originality. The music appears to have been written with unusually little reference to the text for a motet in BQ19, the verbal phrasing implied by the underlay often being contradicted by the musical structure, so that the overall impression given by the piece is one of confusion and stylistic uncertainty only partly ameliorated by the novel close sonority.

The general tenor of 'O rex gentium' (edited in vol. ii, p.147), its low clefs, continuous organic flow, archaic cadences in bb.33 and 51 and strong Dorian flavour, mark it out as a rather old-fashioned motet. Even so, other features, such as the syllabic style of the opening and use of imitation are more forward looking. Formally, there is little in the way of textural contrast to articulate any kind of rhetorical structure, but the piece does at least fall into two clearly defined sections, much as Lupus's 'Miserere...tribulabor' did.

The division comes at b.34, which is the first full cadence of the entire piece, and the parallelism of this and the final close (both have similar distinctive Tenor and Bassus formations) and hence their equivalent functions as closing groups is reinforced by the approaches to each: bb.45-51 are a variation of bb.29-34, especially in the Cantus and Tenor lines. The two parts are quite blatantly different in their text setting, as the second reiterates the last words of the first without any new ones of its own in a much more expansive manner, the prevailing rhythmic motion changing from the *minima* to the *breve*. The intent is evidently to underline the words 'in umbra mortis aeternae' and is successful if unorthodox. The origin of the text is uncertain; it seems to be a pastiche of liturgical items for Advent,[84] although it is possible that it may be a bona-fide item in itself as yet undiscovered, a hypothesis supported by the occasional but tenuous and inconsistent references to fragments of the associated melodies and the imitative style, which seems to have been reserved for paraphrasing chant material (see chapter 5).

This imitation is hardly likely to be confused with anything by Palestrina or Lassus. The motives are very low-profile so that blurred distinctions and ambiguity create a complex fabric of interrelationships rather than a progressive chain, exemplified by bb.5-13. The idea first heard in the Bassus at b.13 actually dominates the whole of the rest of the motet and also corresponds to the original plainchant for these words and the others it sets, the exception being 'veni ad liberandum nos' whose rising motive parallels the beginning. All this gives the piece a deep unity which together with the steady use of imitation and equivalent endings to the two parts compensates for the irregularity and asymmetry of its component details. These

structural elements also make any sort of rhetorical structure
redundant, and indeed there is nothing that can be truly detached and
considered as an *exordium* or *conclusio*. The techniques of
composition thus diverge widely from those of the named authors in
BQ19, and it seems unlikely that this piece is by any of them.

Other anonymous pieces

The 'Felix namque' in FP27 (edited in vol. ii, p.76) presents
something of a puzzle, principally because no text is given beyond the
incipit in the Cantus and Bassus parts. There are a number of possible
continuations, but none can be made to fit the music at all; even the
incipit sits awkwardly and unconvincingly on the opening notes.
Moreover, no contemporaneous settings of any such text survive,
making it impossible to ascertain which, if any of them, was probably
intended.   It is particularly surprising that the scribe, who was
scrupulous to the point of copying out well-known texts such as the
'Ave Maria' in full over and over again, should have permitted this
ambiguity.

The most likely explanation is that he had no choice, and that
the incipit was an invention or corruption, serving here merely as a
title for a piece whose original text had got lost. The character of the
music seems to reflect a verbal conception (unlike the other
incompletely texted motet in FP27, Weerbeke's 'Adonai'), but in
view of the unsuitability of any of the texts implied by the incipit, and
the lack of any recognizable reference to chant material, it is not
possible to establish what the original words may have been.

The transmission of this piece certainly seems to have been a
strange affair altogether. The words '*secunda pars*' appear at the top
of the second page (f.131v.), despite the lack of a double bar or any
musical discontinuity whatsoever, and there is also an alternative
florid Bassus part written out next to the main one, with the words
'alio modo notatio'. This suggests an adaptation for instrumental use,

the second part being the same as the first with its rests replaced by decorative figurations. This alone serves to obliterate the original structure of contrasting textures, and in fact the added sections are often waywardly dissonant with the other voices, so that it barely makes sense even as a sort of showpiece for a bass instrument. It was not, however, a later addition to the manuscript; it was copied in the same hand and at the same time, as is evident from the arrangement of the two parts on the page.

The structural details of this motet are also rather odd. After a regular *exordium* in bb.1-16, the music launches into a series of duets that could be written strictly canonically but are in fact modified in tiny rhythmic details, a procedure carried on through the whole piece. The only exception is the duet at bb.50-61, which is an extraordinary play on just three notes in the Cantus permutated in a seemingly random order. The Tenor meanwhile has a line strangely conspicuous for its repeated notes, so that it is difficult to imagine any text being fitted to the rhythms as they stand. The duet texture is broken up by two 5b. homophonic passages (at bb.35 and 61) into two equal sections of about 20bb. length each, lending a sense of regularity to the *narratio*; the *conclusio* (starting at b.66) is typical in its use of a large scale repeat.

A certain conventionality is thus apparent in the overall form, but eccentricities of detail, text and optional parts mean that this is one of the most mysterious pieces under consideration. A knowledge of the text, so unusually left out by the scribe, might go a long way towards explaining some of these features, but the transmission of the music in such an apparently distorted form does seem to indicate an origin far removed from this one extant version.

'Tenebrae' (edited in vol. ii, p.189), also from FP27, has already been mentioned in the context of Renaldo's work on account of its clarity of form. However, its musical substance is somewhat different, having more of the flavour of the *lauda* to it; the music moves chordally rather than contrapuntally, and the writing betrays a superficial aural grasp of compositional technique rather than any great learning. The cadences (as for example in bb.8-9 and 23-4) imply a perception of the melodic formulae involved and the general harmonic direction as two separate entities, which remain unreconciled into the neatly turned closes taught by theorists. A similar rusticity is evident too in the repeated ending of short phrases on *F*, which actually becomes quite monotonous.

The status of the piece as a motet is still secure due to the effort put into varying the texture, whereby full imitation alternates with homophonic textures throughout in sections of approximately equal length. The imitation is simplicity itself, all the points being triadic or scalar, and this directness matches the formulaic regularity of the alternation scheme with the homophony. What is interesting is that an *exordium* can be discerned in bb.1-15, followed by a duet implying the beginning of a *narratio* and finally a literal repeat as a *conclusio*. These are obviously not as clear as in other motets with more imaginative uses of textural contrast, but it is notable that the sense of form, like that of harmony, seems to have been absorbed aurally and incompletely. The impression thus given of amateurism is not altogether negative; the *frottola*-like style has a certain pastoral charm and is actually turned to great effect in the dramatic setting of 'Deus, Deus meus' in bb.32-7.

Other contemporaneous settings of the 'Tenebrae' text survive by Weerbeke, Pisano and Corteccia,[85] all of them written in a comparably simple style. Corteccia's is one of a series of Responsories for Good Friday and it is likely that the others too were specifically intended for that particular liturgical occasion; however, while their unpretentiousness suggests a popualar usage, possibly by the Florentine *compagnie di laudesi*[86], the music is still sophisticated enough to be distinct from either that of the *lauda* or the more plainly functional works to be discussed in chapter 7.

In a piece as short as the 'Qui seminant in lachrymis' from FP27 (edited in vol. ii, p.159), overall structure is of little concern and coherence is achieved largely by the controlled exploration of the ambitus of the Phrygian mode. Even so, the Cantus pedal E at the beginning recurs exactly half way through (bb.15-16) and again in the Tenor at the end, providing a symmetrical frame for the intervening music.

The function of this brief piece remains obscure. Its use as a polyphonic setting part of a Tract[87] with the verses chanted seems unlikely, as all the surviving forms of the melody are in the eighth mode. It could be conjectured that the music was composed in response to a specific demand for a musical setting of the well-known proverb, but again the occasion or justification for this would be impossible to determine at present.

The structure of 'Vidimus enim stellam' (edited in vol. ii, p.202), again from FP27, is extremely open, the voices at first sight having little in common other than mutual consonance. The governing principle is in fact free decoration of the Tenor by the other two voices, the Cantus invariably forming the cadences with it. The Tenor line is not apparently derived from any chant, and works by the successive attainment of different modal goals, usually by sequence (see bb.3-5, 12-15, 15-19 and 20-24). Around this, the Cantus usually follows the sequences where possible and is more often than not accompanied by the Bassus in tenths, while the Altus is much freer. This hierarchy contrasts with the more predominantly imitative texture of 'Qui seminant' and the two need not be taken to be by the same composer despite their similarities of length and scope.

Motets for three voices

The motets considered thus far in the present chapter are for four or occasionally five or six voices, a preference typical of most of the notated music that survives from around the beginning of the sixteenth century. Most of the three- voiced pieces preserved from this time are either in the by then outmoded Burgundian chanson style or are simple, functional pieces like the minor ritual works to be discussed in chapter 7 of this thesis. Therefore it should not be surprising that of the compositions that can unequivocally be termed 'motets' in FP27, BQ18 and BQ19, only three are for three voices, and they are all stylistically well distinct from the motets examined earlier in this chapter.

In many ways the conservatism of 'Beata Apollonia' (edited in vol. ii, p.43) is inherent in the restrictions of three voiced writing, where the opportunities for textural variation and contrast are limited.[88] The texture is densely packed into a low register and the difference between the homophony and imitation which make it up is minimized by the decoration of the former and the repeated note chordal style of the latter. As in 'O rex gentium' (discussed above), the imitation is not clearly structural as it might be in Palestrina, but is rather a method of spinning material out in a sort of continuous variation form with occasional local repeats, to build up discrete but uncontrasting sections.

These sections are marked off by the only caesuras in the piece, at bb.18, 33, 45, 58, (65) and 75. Apart from the fact that the final section (at b.75) is a literal repeat of that at b.65 there is no repetition of text (with the exception of a single word, to be mentioned below) and the relative lengths of the divisions are thus dictated by verbal rather than musical logic, corresponding as they do to the syntactical units of the prayer.[89]

The reconciliation of unity and variety is achieved in this motet not by the calculated juxtaposition of elements but by their integration, resulting in a nearer proximity to the irrational gothic polyphony of Ockeghem than to the clear lines of true renaissance music. While only the end is literally repeated, the rest of the material is so bland that its character is determined mainly by the unchanging *ductus* of the Mixolydian mode within which it works.

Supplementary to this functions the principle of developing variation, visible to best advantage in the long first and fourth (starting at b.46) sections. In the first, the imitative idea that structures the opening 9bb. gives rise to the 'grave tormentum' motive by the omission of the third note; the rhythm of this latter is then taken up by the Bassus at b.11, which then paraphrases the beginning motive complete in bb.12-14. A local repeat is also used here, bb.16-18 being a variation of the previous three in all voices with the same word of text (the exception to the textual dominance over the music mentioned above), this technique not being used again until the homophony at b.59 and the *conclusio* scheme. The fourth section is run along similar lines, where the music of b.46 yields that at b.50 by rhythmic alteration and omission of the second note, and the imitation at b.50 gives up that at b.54 by expansion of the intervals.

In the second section the music for 'extraxerunt dentes' at b.24 stands out by its uniform parallel chordal motion and is a rare and wincingly graphic instance of word-painting. Nonetheless the rising scale is used to generate bb.28-33, so that both the texture and the motive are sewn into the surrounding polyphony. This integration is visible too in the third section (beginning at b.33) where the imitation at b.34 is chordal, composed of repeated notes and harmonic intervals giving rise to a quasi-homophonic texture also taken up by the following free passage. The material at b.41 is intervallically identical to that in b.34 and the way that the final *C*'s in the top voice (at bb.40 and 45) are harmonized differently has a sort of 'ouvert' and 'clos' effect; this section is evidently binary in construction but is too convoluted to be called a real local repeat.

That the fifth section should be repeated wholesale is no surprise in view of its function as a closing group. Less obvious, but equally typical, is the way that the repeat at b.75 does not recapitulate the beginning of a discrete unit but breaks into the continuous

polyphony at b.65, thus concealing the repetition and integrating it
with the rest of the piece.

While elements of balance can be perceived - the carefully
distributed local repeats being summed up in the final repetition, the
whimsical 'extraxerunt dentes' matching an earlier eccentricity on 'pro
domino' (bb.10-11) - the style is closest to that of the late fifteenth
century, and of course the low register accentuates this. Unity
between the various sections is achieved mainly by a lack of contrast
that inadvertently gives rise to a complex network of relationships
both old-fashioned and at the same time curiously looking forward to
some of those found in the more definitely modern bipartite pieces.

The style of Jo. Touront's 'O gloriosa regina mundi' (edited in
RRMMER, ix/x, p.176) is unique even among the motets from FP27
in its proximity to that of the fifteenth- century chanson. This is
apparent from the disposition of the three-voiced texture and the
independence and angularity of the lowest part, which immediately
distinguish it as a functional Contratenor. Moreover, the tuneful
nature of the Cantus in particular, along with the way in which
fragments of text are set to discrete melodic phrases supported by
well- defined cadences, result in a *cantilena* effect again more
reminiscent of the *rondeaux* of Binchois than the later motet.

Nevertheless, the lack of any *forme fixe* in the Latin text
necessitates the imposition of some kind of external musical structure,
and indeed it is here that the principal originality of the piece lies. It
is divided into three sections of almost exactly equal length, marked
by cadences onto *G*, *D*, and *G* at bb.32, 69 and 101 (i. e. the end).
The closes of the first and third sections are made prominent not only
by their accelerated movement but also by the varied use of the same
material (compare bb.90-101 with bb.22-33), thus clarifying the
structure and enhancing their tonal symmetry; the close of the second
section is also emphasized, by the melodic climax of the piece onto
the high Cantus f'' in b.66. More subtly, while the two upper voices

are uniformly imitative in the first and third sections, in the second the Cantus predominates, while the Altus is relegated to a more subservient harmonic role.

It is of note that this threefold division is implicit in the Latin words; what Touront seems to have done is derive his outline as he would from a *rondeau* text, using a like procedure to obtain a completely different form. This framework then leaves him free to exploit the virtues of courtly refinement associated with the chanson and thus compose a fascinating hybrid whose success and popularity are evident from the wide range of sources that preserve it.[90]

Lastly, 'Quemadmodum desiderat' (edited in vol. ii, p.157), with its dotted rhythms, frequent cadences and the busy sequence at the end is reminiscent of the 'instrumental' motets found in BQ18 and occasionally elsewhere in FP27 (see chapter 8). In fact, although the text is clearly indicated in all three voice parts, the music does not seem to be written round it and any other of about the same length would fit just as well. However, in contrast to the other instrumental pieces the music proceeds purely by local exigency and shows little concern for motivic or even modal unity in its overall construction.

The welding together of simple textures without any clear sense of direction seems the work of a less experienced composer, and while the extensive use of imitation is unusual, the artlessness that attends it again belies a certain insecurity. This is accentuated by the shortwinded cadences and rambling lines, all of which conspire to relegate the piece to the periphery of any discussion of the motets in FP27.

With the possible exceptions of some of the shorter anonymous pieces and Touront's chanson-like 'O gloriosa regina mundi', the motets examined above are all characterized by similar formal procedures. While the quasi-Ciceronian form sometimes found in Renaldo is observed strictly in only a minority of cases, the principle of functional opening, central and closing sections made mutually distinct by the use of different compositional techniques is universal. This is not a feature of earlier fifteenth-century music, nor does it persist long into the sixteenth, when it was superseded by the adoption of increased numbers of voices, structural imitation, word painting and other like devices. Structures based on articulation and contrast are rarely to be found among the four-voiced motets of Willaert, who consistently preferred a fuller texture based on imitation.[91] Likewise, though examples do occur in certain of Costanzo Festa's motets (most notably in his 'Deduc me, Domine'),[92] the tendency is still towards through imitation and textural integration rather than contrast. It appears therefore that the formal principles discussed in the present chapter are a unique property of the peculiar conjunction of humanistic thought and the revival of the motet form in Italy towards the turn of the fifteenth century. The possibilities it offered, even among the relatively minor composers examined in the foregoing chapter, for strongly personal expression make it a fascinating medium through which to study their works and a telling symptom of a new and genuinely renaissance spirit in music.

Notes

[1] These figures are those given in *HammCC*, vol. i, rather than the revised totals in vol. iv, for reasons given in appendices A and B.

[2] Such as are, for example, the majority of the 'Ave Maria' settings at the beginning of FP27, which will be discussed fully in chapter 7.

[3] As with the *laude*, these will be considered separately in chapter 7; see also *KenneyL* for an elaboration of this distinction between types.

[4] All of these were however printed in Petrucci's *Motetti A* of 1502

and one, 'Virgo Maria, non est tibi similis' was published in Ambros's *Geschichte der Musik* (Leipzig, 1882, rev3/1911 by O. Kade), p.183.

[5]See for example *CrollGW* (*passim*) and *AMMM*, xi, p.1.

[6] A great deal of the repertory of FP27, secular pieces as well as motets, seems to have been taken from these earliest printed books; see *HammCC*, i, p.232.

[7]See *JeppG*, pp.15-16.

[8]The argument that the *motetti missales* pieces originated before the assassination of Galeazzo Maria Sforza in 1476 is advanced in chapter 2.

[9]The text can be found transcribed in verse form in *MorelH*, p.115.

[10]On the words 'ut quid dereliquisti me/ Et inclinato capite emisisti spiritum': see *DartIM*, no.1 (p.1).

[11]His one Roman Mass composition, on 'Ave caelorum regina', does use *tempus perfectum* extensively, but is an exceptional work for other reasons, having apparently been written in imitation of Dufay; see *CrollGW*, pp.80-1.

[12]Published in *AMMM*, xi, p.73. Although they appear in the edition as two separate pieces, it is clear from their position and relatively short lengths in the cycle, as well as their common material, that they are two parts of the same motet. Their separation presumably occurred through their copying onto different folia of Librone 1.

[13]*AmbrosG*, v, p.183.

[14]*ReeseMR*, p.218.

[15]They also both appear on consecutive pages in Librone 1, followed by 'Ave stella matutina', though this is probably of little significance

as that order is not maintained in either 1502[1] or FP27.

[16]The text is substantially different after the first line from the versions in *ChevH* (no. 2135), *MoneH* (ii, p.321), *DrevesH* (xlv[a], p.26), *PM* 277 or those set by Brumel, Manchicourt or the anonymous composer of BQ20, no. 48; it has not been possible to locate any other source for it.

[17]The index to BQ19 also gives his name as 'Renaldus' and 'Renaldino'.

[18]This attribution is given in *I-VEcap* 760, though the benefit of the doubt is usually given to Renaldo, as it is for example in *HammCC*; the piece is not included in Lupus's worklist in *Grove*.

[19]For 'O Jesu Christe', see vol. i, p.25; for 'Regina caeli', 'Haec dies' and the two Magnificats see vol. xi, pp.40, 43, 44 and 49 respectively; for 'O Domine Jesu Christe' and 'Ave sanctissima Maria', see vol xii, pp. 3 and 4.

[20]This has already been noted in *ReeseMR*, p.220, note 188.

[21]*Idem*, see also *JeppFR*, i, p.162 and ii, pp.37-42.

[22]Neither *Grove*, *MGG* or any other such work yet consulted has an entry under the name 'Renaldo'.

[23]A. Sacchetti-Sassetti: 'La Cappella Musicale del Duomo di Rieti', *NA*, xvii (1940), p.123.

[24]G. Barblan: 'Vita Musicale alla Corte Sforzesca', in *Storia di Milano*, ix (Milan, 1961), p.826. It should be noted that the relevant document is not actually dated, though Barblan's proposal of 1473 does seem the most likely.

[25]*Idem*, p.830.

[26]L. Lockwood: *Music in Renaissance Ferrara 1400-1505* (Oxford,

1984), pp.319-20.

[27]G. D'Alessi: *La cappella musicale del Duomo di Treviso* (Vedelago, 1954), p.49.

[28]F. D'Accone: 'The Singers of San Giovanni in Florence during the Fifteenth Century', *JAMS*, xiv (1961), p.334.

[29]R. Casimiri: 'Musica e musicisti nella Cattedrale di Padova nei sec. XIV, XV, XVI', *NA*, xviii (1941), p.12.

[30]F. Haberl: Die Römische "Schola Cantorum" und die päpstlichen Kapellsänger bis zur Mitte des 16. Jahrhunderts (Leipzig, 1888), p.56.

[31]*Idem*.

[32]See chapter 1 for the supposed dating of the manuscript.

[33]N. Pelicelli: 'Musicisti in Parma nei secoli XV-XVI', *NA*, viii (1931), p.197.

[34]Jeppesen asserts this quite positively; see *JeppFR*, i, p.162.

[35]For example, one 'Frate Andrea di Giovanni di Fiandra' was identical with a 'Frate Andrea Francioso'; see *D'AccSG*, p.334. Another more famous (though less contemporaneous) example might be Ockeghem, who was variouly referred to as Netherlandish, French, Flemish and Belgian (see *LenC*, p.103).

[36]A complete account of them is given by in *D'AccSG, passim*.

[37]It is unfortunate in this respect that the excellent study of musical life in Treviso in *BlackT* is confined to the later sixteenth century and does not cover documents pertaining to Renaldo's time or mention his name.

[38]Ernoul Caussin, *ca.*1510-?48, who later became *maestro* at Parma:

see *PeliP*, pp.197 and 141, and *Grove*, 'Caussin', (iv, 17).

[39]*Idem*, note 2: Jeppesen appears to derive his information solely from *PeliP*, which does not mention marriage anywhere.

[40]In particular, the apparent move from Milan to Ferrara in 1474 parallels that of Johannes Martini and would be but one of many examples of singers moving between the two courts; see *LockF*, p.133.

[41]Although it would be anachronistic to describe the mode as Ionian transposed to F, this would in fact be a much more telling description of it.

[42]*LU*, p.1570. This kind of arrangement forms the basis also of Symon Ferrariensis's 'Maria ergo' and Lupus's 'In nomine Jesu', which are considered separately in chapter 6 (see pp.167 and 177 respectively) on account of their much greater length and more complex style.

[43]However, a version of the 'O Domine Jesu Christe' text was used as the basis of one of the *laude* in FP27, as will be discussed in chapter 7.

[44]It also sheds an interesting light on the insistence of theorists as diverse as Gaffurius (see *MillerPM*, pp.149-50, also p.147) and Dressler (see the entry under 'Mode' in *Grove*, xii, p.404) that the Phrygian mode was either sad, in its plagal form, or harsh ('morosus et austerus') in its authentic form. This view was obviously not universally held and thus may have owed more to neo-classical nostalgia than actual musical practice, especially at a time when the validity of the modal system for polyphony was being called into serious doubt by Tinctoris, Ramos and their followers.

That the music is in the Phrygian mode at all, despite its tonal centre moving away from E to A at the first cadence, is testified by Pietro

Aaron in his *Trattato della natura e cognizione di tutti gli toni di canto figurato* (Venice, 1525; English translation of chapters 1-7 in *StrunkSR*, pp.205-18). In his fifth chapter he discusses the assignation of polyphonic pieces to the third and fourth modes and concludes that compositions ending on *A* after following the 'correct procedure' belong to the third tone, citing Josquin's 'Miserere mei, Deus' as an example (see *StrunkSR*, p.215).

[45]See bb.31-5. This motet will be discussed on its own merits below; being as yet unpublished, it is included amomg the transcriptions in vol. ii (see p.85).

[46]The Rusconi Codex is the only source to preserve more than one of Sebastiano's four surviving motets as well as being the major source of Renaldo's work.

[47]In other words that on ff.131v.-142r.

[48]The rebus is found at the head of f.55v., in the normal position for a composer attribution.

[49]On a purely conjectural level, the name 'Remi' might imply a connection with the city of Rheims; for other suggestions, see *LowMC*, i, p.52, note 2.

[50]See *ApelGC*, pp.241-4; also *Grove*, 'Invitatory' (ix, p.286).

[51]See *LU*, p.497.

[52]*Grove*, 'Barra' (ii, 178).

[53]*Idem.*

[54]*Idem.*

[55]This motet will be analysed in detail in chapter 6 (see p.180).

[56]See *JeppFR*, i, p.156; also *GuerB*, pp.212-13 and *GuerO*, p.137.

[57] *1502[1]*, f.6v.-7r., ascribed likewise to 'Jo. de Pinarol', or in the index simply as 'Pinarol'.

[58] A. Main: 'Festa, Sebastiano', *Grove,* vi, p.504.

[59] See *LowMC*, iii, p.59, and W. H. Rubsamen: 'Sebastiano Festa and the Early Madrigal', *GfMKB* (Kassel, 1962), p.122.

[60] *Primo Libro Della Croce* (A-R editions, 1978), ed. W. F. Prizer, introduction.

[61] *LowMC*, p.59ff.

[62] *PerkR*, p.265ff.

[63] See K. Jeppesen: 'Festa, Sebastiano', *MGG*, iv, p.102, and H. Albrecht: 'Zwei Quellen zur Musikgeschichte', *MF*, i (1948), pp.242-85 and especially pp.271 and 277.

[64] See D. Mace: 'Pietro Bembo and the literary origins of the Italian Madrigal', *MQ*, lv (1969), p.65.

[65] See *RubsSF*, p.122.

[66] *Idem*, p.123.

[67] *MGG*, iv, p.102.

[68] This point of view is echoed in *JeppIS*, ii, p.x: 'The few sacred works [i.e. the four motets] are especially interesting'. His ranking of them above the secular pieces is obvious but the reasoning is not made clear.

[69] In other words, the expansion of a sixth to an octave, or contraction of a third to a unison, as defined by contemporaneous theorists as late as Zarlino (see *ZarlinC*, chapter liii).

[70] Comparable closing sections based on repeated homophonic passages are also a common feature of the works of Sebastiano's

namesake Costanzo Festa; they appear for example at the ends of 'Helisabeth beatissima' (*FestaO*, v, no. 39), 'O pulcherrima' (*Idem*, no. 40), 'Regem archangelorum' (*Idem*, no. 42) and the *prima pars* of 'Quis dabit' (*Idem*, no. 41), to name only those pieces included in BQ19.

[71]There exists a five-voiced motet by Carpentras entitled 'Haec est illa', which uses the 'Salve Regina' melody as a *cantus firmus* and begins with the first three lines of the present poem; however, the text remains unidentified in *CarpO*, iv (see pp.xvi and 26).

[72]'Festa, Sebastiano', (iv, p.504).

[73]Vol. iii, p.55.

[74]Vol. ii, p.184.

[75]The sole source of this motet is *I-Bc* Q20, no.8.

[76]*RubsSF*, p.122.

[77]B. Blackburn: 'Johannes Lupi and Lupus Hellinck. A Double Portrait', *MQ*, lix (1973), p.548.

[78]*Grove*, 'Lupus' (xi, p.338).

[79]For example the 'Salva nos, Domine' on ff.22v.-23r.

[80]B. Blackburn: 'Lupus', *Grove*, xi, p.338.

[81]Edited in *D'AccFR*, ii, p.59.

[82]See *Grove*, 'Josquin des Prez' (ix, p.718).

[83]Although it is also possible to recognize a variant of Josquin's famous motif in Hutinet's setting of these words (see bb.43-9 of his 'Peccantem'), the probability of any direct influence is somewhat less. Whereas Lupus was (as far as can be ascertained) active in northern Italy around the time when BQ19 was compiled, there is no record of

Hutinet ever visiting Italy, and his works are chiefly preserved in French sources. Besides, the thematic similarity is much less obvious in either its shape or treatment.

[84]See *LU*, p.342.

[85]Weerbeke's piece is published in *DartIM*, p.1, Pisano's in *JeppIS*, iii, p.142, and Corteccia's in *D'AccFR*, ix, p.67.

[86]See *D'AccL* for details of these singers and their activities in Florence, *ca.* 1500; the relationship between the *lauda* and the motet will be discussed in more detail in chapter 7.

[87]*LU*, p.1164; there does not appear to be any other liturgical use of this text.

[88]However it should be noted that while some of the many motets in this medium by Francesco de Layolle show a like restraint in comparison with his own four voiced works, others are more modern and it is possible to find plenty of clear imitative *tricinia* among the works of Costanzo Festa and Willaert.

[89]It has so far proved impossible to locate the exact source of this text, whose peculiarity is surely indicative of some specific local function. There does not seem to be any connection between any of the putative places of origin of BQ19 with the saint (see *BollAS*, Feb.II, Antwerp, 1648, pp.278-82); it is possible that this curious piece may owe its inclusion to a worldly concern with the problem of toothache, of which Apollonia was the patron saint. It is also worth noting that Jacquet of Mantua, credited with seven motets in BQ19, was married to a woman named Appolonia until her death in 1527 (see *FenlonM*, pp.67-8). Though he is unlikely to have written the present work for stylistic reasons, he could have introduced it into the repertory as a tribute.

[90]For a full list of these, see the notes to the edition of the piece in

RRMMER, ix/x, p.176.

[91]Nonetheless, his 'Antoni pastor' may be cited as exceptional in its recognizable *exordium* and *conclusio* sections as well as its greater dependence on duet writing (see *WillO*, i, no. 9).

[92]See *FestaO*, iii, no. 1. Costanzo's functionally distinct closing sections (mentioned above in connection with those of Sebastiano Festa) are also more related to the 'rhetorical' style than that of, for example, Willaert.

CHAPTER 5: CANTUS FIRMUS AND PARAPHRASE MOTETS

Surprisingly few of the motets in the repertories from FP27 and BQ19 under consideration here are based on any kind of pre-composed material. Those that are can be divided into two groups, namely those comparable in scale and ambition with the motets discussed in chapter 4 and those more reminiscent in their simplicity and technique of some of the three-voiced hymn settings of Dufay. The archaic and functional style of the latter type, which are found only in the earlier Florentine manuscript, consigns them to a genre of their own, so that they are of only passing interest to the history of the motet as a formal type. Once these are set aside, a mere eight of the multitude of motets from FP27 and BQ19 by the lesser-known or anonymous composers under consideration here are properly motet-like pieces based on *cantus firmus* or paraphrase procedures, compared to the dozens of free motets in the same sources, a significant tribute to the popularity of the newer forms.[1]

Of these pieces, five are based on a *cantus firmus* in one voice and three on chant paraphrased throughout the texture, the two techniques being clearly distinct. The first of these was inherited from the medieval tradition and already seems obsolescent in the early 1500s, while the second was to remain current for the rest of the century,[2] and indeed embodies some of the most progressive features of the time. The simultaneous and equal use of the same melodies in all voices breaks down all part-hierarchies and results in patterns of consistent and regular imitation. Such writing, so typical of the later part of the century, is wholly original in the context of its first decades but even so is handled confidently and indeed in exactly the same way as might be expected from a later composer. It seems from this that composers such as Renaldo (who wrote a completely assured imitative motet in addition to the works examined in chapter 4; see below) were aware of the possibilities of through- imitation but rejected it in favour of forms based on contrasting textures out of choice. It also seems that the technique of imitation owes its origins less to a need to unify the voices as the overall range expanded, or a rejection of medieval part-hierarchy, than to the extension of a traditional paraphrase technique that was incompatible with the changes of texture expected of a free motet. Certainly, the classic examples of early structural imitation, such as Josquin's 'Ave Maria...virgo serena' are all based to some extent on chant paraphrase.

Renaldo's 'Regina caeli' (edited as 'Regina caeli II' in vol. ii, p.163) is a case in point, made even more interesting by its contrast to his other motets. It is in fact a most original composition, as in addition to its use of chant paraphrase it is one of the few pieces in BQ19 for five voices, the added one being a descant *cantus firmus* high above the other four which repeats the litany 'Sancta Maria ora pro nobis' to rhythmic variations of its traditional plainsong melody.[3] Ostinato *cantus firmi* to different texts from the main motet can be found elsewhere (Josquin's 'Virgo salutiferi' for example) but are rare enough to make this piece quite distinctive on this account alone.

The other voices are based wholly on the Antiphon from which the main text is taken,[4] its principal melodic features being successively worked into regular points of imitation in a consistently full texture. The overall structure is thus open-ended and totally dependent on the original chant, a radically different approach from the architectural balance of Renaldo's other motets. The motet is still unified of course by the high ostinato and also by the considerable symmetries and refrains of the plainsong itself, which are translated directly into the polyphony. Certain features are consciously brought out by Renaldo, such as the relationship of the 'quia quam' tune to that of 'sicut dixit', both of which are isolated and developed into ostinati (bb.19 and 51), but there is nonetheless no trace of any kind of rhetorical structure. Even the placing of the high *cantus firmus* is subordinate to the plainsong, there being no regularity as to the placing of its entries or its rhythmic form, though it usually enters above a cadence in the lower voices, frequently where they embark on an 'alleluia', and occurs twice in each pars, with the 'ora pro nobis' repeated right at the end. This does sound like a concession to the repeating *conclusio* principle and as such rings true with Renaldo's matching his *cantus firmus* to the open structure of the lower voices rather than vice-versa.

Harmonically, the work is centred firmly on F and while cadences are used less frequently than in other works due to the overlapping imitative style, their purpose is the same, marking off sections, textures or entries of the *cantus firmus*. The harmony shares the qualities of 'modern' functionality and clarity with Renaldo's other pieces and combined with the imitative style yields a sonority similar to that of Palestrina and his contemporaries, making an ironic contrast with the archaic bitextuality and ostinato writing.

It is interesting to note that the same recurring ostinato is used in exactly the same way in the Sinfonia of Monteverdi's Vespers of 1610, nearly a century later. The correspondence is indeed most striking, and it is tempting to conjecture that Monteverdi was familiar with this work. However, similar ostinati can also be found elsewhere, for example in Giulio Schiavetto's 'Cantantibus organis',[5] where the same melody and text are used in the Tenor, only with 'Maria' replaced by 'Caecilia'.[6] Such pieces may then represent the tip of the iceberg of a genre of dedicatory motets based on similar principles that lasted throughout the sixteenth century.[7] In this case Monteverdi's example would be part of a continuous tradition rather than an isolated antiquarianism, though his interests certainly extended to the music of the past and his composition of a Mass on the 'In illo tempore' of Renaldo's near-contemporary Gombert assumes an interesting new relevance in this context.

The unusual and individual qualities of this motet should not obscure its significance as an early representative of a distinct and important genre, the imitative paraphrase motet. The fact that its style is so different from the composer's other pieces (though there is no cause to doubt its authenticity) and so similar to that of musicians working fifty years later marks this genre out as an important formative influence on later sixteenth-century style and a vital stage in the evolution of imitative technique.

One motet by Lupus, whose biography has already been discussed in the previous chapter, is based on imitative paraphrase but in an even more unusual way than Renaldo's 'Regina caeli'. His 'In convertendo' (edited in *SmijT*, ix, p.37) is an example of a complete psalm setting, a relatively novel type of motet which will be discussed more fully in chapter 6 (see p.161). However, it is differentiated from others of this type by its use of chant paraphrase, and this not of any extended melody but of a humble psalm tone, whose shape governs every single phrase.[8] With such a limited range of ideas, problems of structural unity are completely irrelevant and in fact the piece is only just rescued from monotony by imaginative rhythmic handling and declamation of the text.

The tone is the eighth, whose intonation and end are actually retrogrades, fortifying still more the already imposing melodic rigidity. However Lupus allows himself the licence of using the intonation wheresoever he likes (formally in a psalm it should come at the beginning of the first verse only) and disregards the original procedure of the chant yet further by using its elements for whichever passages of text take his fancy, regardless of their position in the original verse structure of the psalm. Tonally speaking the tone appears on G and D, with only very occasional excursions to C (e.g. in the Altus in b.113).

This minimal material is incorporated into the fabric of the motet in an interesting way. Instead of being used as the one standard opening to a line whose later portion became free (as might be expected), the tone always appears intact in whole phrases, with only a little melodic decoration though the rhythm is hardly ever the same twice. The four-voiced sections usually have two of their number imitating some part of the tone in this manner, often in strict canon, while the others are free and do their best to vary their material and

hide the repetitions as much as possible, although certain motifs such
as the quick scalar rising fifths first heard in the Tenor at b.7 come
again and again, due partly to the exigencies of the reciting note of the
tone (see bb.33-35, 42, 46-47, 56-57, 65, 70-73, 75, 79, 113-18 and
129-30). The beginning is an example of the psalm melody in one
voice of a duet decorated by the other, which is incorporated into a
grand ostinato scheme by its repeat in the other two voices (at bb.14-
28); this kind of beginning serves as a kind of exordium (see
Sebastiano Festa's 'Angele Dei' or Renaldo's 'Haec dies' for
equivalent duet openings) though the omnipresence of the tone renders
such structural devices obsolete and there is no like passage anywhere
else, as the texture remains resolutely full. Even the quasi-repetitious
end is less a *conclusio* construction than a continuation of the style of
all the previous music.

Thus the functional segregation of the lines into either
'structure' or 'decoration' is thrown into particular prominence, and
the discrete nature of the former results in a composition almost
wholly based on ostinati of various types. These are well
differentiated in character: there are varied local repeats with voices
exchanged (e.g. bb.38-48) but generally even when more than two
voices are charged with the tone the structure is founded on a duet
framework which the others imitate to camouflage its outline.

As in Renaldo's 'Regina caeli', the originality of the imitative
paraphrase technique is somewhat swamped by the more individual
features of this motet. The elaboration of such an extended
composition from such a restricted foundation would appear to be a
conceit or display of virtuosity rather than a pious observance of
liturgical propriety. As such, its introversion and obsession with
contrapuntal craft accord well with Lupus's putatively northern
origins and are well distinct from the simplicity of outline typical of
the 'rhetorical' pieces in the same manuscript.

A more straightforward imitative piece is the anonymous

'Verbum caro panem verum' from FP27 (edited in vol. ii, p.200).
Although it is ostensibly a hymn (it sets the fourth verse of the famous
'Pange lingua' text), it differs from those to be discussed at the end of
this chapter in its length, use of four voices and thoroughly motet-like
imitative technique, making it a composition based on a melody as
distinct from a setting of one.

The technique does not seem as mature as in either of the works
examined above and is in fact more similar to that of the 'O rex
gentium' examined in the previous chapter. Instead of well-profiled
motivic points of imitation, elements of the chant appear in different
guises in different voices as part of an irregular flow (see for example
bb.30-34) and there is a great deal of variation and free writing. This
imparts a rather archaic character which is compounded by the last
vestiges of voice-hierarchy (the Cantus and Tenor seem more closely
tied to the chant, particularly in comparison to the angular Altus line,
and form all the cadences) and the way that each motif is treated as a
separate unit defined by a strong cadence rather than allowed to
overlap with the next.

Despite their markedly individual features, the three motets
described above all share a common dependence on imitative
technique derived from paraphrasing pre-composed material. Such
extensive use of structural imitation is rare among these pieces and
seems to be directly related to the incorporation of external musical
ideas. Only the other motets of Lupus and the anonymous 'Benedicta
mater matris' or 'O rex gentium' follow any comparable procedure
and that to a much lesser extent; the last of these looks as if it may be
based on a melody that has not yet been identified anyway. The
specificity of imitation to paraphrase motets and exordia does not
seem limited to the group of works under scrutiny here and may prove
to be an important factor in the mechanism of its eventual universal
adoption. The fact that it can be seen most clearly here in the works
of Lupus and first became firmly established in those of Gombert also
implies a national bias away from Italy and to the north, though it is

impossible to state anything categorically without a great deal of further research.

The five *cantus firmus* pieces are essentially conservative and display none of the spectacular originality of some of the paraphrase motets. Even so, the two that appear in FP27 were also printed by Petrucci[9] and so were presumably representative of a valid current style. Several of Mouton's motets in BQ19 are moreover based on canonic *cantus firmi*, though these are more typical of him than the rest of the manuscript, being the expression of a more introverted and contrapuntally-minded northern personality; generally speaking, such pieces are uncommon in both sources.

The most straightforward example is the anonymous 'Stella caeli' (edited in vol. ii, p.181) presumably copied into FP27 from 1502[1] where it appears in an identical version. The melody begins as an intonation and then proceeds in even breves without a break. While the other voices are barely integrated with it at all, either by imitation or any other means, they have a mutual coherence which actually lends a stronger outline to the piece than the open-ended Tenor line.

This is achieved principally by the unusual dialogue nature of the free voices, where only one or two sound together with the Tenor for most of the piece and the relationships of successive entries give rise to frequent binary repeat constructions. Thus the Altus in bb.6-11 is the same as the Cantus in bb.1-6, whose bb.13-17 are a repeat of the Bassus in bb.10-14 even though the *cantus firmus* notes are not the same. This ingenious design relaxes into shorter answering phrases and eventually, in bb.30-53, to more orthodox organically associative writing though the dialogue effect is maintained. The style of the opening is resumed at the end, where the long idea begun in the Altus in b.53 and continued in the Cantus at b.56 is repeated in its entirety by the Cantus (starting at b.61) over a different Tenor sequence, before a full tonic cadence marking the transition to a harmonically stable closing section.

This symmetry, and the effort made to work out these repeat schemes are unusual and impressive in a piece of this sort. Although these give way to short cadential *clichés* in the middle, they still make the piece more than the contrapuntal exercise it seems at first sight and may account for its unique inclusion among the majority of works in a very different style in 1502[1] and FP27.

A more ambitious work is the 'Per lignum crucis' by Divitis from BQ19 (edited in *LowMC*, iii, p.188). A full account of the composer's life is given in *Grove*, Picker's article being based on a relatively recent dissertation on the man and his works.[10] Therefore it seems superfluous to mention anything here beyond the fact that he was a Northerner who seems never to have visited Italy, so that his 'Per lignum crucis' was presumably transmitted from another source rather than included on account of the composer's direct intervention. Since Divitis was a composer of some standing whose works include several Masses as well as the motets, since he was not even Italian and since this particular piece has already received attention from Lowinsky due to its inclusion in the Medici Codex, he deserves only a passing mention here as a footnote to the latter commentary.

The motet is shaped by a *cantus firmus* set canonically in two voices, based on a plainsong melody but quite liberally decorated. As Lowinsky points out,[11] Divitis derived this procedure from an eponymous motet by Mouton and indeed he has plainly modelled his own piece on that of the older master, as a comparison of the two readily reveals. The Mouton motet appears alongside that of Divitis in both the Medici Codex and BQ19, so it would seem that they were transmitted together although they are not copied onto adjacent folia: further details of the relationship between the two are given by Lowinsky.

The style of Divitis's free voices is contrapuntal rather than melodic. The restless motion, rhythmic *clichés* and long- winded amorphous phrases are actually reminiscent of the 'instrumental' style found in BQ18, and even the occasional passage free of the canonic pair (e.g. bb.42-48) has little to distinguish it in terms of structural relations between the other voices. Also as in BQ18, passing rhythmic euphony between the lines is favoured, along with parallel motion with the Bassus, and these commonplaces are the only coherent elements apart from the occasional free imitation of the *cantus firmus*. A good example of this, and one of the more interesting passages in the piece, comes when Divitis spurs his *cantus firmus* into a melodic sequence (bb.29-33), resulting in a flurry of activity quite distinct from the sedate processional of the rest of the piece. This consorts well with the end, where at the word 'alleluia' the plainsong is abandoned as the music swings into triple time and a genuinely imaginative five-voiced texture.

Generally speaking though, the *cantus firmus*, canon and dry counterpoint are worlds apart from the clear formal profiles which predominate in BQ19. Lowinsky rightly speaks of a 'ripeness and beauty that matches that of Mouton'[12] in the harmonic texture in his comparison of the two composers' settings of the same text, but goes on to consider that Divitis surpasses his master 'in the elegance and sweep of his melodic phrases, in the variety of rhythmic and metric patterns, in the piquancy of dissonance and in the flow of harmonic progression'. This seems a little unfair on Mouton, whose excellently contrived varied homophony is a much more sumptuous surround to the canon that both composers take as a starting point than Divitis's overlong, directionless lines, whose manner may be gratifyingly original in the context of the Medici Codex but is rather dismally trivial when set against so much other music in a similar vein (that in BQ18 being a case in point). The 'piquance of dissonance' is likewise a property of that rather angular style and the 'flow of harmonic progression' presumably refers to the frequent cadential formulae which contrive to give some kind of articulation to the long lines. The most positive quality of Divitis's motet is to be found right at the end, where he does genuinely look to the future, both in abandoning the plainsong and in subverting the canon into a generator of clear answering phrases instead of contrapuntal embroilment: otherwise the piece seems like an apprentice copy of a master's work, stylistically uncertain and conservative.

The 'Da pacem' in BQ19 (edited as 'Da pacem III' in vol. ii, p.64) is also founded on a canon, but is in fact more like 'Stella caeli' in its plainness and regular Tenor motion in breves. The canon is written out for the Bassus in an F_3 clef, with its resolution lying a fourth higher on G, this latter tonality being adopted as that of the piece as a whole. Above this canon the upper pair are free to spin traceries of scales and figurations untroubled by problems of structure or unity, though they pay occasional lip service to imitation in the form of sequential patterns in the middles of phrases.

The *cantus firmus* melody is simplicity itself, and in fact consists essentially of one phrase repeated twice, as can be seen from the reduction in Ex. 1a below (the opening of the original chant is quoted as Ex. 1b for comparison):

Ex. 1

The variations at the end amount to no more than the sequential extension of the idea on 'in diebus'/'nisi tu' and transposition of the final idea, so that no new material is presented. The inversion and transposition of the beginning of the repeat (bb.29-31 above) are not merely to disguise the want of new musical substance, but also to escape the reference made to the plainsong melody in the first nine notes, which would be textually inappropriate here; it also has the side effect of producing a local repeat and a stable tonal excursion to *F/B flat* and thus happily varying the harmony. The canonic possibilities in the 'Da pacem' Antiphon melody were commonly recognized at the time[13] and it is typical of the unambitious nature of this piece to abandon it as soon as the obvious canon of the first few notes is exhausted. The disruption of the regular rhythmic periods after the careful provision of three notes on 'nostris' to balance the opening phrases is due to the number of syllables in 'quoniam non est alius' and is of marginal significance practically speaking, since the displacement of the canonic resolution by a bar blurs the rhythmic structure anyway. Essentially the motet is a simple exercise in canonic formation and its clothing in routine counterpoint and is not really comparable to the other pieces in BQ19; nevertheless each voice is texted so that it was presumably intended for performance along with the rest of the manuscript, and a modicum of charm must be admitted when considering for example the sequences in bb.36-40.

The FP27 'Da pacem' (edited in *GreyL*, app., nc. 4) places the melody in the top voice rather than the Tenor in a considerably freer paraphrase version. Unlike the paraphrase pieces examined above, however, the lower voices share none of its material or even general style, the impression being of a fairly rigid 'setting' of the tune despite its substantial decoration.

The top voice is also the only one to carry the words, unusually for Latin pieces in FP27.[14] The lower voices compound their textlessness by a restless style characterized by frequent recourse to the conventional cadential figurations associated with the BQ18 motets (see chapter 8), whose distinctive clef configuration they also share, giving the impression that this may be an instrumentally-conceived setting of a vocal chant melody.

The structure is solely that of the *cantus firmus* though cohesion is obtained in the lower voices after the regular opening by sporadic eddy imitation of contrapuntal details. The style is not particularly smooth and there are certain points - such as the sudden void of activity in bb.11-12, the insoluble *musica ficta* problems in bb.3-4, the frequent cadence figurations or general lack of melodic direction throughout - that make this piece seem less than a fully assured masterpiece. All the same, if it was included by Petrucci in 1502[1] it must have been considered to be a viably popular proposition, even if it is quite exceptional in both the print and FP27.

Virtually nothing is known of Ant. Peragulfus Lucensis, to whom the 'Regina caeli' in FP27 (edited as 'Regina caeli I' in vol. ii, p.160) is attributed, except that from the evidence of his name he must have been a native of Lucca, a circumstance quite plausible if the Florentine provenance of the manuscript is accepted.[15] In some ways, the piece belongs as much with the hymn settings to be discussed below as with the more substantial motets, since like the former it is a three-voiced chant setting written out with only a single incipit to indicate the original text. However, its considerably expanded dimensions and use of a non-strophic chant melody make it significantly distinct from what is otherwise a highly consistent and well-defined group of compositions and require that it should be considered separately.

The *cantus firmus* is stated almost continuously in what for the most part is the lowest sounding voice (transcribed as the middle voice in vol. ii) and is a fairly strict presentation of the long version of the melody (*LU*, p.275; see also *AP*, f.62v.). It is occasionally imitated in the Cantus (at bb.1, 44, 62, 72 and 88) and twice in the Bassus (bb.20 and 113) but otherwise provides a structural backbone that the others are content to decorate in a simple and unpretentious manner despite the grandiose scale of the work.

Although the music is notated without any text, it displays none of the florid figuration and sequential passage work characteristic of the BQ18 motets or those pieces from FP27 to be discussed in chapter 8; nor is the way that the *cantus firmus* is set as ambitious as in Divitis's 'Per lignum crucis' or even the 'Da pacem' settings, competent as it may be. Nevertheless it was in emulation of these latter that it seems to have been written rather than as a contribution to the repertory of functional and strophic liturgical pieces, as is evident from its much greater length and its choice of text and *cantus firmus*. The fact that it is one of the very few motets in FP27 by an authentically Italian composer makes it an interesting curiosity from a historical point of view and a representative of a possibly alternative style, even though it has none of the brilliance of Pinarol's 'Surge propera' (see chapter 4).

The simpler chant settings disqualified from consideration as genuine motets in the first paragraph of this chapter are still substantial enough to be distinct from the tiny and crude pieces to be considered in chapter 7, being more conservative than amateurish. There are six such works, all for three voices, potentially strophic in conception (though only the first verse is ever given) and often indistinguishable in style and technique with the exception of the canticle 'Nunc dimittis'.

Most typical are the two 'Lucis creator optime' settings. The first of these (i.e. that on ff.75v.-76r., edited as 'Lucis creator optime I' in vol. ii, p.112) paraphrases the melody freely in the Cantus written in a high C_1 clef as opposed to the C_3 and F_3 clefs of the lower voices. The shape also appears in the Tenor until after 'preferens' (b.26ff.) where it is is taken over solely, but much more clearly in the Cantus. These two voices form all the cadences and are thus distinct as the bearers of the structure, by comparison with which the lower one is a purely decorative contratenor. The melodic liberties taken are generally limited to the filling out and extension of the chant with cadential figures, though at 'optime' (bb.11-14) there is a sequence that is only just related to the original. In this way the *cantus firmus*, though not rigid, governs the progress of the music throughout its short duration. There are details such as the use of brief duets to break up the texture at increasing distances apart (at bb.1, 6 and 26) that give it some additional sense of direction, but in a piece this size, the melody itself is structurally sufficient, particularly in view of its popularity.

The other setting (i.e. on ff.132v.-133r., edited as 'Lucis creator optime II' in vol. ii, p.114) though in a different mensuration and slightly more florid is very similar. The opening is plainly alike, with its one-bar duet and pre-imitation, as is the use of chant paraphrase in both upper voices simultaneously (though they do not imitate) and virtually the same clefs and part-hierarchy. On 'primordiis' (b.14ff.) the melody is then relegated to just one voice in exactly the same way as in the other version; the two also have a Bassus entry on high d' between their second and third lines and a Cantus sequence on 'optime' in common. It is therefore not wholly improbable that one was written in the light of the other, although this is of course purely a matter of conjecture.

'Veni creator spiritus' (edited in vol. ii, p.196) is very much like the 'Lucis creator optime' settings, using the same clefs, free Bassus and chant paraphrase in both upper voices with one predominating at the end. Again, the sense of genre is so strong that the question of common or related authorship seems largely irrelevant, at least in the context of the present thesis.

'Aures ad nostras' (edited in vol. ii, p.13) is if anything in a less confident style than its fellows and the *cantus firmus*, though always present, is so freely treated as to be unrecognizable at times. It comes mainly in the Cantus, though where it rests in bb.15-17, the Tenor fills in the gap. This division is however less artful than the simultaneous paraphrasing of the above works, and implies a less proficient composer at work; such a proposition is borne out by the often dubious counterpoint (for instance the consecutive octaves in b.13 and the odd cadences) and dull melodic motion. The opening words are given as a title above the staves rather than an incipit and it seems that the piece was conceived somewhat differently from the others; the contrasting nature of the free lowest voice is also markedly more pronounced.

'Ave maris stella' (edited in vol. ii, p.31) is rather like 'Aures ad nostras' in almost all repects. The *cantus firmus* is so freely handled that parts of it seem to get completely lost (as with the 'Dei mater alma' line) and the low equal voice-ranges are also the same. The most prominent difference is that the free voice seems to be the middle one here and that cadences are more liberally allocated, occurring between either upper voice and the Bassus; otherwise a similarly tentative manner prevails throughout.

The 'Nunc dimittis' on f.88r. (edited in vol. ii, p.132) is a simple *alternatim* harmonization of the third tone. Following the usual practice, the even-numbered verses are omitted from the source; the others present the melody in a virtually pristine form in the upper voice, decoration being limited to a few minor syncopations at cadences. Underneath, the lower voices are essentially homorhythmic and the harmony has the same kind of functional character as is associated with the frottola, the Bassus frequently moving in perfect intervals. This harmonic accompanying style is very different from the modal independence found in the hymn settings and constitutes the most distinctive feature of the piece, no other Latin work in FP27 being really anything like it.

The two outer polyphonic verses are very similar, both being simple and syllabic arrangements of the same melody. The middle one, on the other hand, is contrasted by a more expansive melismatic style and the use of *tempus imperfectum diminutum*, as opposed to the plain *tempus imperfectum* surrounding it. The use of both these mensurations in the same piece outside of any proportional scheme and without any tempus perfectum sections is highly unusual, and sheds an interesting light on how they should be interpreted. The middle section could as easily been notated in diminished time, with its values halved, but the composer must have been trying to effect a change of tempo to match the more relaxed style of the writing. A direct halving of the *tactus* value was thus surely not intended (and is highly uncomfortable in performance), a more likely proportion being something nearer two thirds. The fact that these temporal relationships were probably not taken at face value is of course well-known,[16] but this is an interesting test case in view of the rarity of direct juxtapositions of *integer valor* and diminished time.

Even among this minority of motets based on some kind of pre-composed material, there is still a wide diversity of style. The small-scale chant harmonizations vary from the traditional 'Lucis creator optime' settings to the transparent and frottola-like 'Nunc dimittis', spanning all degrees of technical competence along the way. Among the full scale motets, approaches vary from the simplicity of Antonius Peragulfus Lucensis's 'Regina caeli' to the intense canonic procedures of Divitis's 'Per lignum crucis'. Moreover, at least two sub-species of motet can be discerned, namely the imitative paraphrase 'Regina caeli' settings and the often canonic 'Da pacem' arrangements, which seem to obey their own rules of genre rather than function as independent pieces within the broader tradition. It is when all these are further set against the 'free' compositions examined in chapter 4 that the inadequacy of the term 'motet' becomes particularly apparent, but even so the range has not yet been fully explored; there are still further distinctions to be made among the pieces in FP27 and BQ19, which will be considered in the following chapters.

Notes

[1]Free pieces similarly predominate over those based on *cantus firmus* or paraphrase techniques among the works by the more established composers in FP27 and BQ19, moreover in approximately the same ratio. Only the 'Regina caeli' settings of Brumel and Compère use such devices in the former source, while in the latter they are largely confined to certain works by Mouton and Moulu.

[2]Palestrina, for example, wrote 35 Masses based on paraphrases of monophonic tunes.

[3]*LU*, p.836; for the original version, see *Grove*, 'Litania Lauretana' (xi, p.75). This melody can be found associated with the same words in several of the *laude* and minor ritual works to be discussed in chapter 7; it is also recognizably similar to that on 'Sancta Maria, Mater Dei, ora pro nobis' in the famous 'Ave Maria' Antiphon (see *LU*, p.1861), from where it may derive.

[4]*LU*, p.275.   This was an immensely popular text in the early sixteenth century, polyphonic versions surviving by Agricola, Arcadelt, Johannes Beauserron (2 settings), Brumel (2 settings), Carpentras (2 settings), Costanzo Festa (4 settings), Eustachius de Monte Regalis, Ghiselin, Gombert (2 settings, one à12), Manchicourt, Andreas Michot, Vincentius Misonne, Silva and Willaert as well as three anonymous works in BQ19, one in FP27 and one in *I-Rvat* C.S.46 (see *JosephP*). Nearly all are based on paraphrase of the melody (Gombert's 12v. version being in fact the only exception) and the majority use it in more than one voice to generate essentially imitative textures. Thus 'Regina caeli' motets can be considered as a distinct genre of some significance, though its deeper study lies outside the scope of this thesis.

---

[5]Published in Schiavetto's *Motetti a cinque et a sei voci* (Venice, G. Scotto, 1564). The piece has not as yet been reprinted in any modern edition and is not even included in the composer's worklist in *Grove*.

[6]A setting of the same text survives by Richafort in the *Motetti del fiore. Secundus liber cum quinque vocibus* (Lyons, J. Moderne, 1532), though it is not an ostinato piece and makes no reference to the litany melody. Like Schiavetto's setting, Richafort's is presently unavailable in any modern edition and absent from his worklist in *Grove*.

[7]Similar words set to a variant of the melody can also be found in certain of the *laude* from FP27 and Petrucci's *Libro secondo* of 1508; these latter are to be discussed more fully in chapter 7.

[8]For another, though considerably less extreme, example of a psalm tone finding its way into a motet setting, see Silva's 'Judica me Deus', also from BQ19 and edited in *SilvaO*, i (no. 3).

[9]'Stella caeli' and 'Da pacem' both exist in identical versions in *1502[1]*, from where they were probably copied.

[10]W. A. Nugent: *The Life and Works of Antonius Divitis*, diss., North Texas State University, 1970.

[11]*LowMC*, iii, pp.188-93.

[12]*Idem.*

[13]All the early sixteenth-century settings known to me - by Agricola, Brumel, Compère (the 'loco Deo gratias' from the 'Ave Domine Jesu Christe' Mass), Costanzo Festa, Francesco de Layolle, Prioris, and the two anonymous pieces in FP27 (ff.31v.-32r.) and BQ18 (ff.30v.-31r.: see chapter 8, pp.285- 6) - make use of the opening of the melody in an imitative manner, as do other settings as late as that of Schiavetto in his book of 1564. Those by Brumel and Prioris are

actually rigorously canonic throughout, and that by Festa is remarkably similar to this one from BQ19 in the disposition of a strict canon in *breves* in the lower voices with decorative figurations above. The resemblance is so strong that it is difficult to quell the suspicion that one was written in imitation of the other. Festa's piece would be the most obvious chioce as the model, being the more competent and interesting piece, if it were not that its sole source, *I-RVat* CS18, dates from as late as 1539, at least two decades after BQ19. Whatever the case may be, it is still clear that 'Da pacem' settings, like those of the 'Regina caeli' text, comprise a homogenous sub-genre firmly distinct from the main body of contemporaneous motets.

[14]This is in fact because the version in *1502¹*, from which this seems to have been copied, is also only partially texted.

[15]In what seems to be the only reference to the composer in modern literature, Jeppesen cites the appearance of 'Antonius peragulfus aus Lucca' in FP27 as an additional argument for the Florentine or at least Tuscan provenance of the manuscript; see *JeppFR*, ii, p.39.

[16]See *ApelN*, pp.192-3.

CHAPTER 6: THE PSALM MOTETS AND RELATED WORKS

The psalm motet was a radically new type of composition at the beginning of the sixteenth century. The earliest dated setting of a complete psalm text is Brumel's 'Laudate Dominum de caelis' (Psalm 148) of 1507,[1] though it is almost certain that Josquin's famous 'Miserere' (Psalm 50) preceded it, probably as early as 1503 or 1504.[2] Thus it is that while there are no examples in FP27, there are five in BQ19, four of them by 'minor' composers[3] and hence eligible for consideration here, a telling reflection of the decade and a half that passed between their respective compilations.

The sheer size of these motets makes it extremely unlikely that they were intended as direct substitutes for any of the psalms in the order of the Mass or Office. On the contrary, their considerable dramatic scope and sophisticated style point to a use either as independent musical recreation, or if in church, as an extra interpolation into the rite rather than a functional part of it. Extremely long motets were of course a consistent feature of the previous century and in a way these works can be seen as the inheritors of that tradition; however the novel use of a complete psalm and freedom from any restraining *cantus firmus* gave rise to one of the most innovative compositional types of its time, as will be seen in more detail below.

The length of these motets generates different problems of organization from those posed by the smaller-scale pieces considered up to now. The fact that they are all divided into two or more distinct movements is one of the more obvious indications that the formal stereotypes discussed in chapter 4 are insufficient to describe fully their more complex procedures. Elements of structural functions do remain, particularly at the opening and closing points of the music, but the graceful formality of the 'rhetorical style' is on the whole severely compromised by a narrative flow parallel to that of a psalm. The way in which the latent drama of the text is calculatedly exploited and the occasionally vivid word painting are all far in advance of other contemporaneous motets and occasionally most unexpected in music of this time.

These motets are sophisticated not only in their overall form but also in the variety and ingenuity of their basic fabrics. Such ambitious projects taxed a composer's invention well beyond the simple provision of neatly balanced contrasting sections and the picturesque responses to some of the more striking verbal images produce some wholly original effects. The demands made on performers are correspondingly higher, in skill as well as stamina; these are pieces by and for professionals, a status again reminiscent of the 'grand manner' of Regis or Ockeghem which had been so recently usurped by the quest for a more direct means of expression.

Settings of other texts aside from psalms exist that are equivalent in length, style and presumed function. The two bipartite *Canticum Canticorum* settings in BQ19,[4] for example, are based on pastiches of the original verses and can have had no functional relation to the divine service. Symon Ferrariensis's 'Maria ergo' and Lupus's 'In nomine' are also based on compound texts, bipartite in structure and in exactly the same style, while Bruhier's ceremonial 'Vivite felices' is similarly broad in scope. These pieces form a group together with the psalm settings whose ambitions and means set them well aside from the other pieces in BQ19 as yet another of the vital tributaries into what was to become the mainstream of the sixteenth-century motet tradition.

Symon Ferrariensis

The two motets in BQ19 by this composer are strikingly similar in style despite their diverse texts and the rare use of *tempus perfectum* in the *prima pars* of 'Maria ergo', the affinity being due not only to the common Phrygian mode but also to the underlying structural procedures. Of Symon's life nothing is known, though Jeppesen has suggested that he might be identical with Simon, *maestro di capella* of the Casa Santa in Loreto *ca.*1510.[5] As well as the pieces in BQ19 there are two other motets in *GB-Lcm 2037*[6] and a further one in *I-TVca 36*,[7] both of which originated in Ferrara *ca.*1530. This source distribution both confirms the activity in northern Italy implied by Symon's second name and supports the thesis that BQ19 originated in that area rather than in France. Unfortunately the London manuscript comprises only two out of four partbooks and likewise the sole other source of Symon's work, *I-Bc Q23*, conserves only three out of four parts of another composition, a set of Lamentations.[8] Thus apart from the example at Treviso 'Maria ergo' and 'Nisi quia' are the only intact remains of Symon's output, which is a great shame in view of the arrestingly distinctive qualities of his writing.

For a work copied into a manuscript of around 1518, 'Nisi quia' (edited in *JeppIS*, ii, p.149) is remarkable for its sensitivity to the text, both in general mood and in specific details of word painting, which in turn gives rise to an impressive musical vocabulary almost unique in BQ19. The text is that of Psalm 123 complete (but without any doxology), whose eight verses are distributed between two *partes* of four each, the *secunda* somewhat shorter than the *prima* according to the lesser length of the lines. This symmetrical division is convenient in terms of the verbal mood too: the first four verses paint a vivid and dramatic picture of the horrors averted by God's deliverance, while the last four give thanks for that deliverance in more placid images, a contrast taken advantage of in the musical structure.

The originality of the piece is patent from the very opening, whose carefully contrived series of intervals is more reminiscent of the later sixteenth century, as is the measured chordal continuation after b.10 and the harmonic logic of the Bassus in bb.13-18. There is no cadence until that in b.18, after which the opening music is repeated (as its text is in the psalm), with a different cadence onto *A* in b.29 to round off what is essentially a long and extraordinarily individual *exordium*. While much of this originality stems from the unusual verbal repeat, which precludes the usual through-composed imitation, Symon must still be credited with an acute grasp of its formal possibilities and also a fine ability to sustain long passages with barely any recourse to cadential formulae.   Moreover, the opening Cantus notes derive from the solmization of 'Nisi' as '*mi - mi*', which is not only a conceit in itself in the tradition of the '*ut - sol*' at the end of Josquin's 'Virgo prudentissima', but may also refer to certain earlier works by Ockeghem and Isaac.[9]

More typically early sixteenth-century in form are the subsequent duet sections, although their content is again decidedly forward-looking.   The powerful rising idea on 'cum exurgerent homines', for example, is a vivid response to the textual image far removed from anything Renaldo or Weerbeke would have attempted, and there are other passages (e.g. bb.42-7) that indicate the same ear for vocal 'orchestration' evident from the opening. The consistent use of imitation is also noteworthy since its structural function is subordinate to its use as a way of introducing a particular dramatic melody into each voice. The entries on 'cum irascerentur' (see b.47 onwards) may be erratic in their pitches and spacing but their profile is always unmistakeable through the texture, especially the waspish semiquaver ending; a similar compromise between pure melody and the demands of counterpoint as observed in the motets of Sebastiano Festa seems to have been effected. A similar technique can be seen on 'torrentem' (see Ex. 2), a dramatic passage whose texturally highlighted falling ninth scales and pedal Bassus preparation would not be unworthy of Lassus.

Ex. 2

    The combination of this idea with that on the subsequent
'pertransivit' into a varied double counterpoint is also novel because it
arises from the exploitation of their dramatic as much as their
structural possibilities; they are created as individual, non-overlapping
melodies, whose very length distinguishes them from more orthodox
imitative points.

    Whereas the verbally aggressive *prima pars* was constructed
out of well-defined sections carefully articulated by cadences, the
secunda establishes a tranquility appropriate to the new textual mood
by a more frequent use of cadence as a tonal stabilizer in the middle of
a section (e.g. at b.101) or in a position where sectional overlap

diminishes its impact (e.g. b.109).   There is only one dramatic passage, on 'anima nostra erepta est' (b.118 onwards), to recall the *prima pars*, and the succeeding 'laqueus contritus est' is made especially gentle by the slow unfolding of a simple idea repeated literally throughout the texture.   Common to both movements though are features such as an answering voice-pairing technique whereby only the first statement is actually heard as a duet, continuation of its component voices masking the repeat of the same material by the second pair.   This occurs at bb.42-7 in the *prima pars* and is again apparent in bb.88-93 and bb.118-23; while it is also found in many works by other composers (such as Weerbeke), it is the consistency of its application here that makes it so remarkable.

The end of this motet is even more peculiar than the beginning. Although the last formal cadence is onto *E* at b.152, a *G* is held in one voice or another in nearly every one of the 15 bars from b.146 to the end as a sort of migrant pedal.   It lies mainly in the Cantus, which thus recites its remaining text to what is essentially a rhythmic monotone; by imitating this through the texture in a curiously static staggering of one- or two-note ideas, the music eventually ends by dissipating its energy rather than concentrating it into a decisive gesture.   The pedal note is additionally unusual in being the third of the mode and resolving onto the tonic as the very last note of the work, another example of the way that the various tonal possibilities of the Phrygian mode are worked out in this piece.[10]

Thus it seems that although the structure of this piece is governed chiefly by a concern for dramatic narrative, elements of rhetorical formal procedure still persist.   The opening seventeen bars are clearly an *exordium*, both in their closed structure and also their contrast with the following duet passages, typical of the transition to the *narratio*.   The opening is balanced by a section of equivalent length at the end of the motet, where the use of a continuous pedal note imbues the music with an appropriately final character.

What is striking is the way that neither the end of the *prima pars* nor the beginning of the *secunda* show any traces of such functional devices. The abruptness of the former and *narratio* character of the latter are most significant in this respect, showing that alternatives to the procedures usually found at opening and closing sections were available; their apparently limited use by contemporaneous motet composers would thus seem to indicate a conscious association of these specific formal functions with particular compositional devices. By avoiding such conventions at the transition from the *prima pars* to the *secunda*, Symon deliberately weakens the sense of hiatus, with the result that the break is smoothed over and the piece cast more as one continuous whole than two separate movements.

Like 'Nisi quia', 'Maria ergo' (edited in *JeppIS*, ii, p.141) relies almost exclusively on imitation for its musical material, though here it is usually arranged as overlapping duets with plentiful rests so that the effect is never Gombert-like, and the texture is frequently broken up by homophonic passages. The characteristically overlapping imitative technique noted in 'Nisi quia' is discernible here too (see for example the Altus entry in bb.8 and 85 over the ends of the previous duets), as is the corollary that when one idea follows another, it first appears as a counterpoint to it, maintaining a seamless continuity despite the thin texture and the sharply profiled motives. Symon moreover consistently bases his imitation on thirds and sixths (e.g. bb.44-55, 85-94, 99-101, 108-110, 124-127 and 148-150) and although this is to some extent encouraged by the Phrygian mode it is not so characteristic of other composers such as Costanzo Festa or Willaert.

For overall structure, the piece takes its cue from the text, as might be expected. The latter is an Antiphon - 'Oremus' - Collect composite in exactly the same way as Renaldo's 'Illuminavit eum' was (see chapter 4, p.89), but here the inflated scale results in a bipartite motet with the first movement considerably shorter than the second, in the exact proportion of the Antiphon to the collect.[11] The music of the two *partes* is only really related by text and mode as in terms of technique they are set well apart, this being highlighted by the use of different metres for each. The *prima pars* is in *tempus perfectum*, and the *secunda* in *tempus imperfectum diminutum*, an odd reference to the motets of Dufay, Regis and Ockeghem particularly surprising in such an otherwise progressive piece. However, the ostensibly outmoded *tempus perfectum* results, as in Lupus's six voiced 'Miserere', in a stately lilt and periodic regularity very different from fifteenth-century usage.[12] Symon goes out of his way to emphasize this regularity by the use of almost canonic writing between his paired voices and an even succession of clearly grouped four-bar phrases broken really only at b.34, though most obvious before the *fermata* sign in b.17. This opening section has the character of an *exordium*, as did that of 'Nisi quia', and although it continues along a different path from the 'rhetorical' pieces the use of a detached, functional opening group betrays a certain kindred spirit.

The *secunda pars*, while not as strictly contrived as the *prima*, maintains a sense of order by the retention of one pair of voices within the texture imitating the other at a distance, so that the music proceeds as a series of varied local repeats, each overlapping with the next in Symon's own characteristic way. The serenity is disrupted at b.119 (prefigured in the Cantus at b.117) by an extrordinary resort to monotone recitation for the closing formula 'pro Dominum Jesum Christum', which has its parallel in the unique ending of 'Nisi quia' and even more closely in the section of Remi's 'Circumdederunt me' starting at b.55, where the Tenor suddenly comes up with a plain psalm tone in the midst of the polyphony (see chapter 4, p.98). In the present instance the collect is particularly amply endowed with stereotyped formalities at the end, and such a setting may well be a wry acknowledgement of that fact, as well as a convenient means of getting through a patch of musically uninspiring verbiage in a short time. After this, a typical homophonic section in triple time leads, via another basically chordal passage, to the long pedal cadence that rounds the work off, so that the quasi-chanting is significant as the last new music before the usual closing group.

Finally it is interesting from a harmonic point of view that within the normal framework of the Phrygian mode there are progressions with all the character of cadences but which lack the normal sixth to octave or third to unison motion, deriving their effect instead solely from a 'leading note' figure in the upper voice and a falling fifth in the Bassus (see bb.36-7 and 67-8).

This deregulation of the concept of cadence recalls the motets of Sebastiano Festa, whose peculiarities may owe their origins to a deliberate play on theoretical orthodoxies. Further cadential subversion is manifest in the peculiar habit of ending a voice line with a melodic cadential progression, even though no other voice completes the cadence and the harmony is not in the least conclusive; the Altus in bb.107-9 and the Tenor in bb.128-30 are examples of this (see Exx. 3a. and b. respectively).

Ex. 3a   *b.*

Symon has already been compared with Sebastiano Festa on account

of his melodic rather than contrapuntal style. It would seem from
these common traits that they both played similar roles in the adaption
of monodic expression to the discipline of polyphony. Their like
recognition of the cadence as a chordal and dramatic device
independent of the melodic formulae in whose terms it was
theoretically defined is just another symptom of this concentration on
melody for its own sake, as is the converse use of cadential figurations
to end individual voice lines without any necessary harmonic
consequence. However, Symon differs from Sebastiano in his much
stronger sense of the pictorial possibilities of his art, and as such his
work is an important precursor of the music of the later sixteenth
century.

Jacopo Fogliano

Two motets survive in BQ19 under the above attribution, both
very different in style and technique. The information given by Slim
in the *Grove* worklist that Fogliano's entire extant sacred output
consists of three motets and a pair of *laude*[13] contradicts a description
of *I-MOd* 11[14] that mentions 10 sacred pieces of his, unfortunately
without specifying what they are;[15] it is still possible that only three
motets survive as the manuscript is mainly made up of psalms and
hymns, along with other specifically liturgical items. Even if there
are a handful more motets, their number would still be small
alongside that of the *frottole* and madrigals that come down to us
under his name: however, while he was also responsible for two *laude*
in addition to a few instrumental pieces these motets are not in a *lauda*
style even if 'Beati omnes' is a good deal more facile than 'De
profundis'. Fogliano's presence in BQ19, like that of Symon
Ferrariensis, confirms the bias towards northern Italian composers: he
appears to have spent almost the entire span of his eighty-year life as
organist in the cathedral at Modena,[16] and while his secular music
survives in several northern European as well as Italian sources, his
motets (none of which ever found their way into print until the present
century) are less far-flun.g and their distribution is consistent with the

biography outlined above.[17]

Slim writes that 'Fogliano's few sacred compositions reveal much use of imitative duets and frequent homophonic episodes: the text setting is workmanlike, although not particularly expressive', a comment that aptly sums up the style of 'Beati omnes' (edited in *JeppIS*, i, p.70) at least. Although this is a setting of an entire psalm text it has none of the drama and excitement found in others of the type, like the 'Nisi quia' described above. This may be due in part to the text, as Psalm 127 abounds in gentle pastoral imagery in contrast to the vivid drama that permeates Psalm 123. Fogliano also includes the first verse of the doxology but the way that he does it and details of the overall design suggest that this was for musical reasons; the piece is certainly far too elaborate to substitute for a psalm in the liturgy.

The first four verses are set in the *prima pars*, the last three and that of the doxology in the *secunda*, so that both are roughly the same length. However the 'Gloria patri' is set most perfunctorily and the end of the piece actually repeats the opening words 'Beati omnes qui timent Dominum', with a reminiscence of the music of bb.1-7 (compare the Cantus in bb.142-45 with that at bb.4-7), which is the most obvious connection between the two *partes*. The 'ouvert' finish of the *prima* cadencing onto the opening of the *secunda pars* and the clear function of the *exordium* in the former and the *conclusio* in the latter also characterize the two movements as related halves rather than separate motets.

The *prima pars* consists of two pairs of duets alternating between the upper and lower voices prefaced, separated and ended by essentially homophonic passages, the first of which is recognisable as an *exordium* by its regularity.[18] The duets are strictly imitative and actually canonic in many cases, which gives rise to a staggered effect that combines with the frequent overlapping and scarcity of formal cadences to produce a continuous flow of music. The homophonic episodes are, except for the first, highly decorated and while the second is held together by binary repeat schemes (see bb.25-31) the third is a formulaic cadence approached in an effectively free style.

The *secunda pars* is similar but typically less rigid. After the short duet at b.99, however, voice-pairing is eschewed in favour of textural variation between three and four voices. The opening duets before this point are for different pairs from those in the *prima pars*, and so a kind of functional complementarity can be seen to unify the movements still further. At the end a *conclusio* is effected by a homophonic local repeat (bb.124-129) before a curious 'Gloria', where the entire text is set to exact repetitions of the same motif starting progressively on *D*, *A* and *E*; this logical series is consistent with the regularity of Fogliano's structures and can be observed too in the canonic entries on *B-E-A-D* starting at b.111.

The text is divided into fragments most of which are repeated naturally with the answering phrases in the music, the latter structure prevailing over the former at certain points (e.g. bb.7-22). Such abstraction leaves little room for expressive writing and the counterpoint is more noticeable for its smoothness (see for example the melodic development in bb.11-30) than its individuality from one idea to the next. Certain elements are also quite carefully fashioned as decorated melodic sequences, another illustration of the tendency to ordered clarity achieved by abstract planning (see bb.75-85).

As stated above, the regularity of this piece, its clear alternations of duets and homophony, and the firm *exordium* and *conclusio* sections are much more reminiscent of the balanced manner epitomized by Renaldo than the involved open progressions of Symon Ferrariensis. The incorporation of the 'Gloria patri' in order to balance out the numbers of verses in each *parte*, reprise of the opening material at the end and complementary courses of the two *partes* are likewise indicators that this is a rare example of a psalm motet constructed along 'rhetorical' rather than narrative or dramatic lines.

A completely different matter is the same composer's 'De profundis' (edited in *JeppIS*, i, p.77), not only structurally but also in the very minutiae of musical style. The limited vocabulary of alternating imitative and chordal textures and well defined sectional articulation is wholly absent, and the music proceeds instead by organic developmental association in a manner reminiscent of, though in fact more pronounced than, the 'northern' style of Lupus (see chapters 4 and 5). The devices used to maintain continuity are much more flexible and along with the developmental spinning out of material recall the side of Francesco de Layolle's personality that surfaces for example in his 'In principio erat verbum'. They include local repeats, parallel motion in tenths between Cantus and Bassus, short passages of canonic imitation between the upper voices, brief double canons, eddy imitation, imitation by inversion or in just two voices with free counterpoints, harmonic sequence and most strikingly a deliberately concealed block repeat of music from the *prima pars* at the end of the *secunda* unconnected with the sense of the text (compare bb.175-80 with bb.37-41); none of these features are found in such concentration anywhere else among these pieces from BQ19 apart from the parallel tenths in Divitis's 'Per lignum crucis'.

A progressive analytical description of 'De profundis' would be in equal measure confusing and futile, as the music deliberately evades firm outlines and categories. Unity is achieved through the maze of connections listed above and also by the frequent incorporation of a falling fourth motif first treated at length, significantly enough, in the block to be repeated, i.e. bb.37-41 (see Ex. 4, particularly the Cantus).

Ex. 4

Its shape is at first glance rather nondescript but it assumes a high profile through frequent and occasionally intense repetition (e.g. bb.65-71, all voices including by inversion; bb.88-91, 195 *et al.*). A further element of overall formal design is discernible in the way that both *partes* start with passages of genuinely regular imitation in the manner of an *exordium* (albeit befuddled in the *prima* by the addition of a decorative free voice), which then give way to comparable falling third patterns (bb.16-23 and 130-36).

There seems to be no overall proportional plan and the durations of the movements are oddly unequal, the *prima pars* being half as long again as the *secunda* through setting vv.1-6 of the text as opposed to vv.7-8 and the two of the doxology. This is a peculiar precompositional decision that seems to be rather arbitrary since it does not particularly benefit the sense of the words. As with 'Beati omnes' the psalm does not readily lend itself to vivid expression and so the two motets share a similar abstraction of style and a detached quality in spite of their utterly diverse surfaces. There is also more tangible evidence for the hand of the same composer at work; the predilection for sporadic canonic imitation, the use of local repeat forms, the identical endings to the *primae partes* of both pieces and a novel texture where the Tenor and Bassus are linked motivically or by local repeat under a free Altus and monotonic Cantus ('De profundis' bb.160-65, 168-70; 'Beati omnes' bb.22-25). It is interesting to stumble upon these cross-references in two works so otherwise opposed, their opposition reaching out beyond their individual cases and representing the poles of the clear formal style on the one hand and the open organic on the other among these bipartite motets. The incongruity is less one of personal style though, than of genre. 'Beati omnes' is the exception in its application of a neat, closed construction to a type of composition more usually characterized by an open narrative approach. 'De profundis' is much more typical in its freer progress and can be considered as formally similar to Symon's 'Nisi quia' even though its more old-fashioned contrapuntal intensity makes it superficially very different.

Lupus

As well as the pieces already examined in chapters 4 and 5, Lupus left two larger-scale motets in BQ19 that require separate consideration. 'Nigra sum' (edited in vol. ii, p.125) lies under the shadow of a conflicting attribution, Lupus's name in the Bolognese source facing a challenge from that of Consilium (i.e. Jean Conseil) in a later Moderne print from Lyons (*1539*[10]). The prior date of BQ19 is usually taken as authoritative of Lupus's authorship, however, and the piece is not even mentioned in the *Grove* worklist for Conseil.[19] Structurally it is unlike any of Lupus's other works in BQ19 and not so far from the world of Conseil, although there are details, such as the occasional passage of florid decorative writing, that are more typical of him and seem to support the given attribution. Besides, the testimony of the sources must take precedence over stylistic considerations until a full study of the music of both composers provides a more representative basis for comparison.

Like so many other motets drawing on the *Canticum Canticorum* for their texts, 'Nigra sum' sets a selection of lines chosen according to the whim of the composer instead of a specific passage, a procedure facilitated by the even style of the book itself. The verses or lines are presented in the order in which they originally occur, thus: I:4-5, 9, 14-15; II:1-3, 5. The apparent logic of this is marred by the substitution of 'ideo dilexit me rex' for the second half of I:4, the phrase being associated with the first part of the Antiphon 'Nigra sum'.[20] However, given the free assembly of the text this seems perfectly legitimate, particularly as the Antiphon text would be by far the more familiar.

The next irregularity is the division into two *partes* of uneven length (the *secunda* is nearly twice as long as the *prima*), which is surprising as the flexible approach to the biblical verse should make it easy to arrange any proportion or symmetry as desired. The reason for this lies, as might be expected, in the text itself again, but in a way not found in other *Canticum Canticorum* settings. The book is in fact written as a drama, or dialogue between two parties complete with a chorus, and Lupus has elected to take advantage of this and even point it up by the selection of several answering pairs of verses, especially in the *secunda pars*. One such pair, 'Ecce...convallium' (I:14-15, II:1), forms a unit whose central position means that any division of the text into two approximately equal parts must come either before it (at b.60, as actually happens), or after (i.e. at b.101), which would result in an even greater discrepancy in the lengths of the two resultant *partes*. The arrangement adopted has also the functional advantage of separating an expository *prima pars* from a more plainly dialectic *secunda*, and of not disrupting a continuous passage from the original book.

The recognition of the dialogue between Sponsa and Sponsus obviously rules out the possibility that the unusually high clef combination was conceived to complement the femininity implied by the opening; perhaps the 'pastoral' subject matter of the *Canticum Canticorum* seemed apt for a higher, clearer texture, such as is found also in the anonymous 'Vulnerasti cor meum' to be discussed at the end of this chapter.[21] It could also be that Lupus had a specific group of singers in mind when he wrote the work; in this case its copying into a source catering principally for more standard voice combinations shows that this would not rule it out of consideration for performance in other circumstances.

The dialogue structure is reflected at a lower level in that each change of character but one (at b.115) is marked by a full caesura, in most cases graced with a *fermata* sign (see bb. 38, 76, 101 and 115). The *fermata* at b.10 fulfils a different purpose, that of articulating what amounts to an *exordium*, though the subsequent design bears no relationship to normal rhetorical form. The sections so defined are then made internally self-sufficient but rarely directly connected to each other. This reliance on dialogue form explains some of the apparent looseness of construction, like the rapid proliferation of ideas in the first ten bars, but there are also some well-handled developmental passages, such as the way that the arch of a fourth at bb.38-45 is contracted in b.47 (in the Bassus) and finally reduced to a simple second at b.52, or the derivation of the duet in bb.92-101 from that in bb.76-85.

The vocabulary of local structural techniques is wider than is usual among these motets from BQ19 and while it is not as extreme as in Fogliano's 'De profundis' the frequent use of decorated homophony, passing hints at melodic sequence, varied local repeat (e.g. bb.108-14 or bb.126-32) and consistent imitation throughout makes it a somewhat different offering technically from the majority of its fellows, more sophisticated in execution if perhaps less in conception. The consequently rather old-fashioned impression is exacerbated by the use of the Mixolydian mode whose inflections, apparent from the first two bars, lend it a peculiar character quite distinct from the incipient 'tonal' manner that was coming into vogue in other music of the time.

Like all Lupus's motets in BQ19, 'In nomine Jesu' (edited in vol. ii, p.104) presents a homogenous surface in preference to the strong contrasts of duets and homophony favoured elsewhere. Here in particular the texture is relentlessly full with every section based on imitation, albeit of a characteristically erratic sort. The only regular full imitation is at the very beginning, after which themes are treated freely in two or three voices, the remainder moving decoratively around them. No structural part-hierarchy exists and the usual cadential procedures appear between any pair of voices at the composer's convenience. This kind of freedom, though in its way equally progressive, is very different from that exercised by Symon Ferrariensis; it is first and foremost a contrapuntal matter and has little bearing on the actual melodic and expressive substance of the music. As in Lupus's 'Miserere...quoniam tribulabor', the free lines are particularly florid with frequent runs in *minimae* and octave leaps, giving a general impression of density and restless activity noticeable also in 'Nigra sum' and reminiscent too of the four-voiced motets of Willaert.

The text is composed of two different items separated by an 'Oremus' and this structure is reflected in its musical setting.[22] The *prima pars* of the motet sets what can only be recognized as a pastiche of an Introit and Gradual[23] (though it is more likely to be a genuine single item as yet unidentified) and the second a prayer; as in 'Maria ergo' and Renaldo's 'Illuminavit eum', the two are of unequal lengths, resulting in a similar musical imbalance. The opening of the Introit melody is used at the beginning of the motet but after this the music is freely invented; although other faint references to fragments of plainchant do occasionally appear, these are not of any structural significance. What is more interesting is that the opening is virtually identical to that of the same composer's 'Miserere...quoniam tribulabor', even in the order of voice entries. Since that of 'In nomine Jesu' is obviously related to chant material, it looks as if it would have been the model for the other, which is more expansive and introduces a fifth voice. Both works are unique to this source, so that the establishment of a relative chronology between them is of little consequence, but the fact that a composer was prepared to paraphrase one of his motets to open another and disregard its liturgical origins in the process has a certain curiosity value.

In spite of this freedom of construction, the music still bears traces of certain of the 'rhetorical' procedures typical of the shorter pieces. The full imitation and self- sufficiency of bb.1-12 qualify the opening passage as an *exordium*, though it fails to end on the modal tonic, and the end of the piece conforms to the principle of reprise, bb.124- 35 being an obvious reworking of the end of the *prima pars*, after which the idea from b.124 is spun out further to the final close. However, the lack of any reduced textures means that the central span of the motet has none of the character of a *narratio* and indeed the rigorously imitative texture throughout this section is not to be found elsewhere in any of the more concise BQ19 motets.

The few 'rhetorical' features apparent in 'In nomine Jesu' are essentially superficial to its construction, being really no more than gestures grafted on to a profoundly different musical substance. The work bears the stamp more of its composer's contrapuntally-orientated personality and preference for consistently full and florid textures than any concern for formal grace or verbal expression, as indeed do all his motets in BQ19 despite their variety of outward forms. This style is of course in marked opposition to the quasi- monodic approach of Sebastiano Festa or Symon Ferrariensis, being more closely aligned with the manner of the northern masters such as Mouton and Gombert. The details of Lupus's life and sojourn in Italy (if any) are completely unknown, the relevant details of his biography resting on purely hypothetical identifications. However, the style of his music as evinced by the BQ19 works, and indeed others too,[24] is decidedly unlike that of the composers known to have been active in Italy at the same time, so that until further investigations of his life and remaining works have been made it is only possible to agree again with Blackburn that he was probably northern by training and habit.[25]

Although Antoine Bruhier was probably of Flemish or Provençal origin, such documentation as concerns him refers to his activities as a singer in the chapel choir of Pope Leo X in the second decade of the sixteenth century.[26] His surviving sacred output consists of a mass and two motets, alongside ten secular pieces, one each in Latin and Italian and eight in French. These latter are not a little puzzling since Bruhier was apparently granted prebends in Lyons and Geneva on account of his ignorance of the French language,[27] but their attributions are not entirely secure anyway, confusion existing between him and one Jean de la Brugière, a genuine Frenchman of a younger generation. No such problems arise with 'Vivite felices' (edited in *DunnVS*, no. 2) however, because of the early date inferred not only from that of the source but also from the fact that the motet is exceptional in having been written for a specific event, the meeting of François I and Leo X in Bologna at the end of 1515. On the strength of this it has already been examined in Dunning's *Die Staatsmotette*[28], where in addition to a historical criticism of the text an analysis of the music is also provided. This analysis points out the declamation, easy homophony, standard cadential progressions and harmonic stability of the piece and comes to the conclusion that it is more in the style of the *frottola* than that of the Netherlands motet.

The influence of Italian secular music is certainly prominent enough in the ways that Dunning states, quite appropriately so in view of the Bacchic text. Nevertheless, even in the most basic terms of length and through-composition it is definitely a motet and moreover one of some contrivance both structurally and, in its closing section, contrapuntally.

The work falls into two *partes* of approximately equal length, the *secunda* being slightly the longer, each of which set one stanza of the verse text. Both *partes* are divided exactly into two (at bb.29 and

91) by musical caesurae corresponding to breaks in the sense of the words rather than their line structure: the entire second half of the *secunda pars* sets one line only as an extended coda of bravura monothematic writing. The word 'coda' is used with intent here as this last section stands quite distinct from the other three while at the same time picking up a motivic thread that has been running through the whole piece. The relationship between the first three sections is that the third (i.e. the secunda pars up to b.91) goes through exactly the same sequence of events as the first two together: homophony (b.1/59), then falling triadic imitation (b.23/65), then duet texture (b.30/71) and finally homophony again, both times in triple time (b.48/82). The fourth section, on the other hand, proceeds quite independently of this structure and is also based on another series of contrapuntal textures altogether.

The 'motivic thread' is something that Dunning overlooked and along with the ordering outlined above makes it impossible to dismiss the work as a facile essay in *frottola* style. The piece is unified from start to finish by the varied thematic use of falling thirds, either interlocking in a stepwise pattern or conjunct. Their first obvious appearance is as the substance of the simple triadic imitation at b.23, and then they are taken up sequentially by the duet starting at b.41. In the *secunda pars* they can be found again in the corresponding triadic imitation at b.65 and as the basic constituents of the whole closing section from b.91; the idea expressed at b.91 itself comes back augmented at b.99, diminished at bb.107 and 113, and conjunct thirds reappear as a sort of *cantus firmus* in the Tenor at b.115 surrounded by their own diminutions, a particularly effective climax to the work. Not only is the interval consistent throughout but the use of syncopation in the duets makes it very prominent: it is also perhaps not too fanciful to see a constructive falling third in the way that the harmony of the opening four bars lurch arrestingly from F down to D, and indeed this movement is stated in the very first chord change of the entire piece, in b.2. Thus through the accumulation of detail into larger patterns 'Vivite felices' can be seen as a highly original construction where the *secunda pars* sums up the *prima* in two different ways, firstly condensing its sequence of events and then developing an inherent motif and in doing so producing a 34 bar section on a single idea treated with such imagination and assurance as to be quite unique in the repertory.

Aside from this the style is as Dunning describes: a clearly defined alternation of homophony and duet textures with the emphasis on the former, whose lively rhythmic decorations and even dialogue (e.g. bb.32-35 and parts of the closing section) do belong to the *frottola* rather than the motet tradition. The harmonic stability mentioned by Dunning is as equally typical of the motet as the *frottola* at this point in its evolution and monotony is carefully avoided by the peculiar opening mentioned above and the corresponding veer into *B-flat/G* at the beginning of the *secunda pars*, these chords having been scrupulously left out of the *prima*.

It is worth pointing out that the final section has an internal structure of its own, falling as it does into three smaller units all based on falling thirds and ended by similar 'codette' whose function is purely harmonic, at bb.105-6, 111-12 and 121-22 (Dunning's stereotyped *Schlussformelle*). These passages, which are rhythmically as well as harmonically alike, serve to regulate the flow of the music and provide a haven from the motivic insistence: the short middle section (bb.107-12) acts in the same way, paying lip-service to the falling thirds before turning into the only three-voiced part of the piece before its 'codetta'.

Such attention to detail in the interest of more far-reaching structural concerns along with the other elements mentioned above demonstrate the seriousness and competence of the work, which is well worthy of the Netherlands motet tradition. The contrast between this and its superficial frivolity is a typically renaissance compromise that not only suits the quaint admixture of *récherché* humanism and extrovert drinking song of the text, but is ideally appropriate for the coalescence of Church and State, religious service and secular celebration, that is implicit in the occasion for which it was written.

Like so many other *Canticum Canticorum* settings, the text of the anonymous 'Vulnerasti cor meum' (edited in vol. ii, p.212) is based not on a particular passage, but on a pastiche of favourite phrases taken from various places in the original book, whose uniformity of idea makes it peculiarly suitable for this kind of treatment. The element of choice is important both as a manifestation of the new humanistic subjectivity associated with music in Italy at the turn of the sixteenth century and, more specifically, because a composer would choose those particular phrases that he wanted to set to music, or that he found in some way congenial to his imagination; it is no accident that some of the most 'expressive' music of the time was composed in response to *Canticum Canticorum* texts.

The text under consideration is unusual in that the first three words are used as a refrain, regularly in the *prima pars* and more sporadically in the *secunda* too, because it is associated with a motif which thus returns as a kind of ostinato. This is a distinctively profiled melody first heard in bb.1-2 and its subsequent imitations, which usually comes back in the Bassus alone, in this way subtly concealed under the rest of the texture. The main exception to this is its imitation at the opening of the *secunda pars*, matching that in the *prima* and causing it to act as a linking headmotif as well as an ostinato. The strong character of this phrase also means that it appropriates anything that sounds similar, so that otherwise innocuous phrases like that of the Cantus in bb.96/98 assume a greater significance as parts of the close structure of the piece. There is in addition another unifying sub-motif at bb.12/13 (Altus), 13-16 and 57 (Cantus), 64/65 (Altus) and 66/67 (Cantus) although its force is diminished as it always arises as a counterpoint to a pedal point and is highly formulaic anyway.

The ostinato function of the main motif is most apparent in the *prima pars*, where after a nine-bar *exordium* it recurs after every cadence as an introduction to a passage of six or seven bars setting different words (at bb.10, 17, 25, 31, 37 and 44).   The only aberration is at b.17 where it is varied and extended into a long range imitation figure (repeated at b.21 in the Tenor) with diverse accompaniments, retaining the 'Vulnerasti cor meum' text.   This disruption so early on aids the concealment of its structural function, along with its restriction to the lowest voice.

There is regularity too in the five intervening episodes, which are all based on relatively long repeated notes in the manner of a *cantus firmus* in the Tenor (at bb.10, [17], 26, 32, 38 and 45), which is paralleled by the Cantus in all cases except the first. The functional nature of these two voices is further evident in that they form all the cadences, the Altus and Bassus being decorative apart from the ostinato; this part-hierarchy is surprisingly anachronistic in a work so very forward-looking in many other ways. The quasi-*cantus firmi* are obviously not chant-derived and are unrelated save that they all share a common logic in being either decorated falling fifths or rising fifth arch patterns. That at b.38 is notable as the Tenor reaches its highest note as a deliberate expressive climax (all the other voices do likewise at the same time) shortly before the end of the movement.

The *secunda pars*, though freer, is in a similar style and opens with the same ostinato motif in the Bassus. The pairing of the Cantus with a quasi-*cantus firmus* in the Tenor appears at b.55 and leads on to two long-range imitation patterns (Tenor b.66 = Bass b.62, then Tenor b.76 = Bass b.71) before the motif recurs at the significant moment just after the first and only cadence on A in the piece, at b.84. The idea of a rising climax noted near the end of the *prima pars* comes back again more obviously at b.86 and is matched at b.93 by a peculiar passage where each voice is motivically different but all decorate a falling fifth or octave: the motif crops up in the Bassus at b.93 as one of these phrases.

From here on the motet becomes more 'normal'; answering duet phrases and homophony lead, via a rare (for this time) and beautiful double suspension in b.110 to a closing passage whose slower motion and homophony characterize it as a *conclusio* despite the unusual quasi-duet texture in bb.111-113. It is in fact justifiable to see the section after b.100 as an added coda, since up to that point the *secunda pars* is not only almost exactly the same length as the *prima*, but also progresses through the same sequence of events, namely headmotif - quasi-*cantus firmus* in Tenor and Cantus - long-range imitation - climax. After b.100 this unity is abandoned and the entire style radically changes, homophony and matching voice pairs are used for the first time and even the motif is discarded: furthermore nearly all of the final text has been stated already in the main part of the piece.

The parallel courses of the two movements can be found elsewhere, for example in 'Vivite felices', but the tacking on of an ending that looks for all the world as if it had been written by a completely different composer is most unusual. Again, 'Vivite felices' furnishes another instance of a long closing section, but there it is highly integrated motivically with the previous music and does not disturb the isometry of the two movements. There are other surprising juxtapositions too: while the part-hierarchy, quasi-*cantus firmus* and lack of homophony or voice pairing (until the end) are definitely old-fashioned, the expressive style and especially the carefully arranged climaxes are very much part of the sixteenth century, as is the well-defined motif and strong sense of unity. Despite the features shared with 'Vivite felices' there do not seem to be any grounds for attributing the piece to any of the other named composers in BQ19, as both the structural and textural techniques are extraordinarily original and combine to make this one of the most individual works in the codex, and one moreover of outstandingly high quality.

The long bipartite pieces discussed above are much more varied, as a group, in their structures and styles than the shorter motets. This is partly due to the greater complexity inherent in the larger scale, but is also symptomatic of the wider possibilities for personal expression and constructive originality in an open form unbound by convention. The mere division into two *partes* involves all sorts of problems as to the complementary relationship between them that simply do not arise with the single-movement works. The various solutions to these, and their reconciliation with a deliberately greater emphasis on text setting in both overall structure and local details, are what give each piece its own particular character. These are to a certain extent pre-compositional decisions and thus affect a piece rather as the choice of a *cantus firmus* might have, exerting an influence that transcends in most cases the limitations of personal style.

Common procedures can be seen to occur, however, in pieces based on similar texts. For all their differences of outward personality, Symon's 'Nisi quia' and Fogliano's 'De profundis' both follow similar narrative courses and the survival in the former of the rhetorical opening and closing functions relates it also to Fogliano's 'Beati omnes'. The compromise made betweem psalmodic rhapsody and closed musical structures here are significant indicators of how important such considerations could be to a musician and how he clung to them even when embarking on a decisively original type of composition.

The two lyric pieces based on the *Canticum Canticorum* are on the other hand rather less uniform in their approaches. The complete freedom of a composer in the compilation of his text elicits a highly original dialogue form from Lupus, a sense of unity being lent by dramatic rather than musical means. More obvious as a constructive device is the ostinato of 'Vulnerasti cor meum', though its camouflaging and support by parallel series of events in both *partes* result in a musical structure of some sophistication. It is of note that some of the most original of the shorter motets were composed on similar texts, for example Weerbeke's 'Ibo mihi' or Pinarol's 'Surge propera'. The unique form of the *Canticum Canticorum* and its poetry, a combination of the erotic and the spiritual typical of the fifteenth-century courtly love tradition and also the contemporaneous cult of Marian worship, seems to have elicited a deeply personal response from composers that sets their workings of it apart from those of any other texts, as one of the most interesting genres of the time.

The secular 'Vivite felices' again uses a motivic device to unify its two movements, but the sparkling surface of the music and ceremonial function mark it out as being quite different in conception from 'Vulnerasti cor meum'. The sheer intensity of the thematic process, short phrases and witty textural dialogues are indeed as typical of the later Parisian chanson as the *frottola*, the music seeming to belong to a particularly French vein of composition unique in BQ19.

Less original are the composite 'Maria ergo' and 'In nomine Jesu' settings, which have neither narrative or lyric spirit to guide them. As might be expected, elements of functional form survive in both, their appearance being more of loosely overgrown single-movement motets than any distinct genre; Lupus's piece is a typical example of his densely imitative style, while Symon's is likewise consistent with the melodic approach of his 'Nisi quia', though without the prop of the psalm narrative.

Lacking from both is the verbal sensitivity apparent in the other long pieces, partly due of course to the neutrality of the texts in question. It is, however, exactly this sense of the dramatic and picturesque that distinguishes the more radical bipartite motets from their shorter counterparts. The dialogue structure of 'Nigra sum' or more particularly the vivid word painting of 'Nisi quia' are extraordinarily prescient of later sixteenth-century innovations, all the more so considering the early date of their manuscript source. These features were a most original and surely influential contribution to the motet tradition and would seem also to have played a leading role in the evolution of the later madrigalian repertory, in technique as well as spirit.

Notes

[1]See *ReeseMR*, p.246.

[2]See *LockF*, p.206, or *MaceyS*, p.449.

[3]This number includes Lupus's 'In convertendo', which has already been examined seperately in chapter 5, on account of its unique dependance on a *cantus prius factus*, namely the eighth psalm tone. The single piece by a 'major' composer is the 'Judica me Deus' by Andreas de Silva, (f.111v.-112r.), a setting in two *partes* of the full six verses of Psalm 42, without any doxology. Kirsch states that it is based on the fourth psalm tone (see *SilvaO*, i, no. 3), but the references are inconsistent and very vague; certainly the piece displays none of the calculated minimalism of 'In convertendo'.

[4]Lupus's 'Nigra sum' and the anonymous 'Vulnerasti cor meum'; see vol.ii, pp.125 and 212 respectively.

[5]*JeppIS*, ii, p.x.

[6]Nos. 21, 'Sub tuum praesidium' (f.33v.) and 35, 'Surgens Jesus Dominus noster' (ff.53v.-55r.), both for four voices; see *LowMC*, iii, pp.116-17.

[7]No. 15, 'Hebe potens cythara', for five voices. See *D'AllM*, pp. 148-55 and *D'AllT*, p.115.

[8]Literature on this set of partbooks seems confined at present to the merest of passing references, usually via concordances with other sources; it is hardly even mentioned in *GaspaCB* (ii, p.169).

[9]This latter is of course purely hypothetical, but it is worth noting that the '*mi - mi*' idea seems to have had a peculiar significance for fifteenth-century musicians, being prominent in Isaac's 'My - my' (textless apart from the incipit, though possibly a *rondeau*; see *BrownFC*, vii, no. 14) as well as Ockeghem's *bergerette* 'Presque transi', his famous Mass based on it (generally known as the 'Missa Mi - mi') and motet 'Intemerata Dei mater' (see *MiyazO*).

[10]It is of note that a rather similar passage occurs at the very end of Costanzo Festa's 'Quis dabit', which is also in the Phrygian Mode, on the words 'requiescat in pace' (see *FestaO*, v, no. 41, bb.126-30). Since this motet is also preserved in BQ19, it is tempting to conjecture some kind of direct influence or tribute, though this can naturally be no more than speculation at present.

[11]This procedure likewise occurs in Lupus's 'In nomine Jesu', to be examined on p.177 below.

[12]Coppini's 'Hodie nobis' can be cited again as a similar late example of both the quasi-archaic mensural progression and a regular periodic use of *tempus perfectum* quite different from the irrationality characteristic of Ockeghem.

[13]One of these is the 'Ave Maria' from FP27 to be examined in chapter 7; it is classified as a motet in *HammCC*, i.

[14]*HammCC*, ii, p.160, which credits Fogliano with 10 pieces in what it describes as a purely sacred manuscript.

---

[15]Although the present author has made contact with the archive in Modena, a request for a microfilm of the manuscript or information concerning its contents was unfortunately refused.

[16]Not quite as long, however, as appears from the article on Fogliano in *Grove*, which misprints the date of his appointment ten years too early; see *JeppIS*, i, p.xiv for the correct date.

[17]The third motet is found in *I-BGc* 1208 D (f.110v.- 111r., 'Adoramus te': see *JeppIS*, i, p.64). Another appears in *I-Ma* Trotti 519 (title unknown: *HammCC*, ii, p.143 states that there is 'no literature' on the manuscript), while there are three sacred pieces firmly attributed to Fogliano and two more possibly by him in *I-MOd* 4. It is impossible to determine their titles and forms from the available literature, even though Jeppesen implies that BQ19 is the unique source of 'Beati omnes' and 'De profundis' in his introduction to *JeppIS*, i. A written request to the archive in Modena for either information about the pieces in *I-MOd* 4 and 11 or microfilms of the manuscripts was unfortunately refused: another to the Biblioteca Ambrosiana for the title of the work in *I-Ma* Trotti 519 received no response.

[18]See Renaldo's 'Haec dies' or Sebastiano Festa's 'Angele Dei' for similar instances of duet *exordia*.

[19]Not to be confused with another 'Nigra sum' definitely by Conseil found in 1534^4 and published in *SmijT*, iv (not ii, as stated in *Grove*), p.152.

[20]See *LU*, p.1259.

[21]See also Costanzo Festa's 'Quam pulchra es', another *Canticum Canticorum* motet using a C_1, C_1, C_1, C_4 clef combination (published in *FestaO*, v, no. 46).

[22]See also Symon's 'Maria ergo' above and Renaldo's 'Paradisi

portas aperuit' in chapter 4 (p.90) for comparable arrangements.

[23]See *LU*, pp.446 and 669 respectively.

[24]Lupus's style is described in similar terms with respect to his 'Esto nobis, Domine, turris fortitudinis' in *LowMC*, iii, p.235. Lowinsky also recognizes the same traits of careless text setting, melismatic melody, free dissonance treatment and pervading imitation in another motet, 'Postquam consummati sunt dies octo'; together with those considered in this thesis, these constitute nearly all of his pieces in this medium, so that a fairly well-defined stylistic portrait of the composer can be drawn.

[25]See *BlackL*, p.548.

[26]See A. Dunning: *Die Staatsmotette* (Utrecht, 1970), p.116.

[27]See *Grove*, 'Bruhier' (iii, p.374).

[28]There is a substantial discussion and analysis of the piece on pp.116-20.

CHAPTER 7: LATIN LAUDE AND MINOR RITUAL WORKS

Nowhere is the loose definition of the term 'motet' more apparent than in its application to the pieces to be examined in the present chapter. These, all from FP27, are counted as motets in the most recent survey of the manuscript[1] solely by virtue of their Latin religious texts. In contrast, their music bears little relation to that of the works seen in the preceding chapters, the stylistic gulf in some cases being so tremendous as to make a mockery of any serious attempt to join them together under the same heading.

The most curious anomaly in the designations given in *HammCC*, i, is the failure to isolate the various *laude* as a separate group, as is done in the case of other manuscripts. Those in Italian are counted among the 'Italian secular pieces' and those in Latin among the motets[2] in a direct negation of distinctions quite clearly made as early as the anthologies of Petrucci in which certain of them also appear.[3]

There is besides these another group of works that can properly be described neither as motets nor *laude*. These are bound together by a common emphasis on purely functional fragments of the rite; texts include the 'Benedicamus Domino', 'Sancta Maria, ora pro nobis', various strophic sequences and some excerpts from the Requiem Mass service. All these receive perfunctory and extremely simple amateur settings, making it plain that they were fashioned as specific parts of a ritual, outside of which they make little sense. It would be inaccurate to consider them as liturgical, as the style of the music indicates that it was most likely performed in the course of the popular services conducted by the Florentine compagnie di laudesi,[4] rather than in any formal ecclesiastical context. Therefore the term 'minor ritual works' has been adopted for their generic description, in the absence of any other definitions or precise knowledge of their original use.

The 'Ave Maria' settings

It is quite plain from their musical style that six of the eight 'Ave Maria' settings in FP27[5] are in fact *laude* rather than motets,[6] and indeed three of them came to be published in Petrucci's *Laude libro secondo* of 1508.[7] The latter preserves a further three alongside these[8] and yet another one, by Innocentius Dammonis, survives in the *libro primo*.[9] It seems, then, that the FP27 pieces are part of a distinctive sub-genre even among the *laude*, and in fact there is a consistency of musical style running through all these pieces that sets them slightly apart from the common ru,[10] an in either the manuscript or printed sources.

The recognition of these works as *laude* should technically disqualify them from consideration in a thesis devoted to the motet. However, they are unusual in setting a text that was also a popular basis for genuine motet compositionsnd which in its length and non-strophic form differs from other *laude*.[11] This means that similar problems of organization arise as with the motet, a factor reflected in a generally (though not universally) more elaborate musical treatment. The pieces are all similar enough to each other to be accounted for as the same genre, which in several individual cases is clearly designated by Petrucci (and most modern writers) as the *lauda*; however, some also encroach on the more elevated territory of the motet and there is certainly enough scope for individuality to render each quite distinct. The result is something of a hybrid type whose study is thus particularly relevant as part of the closer context in which the motet tradition was set.

Six of the eight pieces from FP27 are found on adjacent pages at the front of the book, indicating a conscious grouping on the part of the scribe. Apart from the putatively instrumental no. V[12] (on ff.5v.-7r.), they make up a closely- knit stylistic group, to which belongs also no. VIII (on ff.146v.-147r.), whose separation is probably due solely to the composite structure of the manuscript.[13] This group therefore comprises six compositions, nos. I-IV, VI and VIII, that are notably similar in their musical procedures.[14] Nevertheless, each adopts a different solution to the problem of setting the given text in a manner compatible with the confines of *lauda* style. Thus while they are all of similar length and divide into two parts after the word 'Jesus', which is invariably set chordally, no two make the same divisions between phrases or use the same succession of textures and each attempts to cast a different light on the meaning and dramatic import of the words. Three of them, nos. III, VI and VIII, are further distinguished by a seemingly earlier style, characterized by rising octave cadences, angular partwriting, more modal harmony and irregular imitations, which makes it possible to isolate them as a group.

Tromboncino's composition (edited as 'Ave Maria VI' in vol. ii, p.25) is one such piece. It is extremely sectional, being principally composed of short chordal passages articulated by fermata signs. Nevertheless, continuity is maintained by the careful arrangement of these sections into what are essentially binary pairs, to make up the following pattern (the two lines indicating the *prima* and *secunda partes* repectively):

A A'   B B'   C   (bb. 13-17)   B'' D   (bb.22-7)

E E'   F   (bb. 37-42)   D'/C'   (bb.43-53)   C'' ('Amen')

Thus variations of the same 'D' material round off both main sections, establishing a closed structure emphasized by the way that the very end refers back to 'C', which was significant as the only tonic cadence in the first half. The most interesting passage is 'F', where the consistent homophony gives way to imitative writing. This was surely a calculated move, especially as it is textually appropriate; its conjunction with the imploration 'ora pro nobis' immediately brings to mind the rhetorical *ephodos*,[15] whose pleading effect is here used outside the context of any structural function. Moreover, the subsequent return to plain homophony on 'peccatoribus' comes across almost dramatically as a frank admission of guilt, so that the change of texture is clearly manipulated and not random. This latter, together with the closed structure, typify a sophistication in the use of simple means that is the most telling difference between the 'Ave Maria' settings and the more traditional *laude*.

Cara's piece (edited as 'Ave Maria III' in vol. ii, p.19) has a more continuous contrapuntal texture and replaces the cohesive device of recurring sections with a reliance on similar modal figures in the Cantus, principally a falling fourth such as is found in the opening phrase. However, the first twelve bars do also form an *exordium* of a sort, defined by the completed modal circumnavigation in the Cantus and tonic cadence in b.12. The following reduction and variations of texture are almost reminiscent of the *narratio* of a motet, but their vagueness and the absence of any clear *conclusio* indicate a relationship to rhetorical form more coincidental than considered.

The setting of 'Sancta Maria, Mater Dei' is very like Tromboncino's in its sequential Cantus falling fourths and accompanying harmonies, though Cara extends his by using a Bassus ostinato derived from the falling fourth motif (bb.25- 9), resulting in some unusual repetitions of the text. However, he completely eschews the drama of 'ora pro nobis peccatoribus', setting it briefly as a cadential approach before the final section. Thus despite the possibility of mutual influence, the approaches of the two frottolists are markedly different and it is of note that Tromboncino's seems to have been the most popular, as will be seen presently.

The anonymous no. VIII (edited in vol. ii, p.29) is distinguished by its consistent use of pedal harmonies filled out by irregular triadic imitation. This technique, evident for example in bb.10-15, has already been noted as typical of Weerbeke's motets in chapter 4; were there anything to suggest his authorship on documentary grounds, this piece would fit neatly into his canon of works, given that it is a *lauda* and not a motet.[16]

As with Cara's piece, there is a definite homophonic *exordium* culminating in the cadence at b.15, after which contrasting *narratio* techniques take over before the return to chordal textures for 'Jesus'. The way that the duet of bb.16- 17 is repeated in the other two voices, disguised by new material in the original pair, has also been noted as typical of Weerbeke and comes again as the basis of bb.27-35. This whole section is repeated note for note, requiring a considerable licence with the text so that the dramatic possibilities of 'ora pro nobis peccatoribus' are not exploited, though the melodic climax on 'peccatoribus' (in the Altus) is still effective.

At b.48, the opening material is resumed and extended to the end to form a closed structure, again recalling the work of Weerbeke. Essentially, though, the piece comes from the same tradition as those found on the opening pages of the manuscript and while it may have certain features of Weerbeke's motet style it is firmly a *lauda*. The repeated passages may be exceptional but the closed form is also found in Tromboncino's setting (and others too), compared to which it seems actually less rather than more carefully crafted.

The more modern style of the anonymous no. IV (edited in vol. ii, p.21) is immediately apparent in its clearly Ionian mode on F and its smooth homophony uncluttered by any angular rhythms or intervals. In terms of its construction, however, it is still very similar to Tromboncino's setting; the music is even more uniformly sectionalized and chordal, without even the change of texture at 'ora pro nobis'. As with Tromboncino the opening two phrases (bb.1-4 and 5-8) are complimentary, the second being a melodic variation and a harmonic consequence of the first; almost exactly the same passage reappears towards the end, at bb.27-36, resulting in a similarly relaxed closed structure.

Fogliano's piece (edited as 'Ave Maria II' in vol. ii, p.17) is in the same Ionian mode and augments the refined style of no. IV with motet-like devices such as voice-pairing and imitation, its ambition even extending to paraphrasing the antiphon melody as an opening ostinato. This four-bar motif comes first in the Bassus and then appears surreptitiously in each voice, under the cover of a consistently full homophonic texture. A similarly regular imitative technique recurs at the end, from b.29 onwards, but between these symmetrical extremes the texture is homophonic and mainly in paired voices. It is the smoothness of these passages that show most clearly the influence of the motet, especially in their rhythmic adaption to the text (see bb.8-9, for example); such writing would not be out of place in a motet by Renaldo or indeed one of the psalm settings by Fogliano himself.

Tromboncino's arrangement of 'ora pro nobis peccatoribus' is slyly inverted here, the rhetorical *ephodos* falling on the last word, set as a pair of duets. The dramatic effect is not destroyed, but merely reversed in order to stress the individual nature of penitence. Similarly expressive through structural means is the closing ostinato setting of 'mortis eternae', whose repetition and eventual development into a sequential melisma on the word 'nostrae' provide a succinct meditation on eternity.

The musical style of this piece is genuinely closer to that of the motet than the *lauda* and its designation as the latter type rests only on its text and association with the other settings in FP27. Fogliano was also a composer of large-scale motets and the training evinced by his 'De profundis', for example (see chapter 6, p.173) may account for an ingrained tendency towards a more refined idiom. Nevertheless, comparison with even the simpler 'Beati omnnes' reveals that concessions are indeed made to the greater simplicity required of the *lauda*, and the reduced lengths of melismas, phrases and sections clearly distinguish the work from Fogliano's other motet settings.

The composer of no. I, Laurentius Bergomotius mut., has been identified by Jeppesen as a native of Modena (as implied by the abbreviation 'mut.'), born in 1480 and later a private singer to Leo X.[17] His setting (edited as 'Ave Maria I' in vol ii, p.16) is, like Fogliano's, a compromise between homophony and imitation. Bergomotius conceals his entries by doubling them wherever possible with another homorhythmic voice and making each idea brief and evenly syllabic. The combination of these results in a uniformly thick but distinctive texture that is the most striking feature of the piece.

The structure is open-ended, being no more than a succession of similarly cramped ideas, most of which are unified by the use of a falling third. As in both Cara's and Tromboncino's versions (nos. III and VI), 'Mater Dei' is set as a falling fourth in the Cantus, harmonized by parallel tenths in the Bassus. Bergomotius also uses an *ephodos* like Tromboncino's on 'ora pro nobis' and a melismatic expansion right at the end like Fogliano's. In neither case is the effect as forceful, however, and it seems most likely that the author of this piece would have been an imitator, not an originator; the material is otherwise generally bland and inexpressive, with little attention paid to the declamation of the words.

It is of note that of these six, the three more old- fashioned pieces were those that appeared in the *Laude libro secondo*. Their companions there conform to this standard, being again characterized by a more archaic contrapuntal and harmonic style. The piece by Tromboncino (*JeppL* no. 47) is less interesting than his offering in FP27, being texturally unvaried and in fact musically indistinct from other *laude* in the volume. Cara's piece (*JeppL* no.42) is unusual in being for five voices and alternating between typically homophonic full passages and more subtle duets, including a substantial *ephodos* on 'Sancta Maria, ora pro nobis'.

The anonymous version (*JeppL* no. 46) is most original in starting with an intonation, though the melody is unidentifiable and cannot be traced in any of the other settings. However, the Altus at b.31, imitated exactly by the Bassus at b.37, presents a version of the plainsong litany melody on 'Sancta Maria, ora pro nobis'[18] that is recognizable too at the same point in the Cantus of Fogliano's setting, in the imitations of bb.27-44 of the anonymous no. VIII and also, to a certain extent, in the tiny four-voiced litany in FP27, f.102v.[19] Whether the intonation to the present piece is part of an established popular 'Ave Maria' tune, of which the 'Sancta Maria, ora pro nobis' is a fragment, or whether their use together is coincidental, is unfortunately impossible to determine until any more coherent versions of the melody should come to light.

The setting by Dammonis in the *Laude libro primo* (*JeppL* no. 67) is unusually based on a Tenor made distinct from the other voices by its long notes and rhythmic simplicity. Such *cantus firmus* treatment implies a pre-composed melody, but it is not identifiable with any other version. However, like the motif discussed above, it bears occasional similarities to the antiphon, as for instance at 'gratia plena'; such references, along with simplistic features such as the repetitions at the start of the *secunda pars*, invite the proposal that it originated in a popular adaptation. If so, it may belong to the same tradition as the melody of *JeppL* no. 46 or the various 'Sancta Maria, ora pro nobis' settings, a tradition that has otherwise been almost completely obscured by the passage of time.

The polyphonic arrangement of older melodies is quite a common feature of Petrucci's two books of *laude*. The use of *cantus firmus*, five-voiced texture and intonations, on the other hand, is not. Thus although none of the printed 'Ave Maria' settings are as motet-like even as those by Bergomotius or Fogliano, they still represent a slightly more complex form than their companion pieces. This, and their generally uniform style, distinguishes them as a separate genre on the borderline between motet and *lauda* styles, whose simplicity conceals a lively and creative background culture.

Other laude

The anonymous 'Ave sanctissima Maria' (edited as 'Ave sanctissima Maria I' in vol ii, p.34) and 'O Domine Jesu Christe' (edited as 'O Domine Jesu Christe I' in vol. ii, p.139) are both examples of the four-voiced type of *lauda* favoured by Petrucci in his publications. The text of the second of these is one of a series of prayers starting with the same words,[20] five of which were set by Josquin,[21] four by Willaert[22] and one each by Renaldo (see chapter 4, p.92) and Brumel.[23] These, though uniformly chordal and unpretentious, are genuine motet settings, where the lines are simple but smooth and given substance by a controlled sense of direction and overall structure. The present example is plainly different, however, in its jerky, angular manner and the way that its contrapuntal interest is limited to syncopations and passing notes within simple chords. Such an energetic but undisciplined approach is very different from the calculated restraint of the motets and typical of the *lauda*, thus clearly and positively marking the piece out as belonging to the latter rather than the former tradition. Renaldo also made a motet setting of the same 'Ave sanctissima Maria' text (see chapter 3, p.60), but there his artfulness is much more apparent and the difference between *lauda* and motet styles more immediately obvious.

The other Latin *laude* in FP27 are much simpler, often conforming to the three-voiced type familiar from earlier fifteenth-century manuscripts. They are generally brief settings of single strophes, without textural contrasts or contrapuntal elaboration and are often based on traditional melodies. Because of this, the musical issues involved are very different from those discussed with respect to the motets or even the 'Ave Maria' settings above. Nevertheless, their classification as motets in *HammCC* means that they deserve at least a mention here for the sake of completeness.

The four 'Verbum caro' settings (all anonymous) belong to a long tradition, each using the same words and tune as can be found in

numerous earlier sources.[24]   The two on ff.56r. and 109v. (both
edited in *LuisiL*, p.201) are in fact virtually identical (though not
absolutely, as implied in *JeppFR*, p.39) though it is not possible to
make much of this concordance; the two versions can be interpreted as
different notations of a piece more usually transmitted orally.[25]
Whereas these, along with the two-voiced version on f.110r. (edited
in *LuisiL*, p.202), are simple to the point of an almost modal
homorhythmic technique[26] (which will be seen again in connection
with certain of the sequences among the minor ritual works), the
setting on f.104r. (edited in *LuisiL*, p.200) is more in line with the
type of *lauda* championed by Petrucci, despite being for only three
voices. The tune is here set more or less as a *cantus firmus* around
which the other two voices weave decorative patterns, recalling the
manner of the hymns examined in chapter 5, as well as Dammonis's
'Ave Maria'. This piece thus represents a more advanced stage in
what Damilano terms the 'arricchimento graduale della intonazione
monodica tradizionale',[27] although it is still well within the limits of
lauda style and makes no attempt at textural variation.[28] Its greatest
curiosity is in fact that while it notates the ternary metre of its *cantus
firmus* accurately, it does so in *tempus imperfectum*; this anomaly is
reminiscent of the same procedure reversed in Lupus's six-voiced
'Miserere' (see chapter 4, p.115).

'Cum autem venissem', attributed to Johannes de Quadris in
1506[1] (though anonymous in all previous manuscripts), belongs to a
similar sort of repertory, examples surviving with the same text and
melody in a variety of sources.[29] Similar in style is the anonymous
'Memento mei', counted as a motet in *HammCC* on account of its
Latin incipit, but surely intended to continue with the macaronic text
that after the Latin 'o sacra virgo pia' breaks into Italian, this being
familiar from other *laude*.[30] The anonymous 'Miserere' in FP27, ff.
48v. - 49r., has already been published and discussed at some length
in *GreyL*, p.xxx, so that no further comment is necessary here; which
leaves as the only remaining piece of this type the anonymous 'Utile
conscilium' (edited in vol. ii, p.195). Though these words are

unusually given as an incipit in all four voices, it has so far proved impossible to relate it to any known text. The musical style, on the other hand, is exactly like that of the pieces in Petrucci's two books and there seems little to challenge its acceptance as a typical *lauda* whose text has gone astray.

FP27 also contains three longer Latin works which are certainly not motets and whose designation as *laude* is supported by the appearance of similar pieces in Petrucci's books.[31] The shortest and in fact least typical of these is the anonymous 'Ave gratia plena'[32] (edited in vol. ii, p.14) which stands apart on account of its generally smaller and more varied rhythmic values and their syllabic mismatch with the text. This is not a matter of melismatic expansion; rather the *breves* that define the harmonic rhythm are almost invariably divided into two, resulting in repeated chords whether warranted by the words or not. The simplicity of the style stands in direct contrast to the relative sophistication of the 'Ave Maria' settings or even of the other *laude*, and shows it to have been somewhat different in conception.

Though the text of 'Rex autem David' (edited in vol. ii, p.169) is unique, its musical style is quite typical of the Petruccian *lauda* repertory in its constantly full and chordal texture, enlivened by angular decorations in the inner parts. Less easily definable is the three-voiced 'Christi corpus ave' (edited in vol. ii, p.54), whose homorhythmic simplicity could equally well have been expressed in plainsong notation (a feature also of some of the minor ritual works). However, the absence of the original hymn melody and incorporation of a certain degree of homophonic melisma indicate that the piece was freely composed. Corroborative evidence is supplied by a rigid musical repeat structure,[33] although the way that it is independent of and in fact often contrary to the sense of the words is something of a mystery. The given text may of course be a *contrafactum*, but that still begs the question of the form of the original, which must have been unusual indeed to have spawned such a structure with such short phrases.

Minor ritual works

As might be expected, these pieces fall neatly into stylistic groups according to the texts they set. Two pieces, however, require separate consideration because of their music, which despite its great length and four-voiced texture is actually no more than harmonized recitation of a chant. Like the 'Christi corpus ave' above, they could have been as effectively written in unmeasured notation and owe their length solely to that of the pre-composed text and melody.

'Altera autem die' (edited in vol. ii, p.8) sets a Gospel narrative syllabically, to variations on a monotone that are in keeping with the original recitation formulae (see *LU*, p.106). The piece could therefore have been used liturgically without substantially interfering with the length of the service as a whole; another possibility is that it might have been used in a procession or even a dramatic performance, as indeed may have been 'Christi Corpus ave'. Likewise, the 'Requiem aeternam' (edited in vol. ii, p.167), which quotes the original chant exactly in the Tenor, seems to be a decoration of a part of the liturgy rather than any truly independent composition.[34] The piece is copied into FP27 as part of a group of extracts from the Requiem mass (from f.209v. to the end) and although longer and for more voices is essentially equivalent in style and purpose to the shorter *bicinia* which will be discussed presently.

Though the revised entry for FP27 in *HammCC*, iv (p.375) rightly recategorizes the two pieces beginning 'Incipit oratio Jeremie' as Lamentations, their original classification as motets (in *HammCC*, i, p.232) merits their inclusion here. In the case of the three-voiced setting (edited as no. I in vol. ii, p.95), the music gives the impression of being a chant harmonization like those discussed above, although the melody does not correspond to any known plainsong original.[35] However, the possibilities of mensural notation are not exploited to any great extent and it is clearly a functional piece and less complex even than contemporaneous settings of the *lamentatio*.[36]

More akin to these latter, in its counterpoint and variations of rhythm
and texture, is the version for four voices (edited in vol. ii, p.99).
The peculiarities of the text, which translate into a sectional style
whose structure is completely predetermined, mean that it stands well
apart from the repertory of genuine motets, though details of its
writing are similar and even call to mind the works of Weerbeke
examined in chapter 4. This division into small units is also
characteristic of the many *lamentatio* settings, a body of work yet to
be investigated exhaustively and against whose context it could be far
more realistically assessed than in the present study of the motet.

The Requiem *bicinium* on f.103v. (edited as 'Dies illa I' in vol.
ii, p.70) is virtually the same as the first three on ff.210v.-211r. put
together (these are edited as 'Dies illa II' in vol. ii, p.72), differing
only in a few notational details and the omission of the short
'Amen'.[37] They both comprise three sections, beginning 'Dies illa',
'Tremens factus sum' and 'Requiem aeternam', these texts being the
three verses of the Reponsory 'Libera me'.[38] They were thus
presumably intended for performance in a liturgical context as part of
the complete chant and can hardly be considered as independent
motets. The music is extremely simple, a decorated version of the
original chant appearing split between the two equal and essentially
homorhythmic voices, thus confirming the functional nature of the
pieces. It is possible that they are vestigial of a tradition of what
Fallows has called 'sheer *Gebrauchsmusik*'[39] stretching well back into
the fifteenth century; similar compositions are attributed to Binchois
in various Italian sources from the 1450s and 1470s.[40] In addition to
these and a 'Kyrie eleison' on ff.210v.-211r., there is also a 'Dies
irae' (edited as 'Dies irae II' in vol. ii, p.75), which although based
on the famous Requiem sequence (see *LU*, p.1810) rather than the
Responsory, paraphrases the melody in the same way and would have
served likewise as a polyphonic alternative to certain strophes of the
plainsong.

Similar in purpose if a little more elaborate are the two four-voiced 'Dies irae' settings (edited as nos. I and III in vol. ii, pp.74 and 75 respectively). In both, the chant is freely paraphrased in the Cantus and Tenor after the fashion of the motet, but there are no variations of texture and the counterpoint is generally awkward and insecure. Their function as parts of a strophic whole is apparent from their brevity and the inclusion of the incipits to two other verses of the sequence (beginning 'Quid sum miser' and 'Qui Mariam'; see *LU*, pp.1811 and 1812) in the piece on ff.212v.-213r. Although no such hints are given in the other setting, its parallel style makes it reasonable to assume that it was intended to fulfil the same function.

This supposition can also be extended to 'Gaude virgo, mater Christi' (edited in vol. ii, p.80), 'Lauda Syon' (edited in vol. ii, p.112) and 'O gloriosa domina' (edited in vol. ii, p.142), which likewise set single verses of their original sequence texts. The music in each case is homophonic, syllabic and rhythmically reduced to a simple iambic alternation of *breves* and *minimae*, giving a lilting effect already noted in certain of the 'Verbum caro' settings discussed above. The main difference between these and the Requiem pieces is the lack of any reference to the original melodies, which makes it unlikely that they would have been performed in alternation with chanted verses, especially since only 'Lauda Syon' conforms even to the mode of the original.[41] Nevertheless, on account of their length and extremely limited scope they are still best considered as adjuncts to the liturgy rather than as independent works in the manner of genuine motets.

There are two remaining *bicinia* in FP27 that do not seem to be connected with the Requiem Mass service, though they share exactly the same musical style. One (edited as 'Ave Maria VII' in vol. ii, p.28) is supplied with the incipit 'Ave Maria' in both voices but is not long enough to set the full Antiphon text, whose opening sits uncomfortably on the rhythms and caesurae of the music anyway. The other (edited in vol. ii, p.158) carries the 'Benedicamus Domino' trope 'Qui nos fecit ex nihilo / Deo patri et filio' in one voice only, the music being repeated for the two phrases with the voices exchanged. A variant of this piece from a Dalmatian manuscript using the same *rondellus* technique is discussed in *BujicR*; the disparate origins of these two sources suggest a widespread practice of which only isolated fragments remain.[42]

The five 'Benedicamus Domino' pieces grouped all together on ff. 18v.-19r. likewise belong to a tradition of polyphonic settings of the conclusion of the Mass that can be traced back as far as the fourteenth century.[43] Two of them, nos. III and IV (both edited in vol. ii, p.47), quote the original tones in their Cantus and Tenor voices respectively (see *LU*, pp.124 and 125), while the others (nos. I and II edited in vol. ii, p.46, no. V in vol. ii, p.48) appear to be freely composed. This distinction of type can be found also in the two settings by Dufay,[44] but here the similarity ends; whereas the older master brings his full contrapuntal resources to bear in each case to create artful works of comparatively generous length, the five in question are cursory, dissonant and technically insecure. All are homophonic, with nos. I and II displaying the iambic rhythm already noted in the some of the sequences and 'Verbum caro' settings elsewhere; no. IV is a little more complex, but its busy surface belies an essentially chordal basis, crudely filled out with figurations and passing notes.

Lastly, there are two tiny compositions on the litany 'Sancta Maria, ora pro nobis ad Dominum nostrum Jesum Christum' (edited in vol. ii, p.174), both syllabically homophonic except for a gentle decoration at the end. That for four voices briefly alludes to the litany melody in its opening phrase, but otherwise both appear to have been freely composed. As with so many of the works examined above, their succinct and businesslike manner point to a restricted use as part of a service rather than to any independent musical standing.

The Latin *laude* and the minor ritual works have been considered together in the present chapter principally on account of their common misidentification with the motet repertory. However, a comparison of each with the other reveals a number of more direct similarities despite their uses of very different texts. Both were conceived as parts of a religious ceremony and share a pious austerity of style in marked contrast to the musical sophistry of certain other forms. This in turn gives the impression that both were intended for use in the popular, or at least less solemn, services rather than in the rarified surroundings of any aristocratic chapel. Moreover, the music to both types seems to have originated in a partly improvisatory practice whose traditionally oral propagation accounts for the various different versions of particular pieces such as the 'Verbum caro' settings or 'Requiem' *bicinia*.

A designation of the four-voiced *lauda* as distinct from the motet was made by Petrucci, and has been clarified by successive generations of scholars after Jeppesen, to whose collective work the comments on the Latin pieces above are no more than a footnote. On the other hand, no identification of the minor ritual works as a separate type with a long history of its own has yet been made due to a combination of circumstances, the main culprits being the lack of allusions to a separate genre in any source writings, the rarity of notated examples, the indiscriminate use of the term 'motet' to cover those that do survive and the primarily liturgical, rather than musical, impulse behind them. This last is the key to its most profound difference from the other forms of its time; such an orientation relates it not to the artful intricacies of the motet or even any other renaissance polyphony, but to the plainsong repertory. Although the composition and establishment of the chants themselves are associated with a much earlier period, such elaborations as the present examples follow similar principles and are furthermore a continuation of the familiar process of troping. Their medievalism thus goes beyond niceties of style to their very conception, which shows them to be even further from the contemporaneous motet than even the glaring differences of brevity or dissonance treatment suggest. If the word 'motet' is to have any meaning at all in this period, the exclusion of these minor ritual works from the category is an essential prerequisite, as they stand diametrically opposed not only in technique but also in spirit to the music considered in the preceding chapters.

Notes

[1]*HammCC*, i, p.232. See chapter 1 for a more detailed discussion of the use of the word 'motet' both generally and in the context of *HammCC* in particular.

[2]While the compilers of *HammCC* are clear in their reservation of the term *lauda* only 'if this seems appropriate for a given manuscript', there is no provision made in their definition of *secular pieces* for vernacular works of religious sentiment (see p.xix).

[3]Despite the influence of the motet over the *lauda* as evinced by Petrucci's standardization of the form in his two books of 1508 (see chapter 2), he was scrupulously conscientious in distinguishing between the two types. This is particularly clear in the six adaptions of motets from his *Motetti B* of 1503 into *laude* for his *libro secondo* (*JeppL* nos. 6, 8, 9, 25, 52 and 55). Most significantly, all have different texts, and they are furthermore musically abbreviated and simplified to varying degrees. There is only one straightforward *contrafactum* (*JeppL* no.8, a short and simple piece anyway); two others use isolated movements of the original motets (*JeppL* nos.6 and 25, the models again notable for their simplicity) and the remainder are more substantially altered in the direction of reduced complexity.

[4]A full account of these singers and their activities is given in *D'AccL*.

[5]For the sake of convenience, these have been numbered from I-VIII, in the order of their appearance in the manuscript. Those considered

with the *laude* in the present chapter are nos. I-IV, VI and VIII; no. VII is discussed below with the minor ritual works and no. V with the instrumental pieces in chapter 8.

[6]Of the other two, that attributed to Musipula on ff.5v.-7r. carries a textual incipit only, whereas the *laude* are all fully texted. This circumstance is compounded by its much greater length and a very different style to make it more appropriately considered among the 'wordless' pieces further below. The second, on f.19v., is a tiny two-voiced piece, whose text is again limited to an 'Ave Maria' incipit. The brevity and naïvety of the latter is such that it could not possibly have set the full text and its style is that of the minor ritual works, with which it will be discussed in due course. Mention should also be made of the 'Ave gratia plena' on ff.143v.-144r., which is in fact textually identical apart from the omission of the word 'Maria'. However, although it is clearly also a *lauda*, it is in a sufficiently simpler style to be considered separately.

[7]These are nos. III (ff.3v.-4r., attributed to 'Marcetus' [= Cara]), VI (7v.-8r., attributed to 'B.T.' [= Tromboncino]) and VII (146v.-147r., anon), corresponding to nos. 48, 40 and 34 respectively in *JeppL*. The printed and manuscript versions differ in a number of details, so that it is certain that neither was a direct copy from the other.

[8]Published in *JeppL* as nos. 42, 46 and 47.

[9]Also published in 1508; the piece is transcribed in *JeppL*, no. 68.

[10]These are easily distinguishable from the *laude* by their much greater length and complexity; contemporaneous settings survive by Compère, De Orto (from the *Odhecaton A* and edited in *HewO*, p.219), Gombert, Josquin, Layolle, Lhéritier, Regis, Verdelot and Willaert.

[11]The practice of setting of the 'Ave Maria' as a *lauda* was not traditional and seems to be confined to around the early 1500s; the oldest example seems to be that for three voices in MS Cape Town, South African Public Library, Grey 3.b.12 (edited in *GreyL*, no. [6]), which is generally similar to the simpler examples from FP27 though without the variations of texture possible with four voices.

[12]To be discussed in chapter 8.

[13]The details of its present form being a combination of two smaller books, the first comprising ff.1-120, are dealt with in chapter 1.

[14]Like no. V, the two-voiced no. VII (on f.19v.) is rather different and will be considered with the minor ritual works below.

[15]See chapter 3 for a discussion of Cicero's use of this term to mean a subtle approach in a rhetorical *exordium* as opposed to the direct *prooimion*, and the proposed correspondance of the two with imitative and chordal musical openings respectively.

[16]The distinction is important even with a composer with a reputation for simplicity like Weerbeke's, as is borne witness by the considerable alterations made to three of his motets from the *Motetti B* in order to include them in the *Laude libro primo*; see *JeppL*, nos. 9, 52 and 55.

[17]See *JeppL*, p.lxiii.

[18]See *LU*, p.836.

[19]Its use in *JeppL*, no. 46 is acknowledged in the introduction, on p.lxi. A further use of the same litany motif to set these words has already been noted in chapter 5, in connection with the ostinato in Renaldo's 'Regina caeli'.

[20]The origin and function of the text is discussed in *BrumelO*, v, p.xxxix.

[21]See *JosqM*, ii, pp.35-40.

[22]*WillO*, i, pp.10-16.

[23]*BrumelO*, v, p.86.

[24]Sixteen such pieces have been edited in *LuisiL*, ii (nos. 42*-57*), along with another one (no. 58*) based on the same text but from Serafino Razzi's later collection of 1563. Seven more are documented, with their musical incipits, in *DamilL* (pp.70-71 and incipit nos. 77-8 and 81-5 on pp.87-8: nos. 76 and 79-80 are the same pieces as are printed in full in *LuisiL*, as nos. 43*, 46* and 42* respectively). Luisi includes a discussion of the text, its melody and all concordances and other modern editions in his notes (pp.lxxix-lxxxiii), to which can be added the comments of Cattin on its origins in *GreyL*, p.xxi, concerning the setting in that source (published both there as no. 16 and in *LuisiL* as no. 51*). In addition, an as yet unpublished four-voiced piece exists in *I- Fr* 2356, f.120r., with the incipit 'Verbum caro fatu' [*sic*]. However, the music makes no reference to the traditional melody and indeed is closer in style to the *frottola*; moreover its length and binary repeat form are clear evidence that it was not originally intended for the 'Verbum caro' text.

[25]The differences between them are given in the relevant critical apparatus to no. 49* in *LuisiL*.

[26]This is apparent also in the setting published as *LuisiL*, no.47*.

[27]*DamilL*, p.70.

[28]The most complex version of all appears to be one of the two by Dammonis in the *Laude libro primo*, which works through an elaborate series of variations over the basic melody, set as a *cantus firmus* in the Tenor. This is one of the pieces not printed in full in *JeppL* (though an incipit is given on p.lxii); there is however a full edition in *LuisiL*, no. 57*.

[29]The incipits to three of these are given in *DamilL*, p.79, and an edition of the piece from a different source can be found in *AMP*, xiv, p.467, with extensive notes and a full list of concordances on p.156. There is moreover a discussion of the text and its significance in a Florentine context in *CattinPA*, pp.5-6, which also contains an edition of a two- voiced version on p.14.

[30]The edition of the piece in *LuisiL* (ii, no. 51) is supplied with the Italian continuation, which can be traced back well into the thirteenth century (see *LiuzziL*, p.xxv), although the tune in the present case seems completely original and the words do not fit it particularly obviously. The only other continuation that suggests itself is the plea of one of the robbers crucified alongside Christ as related in Luke 23:42-3. This can be made to fit the music equally effectively (and indeed more so than the Antiphon or Responsory texts with this incipit; see *LU*, p.718 and 1791) and its abstraction seems almost plausible on account of its dramatic and personal content. However, the dialogue form of this fragment would be unusual for a *lauda* and the popularity of the Italian text makes it still the most likely alternative.

[31]See for example *JeppL*, nos. 3, 32, 33, 44, 54, 55, 66 and 78, all through-composed settings of mainly, but not exclusively, Latin texts.

[32]The oddity of this text has already received comment in the discussion of the 'Ave Maria' settings above. The omission of the word 'Maria' does have a precedent, however, in an Offertory chant (*LU*, p.1379), though here the text stops short at 'mulieribus'. There is also a polyphonic setting by Verdelot of an unidentified troped version of the same text (see *VerdO*, ii, p.166).

[33]This can be expressed as an ABACA sheme, where A is bb.1-18, 30-47 and 56-73 (the end), and B is the same as the last three phrases of A (bb.11-18).

[34]It is interesting to note that a similar piece is attributed to Josquin in Petrucci's first book of five-voiced motets (see *JosqM*, i, no 29). Although a little more sophisticated than the present example, it is essentially a plain note-against-note chant harmonization; the style may well have been in imitation of Ockeghem's Requiem Mass, which is similarly austere and subservient to the original chants.

[35]The melody is clearly different from those in *LU*, pp.758 and 760, even though it has a similar strophic structure. The style of the piece is however very similar to that of another polyphonic setting of the same text from the Cape Town manuscript Grey 3. b. 12 (edited in *GreyL*, no. 38), which also appears, with a different Contratenor and the text altered to that of the Lamentations, in Petrucci's *Lamentationes Jeremie prophete liber primus* of 1506 (edited in *MassenL*, pp.14-18).

[36]A selective anthology of roughly contemporaneous Lamentations has been published as *MassenL*; the simplest are the anonymous pieces starting on pp.14, 140 and 142 (the last from FP27).

[37]As with the 'Verbum caro' settings discussed above, the impression is again one of two different notations of a simple piece more usually transmitted orally.

[38]See *LU*, p.1767. While these sections are laid out continuously on f.103v., on ff.210v.-211r. they are written as if they were separate entities together with a 'Dies irae' and a 'Kyrie eleison' in the same style. Faced with this, *BecherC* curiously catalogues one piece on f.103v. and three on ff.210v.-211r. (the 'Tremens factus sum', 'Dies illa' and 'Kyrie eleison'; he unaccountably omits to mention the 'Dies irae' or the 'Requiem eternae'). This imbalance is retained by Jeppesen, though he corrects the omission of the 'Dies irae' and 'Kyrie eleison' (see *JeppFR*, ii, p.37), bringing the number of pieces on ff.210v.-211r. up to five. In doing so, however, he still fails to

acknowledge firstly that the three successive verses of the same Responsary text are surely parts of the same piece (from which the 'Dies irae' and 'Requiem' are firmly distinct, being based on completely different parts of the Mass), and secondly that the resultant single item is almost exactly the same piece as that on f.103v. It seems more accurate, therefore, to consider ff.210v.-211r. as containing three pieces, namely a tripartite Responsary concordant with that on f.103v., a 'Kyrie eleison' and a 'Dies irae'. It is for this reason that the total number of pieces in FP27 is reckoned as 185 in chapter 1, rather than 187 as given in *HammCC*, i, p.232.

[39]See *Grove*, 'Binchois' (ii, p.714).

[40]Notably *I-MOe* X. I. II and the first Gaffurius codex. The pieces are edited in *MarixB*, as motet nos. 4 (p.192), 13 (p.218), 14 (p.219) and 15 (p.226); there are also sections in a similar style in nos. 7 (p.194) and 11 (p.212). For some earlier examples, see the processional pieces for the feast of the Ascension in *PMFC* (nos. 31a, b and c).

[41]It has not proved possible so far to find out the mode of 'Gaude virgo', even though it seems certain that its music survives. There is a reference by Besseler in *DufayO*, v, p.ix, to five melodies with this text in 'the Bruno Stäblein collection' (without any further details), but they are not to be found in *StäbH*; presumably he is referring to a private collection, especially since he acknowledges Stäblein's personal help in the introduction to the volume (see p.v).

[42]The derivation of both text and melody are discussed in some detail in *BujicR*; see also *GalloCP* and *PMFC*, xii, nos. 28 and 29 for examples of similar pieces.

[43]Examples can be found in *PMFC*, xii, nos. 21-7; nos. 21, 22 and 25 in particular exhibit a simplicity of style comparable to that of the works under consideration here.

[44]See *DufayO*, v, pp.35 and 36.

CHAPTER 8: 'SONGS WITHOUT WORDS'

There are a number of polyphonic sources from around the turn of the fifteenth century that preserve their contents with no text whatsoever beyond the briefest of titles or incipits. These sources are all North Italian in origin and include Petrucci's *Odhecaton* series as well as several manuscripts generally referred to as 'chansonniers'. A series of recent studies has now established beyond any reasonable doubt that they were primarily intended for use by the instrumental ensembles whose existence in Italy at the time is confirmed by numerous documentary accounts.[1]

These same studies have also noted the way that the uniquely Italian repertory they preserve derives to a great extent from the fifteenth-century French chanson and the various mechanisms by which this took place.[2] Some pieces are indeed recognizable from concordances as copies of a chanson or some other model that have simply been made without the words; the title in such cases is usually the the opening of the original text. Others adapt one or more lines of a preexistent work as the basis for a new set of counterpoints, again retaining its incipit as a title.[3] There is, however, yet another group that bear no relation to any model (although textless concordances may exist) and whose incipits are frequently unrelated to any known text, often taking the form of a catch-phrase or motto.[4]

While some of the last category may well be versions of motets or chansons that have not otherwise been preserved, a substantial number of others have been observed to exhibit traits that suggest they were actually conceived from the start as wordless structures. These take the form of a certain musical self-sufficiency, discernible in features such as a the repetitive working of well-profiled motifs or a marked tendency to florid, restless passage-work,[5] as if the music had been composed independently of any external patterns of verbal rhythm or structure. This is not to say that they are idiomatically instrumental, as the lines are as singable as any others of the time, so that the phrase 'songs without words', as coined by Edwards[6] to describe this type, seems preferable to the expression 'instrumental chansons' invented by Kämper and taken up by Litterick.[7]

The recognition of a given piece as a 'song without words' depends on an assessment of its musical style and the nature of its title. Because certain fully texted pieces exhibit 'wordless' features and titular incipits can be misleading, those in a language foreign to the supposed scribe being notoriously prone to alteration or distortion, scholars have exercised extreme caution in the use of the term as a definition.[8] However, the high coincidence of unrecognizable incipits with 'non-verbal' musical techniques and the use of the latter predominantly in melismatic passages in the course of actual text settings[9] make it possible to think in terms of a genre or tradition of some consistency.[10]

If the 'song without words' is compared not to the chanson but to the motet as described in chapter 4, the differences are even more salient. Not only is the writing on the whole more florid and motivic, but the characteristics of motet technique, such as voice-pairing, contrast of polyphonic and homophonic textures, rhythmic chordal declamation and rhetorical structure are entirely absent. Nonetheless, a number of such pieces have come to be categorized as motets simply on account of their Latin incipits, despite their far greater affinity with similarly textless works with vernacular titles.

A case in point is the 'chansonnier' BQ18 which is reckoned in the *Census-Catalogue* as including 26 motets among its 93 items,[11] a figure that is acknowledged in a recent detailed study of the manuscript by Susan Weiss.[12] In common with all but six of the pieces in the book, these 'motets' are supplied with an aphoristic incipit only by way of a text. Eight of them can be identified as textless versions of motets known from other sources,[13] namely:

Semper	('G. F.')	f.38v.-39r.[14]
Noe noe	(Brumel)	f.22v.-23r.
Alma redemptoris	(Josquin)	f.55v.-57r.[15]
Sy dedero	(Agricola)	f.70v.-71r.
Mater patris	(Brumel)	f.75v.-76r.
Byblis	(anon)	f.77v.-78r.[16]
Thysis	(Isaac)	f.79v.-80r.[17]
Parce domine	(Obrecht)	f.84v.-85r.

(All items are anonymous in BQ18; the composer attributions have been deduced from concordances.)

However, on the same basis, two other pieces can be immediately discounted from the canon of motets. The 'Ave Maria' on f.19v.-20r., can be recognized as a *lauda* by Tromboncino,[18] while the 'Absque verbis' on f.63v.-64r. is a version of the 'Benedictus' from Isaac's 'Quant j'ay au cour' Mass.[19]

The remaining 16 'motets' are all *unica* and many of them, like 'Semper' and 'Byblis' above, are decidedly non-verbal in style.[20] With a very few exceptions they are devoid of voice- pairing, homophony, changes of meter or articulated rhetorical structure. Instead, the music proceeds by busy motivic work, sequences, 'harmonic' bass lines moving in perfect intervals, restless upper voices incorporating frequent cadential figures (though rarely pausing on them) and florid scales, these last often set in one voice against a long held note in the middle of a phrase in another, giving rise to an unequal, asymmetrical effect. All have self-contained 'motto' incipits, few of which are positively identifiable with any known text; in addition the pieces also share the same clefs and even lengths, thus presenting a remarkably coherent group even by purely external standards. In the face of this the only useful distinctions that can be made among them concern the extent to which *cantus firmus* technique is used in their constructions, which are otherwise all based on the same type of motivic work and full textures.

Most noteworthy in this respect are a group of five pieces ('Adiuva me deus', 'In te domine sperabo', 'Surge', 'Ave regina celorum' and 'Speciosa', edited in vol. ii on pp.1, 109, 183, 32 and 176 respectively) which, while ostensibly freely composed, resort to what might be called a partial *cantus firmus*, a practice not found in any known examples of genuine motet writing. In each case, long held notes appear unobtrusively in the middle of the piece, forming a regular descending scalar pattern accompanied by more lively lines in the other voices (see 'Adiuva me deus', bb.18-39, 'In te domine sperabo', bb.35-41, 'Surge', bb.17-38, 'Ave regina celorum',[21] bb.24-32 and 37-42 and 'Speciosa', bb.45-53).[22] The latter two instances are actually sequential in all voices, such that it could be argued that the *cantus firmus* effect is no more than a by-product, where the composer has simply taken advantage of the harmonic stability inherent in such passages. However, the others are not in the least sequential and neither is a secondary long-note section in 'Speciosa' (at bb.24-32); these seem to require interpretation in the context of a distinct sub-genre even within the 'songs without words' group to which all five pieces belong.[23]

Although 'Ave regina celorum' is unusual in that the incipit can be identified with a text, there is apparently no musical reference to the famous Antiphon whatsoever. Indeed, the piece extends the partial *cantus firmus* principle by opening with what looks like the the beginning of the 'Regina caeli' Antiphon melody in long notes in its uppermost voice. If anything this directly contradicts the given title, though the use of both chants as seasonal alternatives in the same liturgical context may well be at the root of the confusion.[24] This passage is also notable for the motivic single-mindedness of the lower parts, whose first 14 bars (and later, bb.25-32 and 36-42) are a particularly forthright manifestation of the non-verbal style.

'Surge' is also worth singling out for attention as it is one of only two 'motets' in BQ18 to make use of genuinely motet-like duet and chordal textures (see bb.39-52).[25] This is not a serious challenge to the assumption that it was conceived for instruments, however; apart from this one brief section, the writing is characteristically non-verbal throughout, rather giving the impression that the composer was making a deliberate allusion to contemporaneous motet style while remaining well within the confines of the wordless tradition.

Of the five other pieces more immediately recognizable as being based on *cantus firmi*, three are built around short and plainly artificial ostinato motifs repeated in progressive rhythmic diminution, around which the other voices weave a typically 'wordless' texture. It has been suggested that the title of 'Spes mea' (edited in vol. ii, p.179) alludes to the motto of Ginevra Sforza Bentivoglio and thence that the ostinato is a *soggetto cavato*, derived by solmization from the name of his daughter Francesca.[26] Similarly, the title of 'Deus fortitudo mea' (edited in vol. ii, p.68), which was a motto of the Este family, has been associated circumstantially with the marriage of Lucrezia d'Este and Annibale Bentivoglio in 1487[27] and musically with the Mazzola family,[28] the two possibilities not necessarily being mutually exclusive. In the case of 'De ramo in ramo' (edited in vol. ii, p.66), however, it has so far proved impossible to conjecture a source either for the title or Tenor, though the general similarity of the piece to 'Spes mea' and 'Deus fortitudo mea' suggests some comparable origin for the curious nine-note subject.

'Bonus et misereator dominus' (edited in vol. ii, p.51) is slightly different in that as well as being in *tempus perfectum* and moreover the only piece in BQ18 for five voices, it uses a simple scale as a *cantus firmus*, descending in even long notes through an octave and then reascending symmetrically.[29] The overriding regularity of this structure would seem to preclude any arcane verbal origin but the relationship of its purely musical logic to that of the accelerated ostinato pieces is still clear, as are the similar styles of their respective free voices.

Somewhat more puzzling is the Tenor of 'Probasti cor meum' (edited in vol. ii, p.155), which combines elements of abstract design, such as the similar configurations of bb.27- 41 and 52-66 or the regular scalar passages at bb.12-24, with unpredictable rhythms and erratic intervallic motion.   It hardly looks like a pre-composed melody, yet its vagaries defy any attempt to construe a rational basis so that it must necessarily be left as a case unsolved. Less mysterious, though, is the style of writing in the voices around the enigmatic Tenor, which is plainly that of the other works based on more easily comprehensible *cantus firmi*.

The remaining six pieces require a certain amount of qualification in their assessment as possible 'songs without words'. 'Nunc scio vere', 'Salva nos' and 'Da pacem' are quite explicitly connected to the texts implied by their titles by the incorporation of the appropriate plainsong material. In 'Nunc scio vere' (edited in vol. ii, p.135), the Introit melody is very freely paraphrased in the Cantus, though phrases also appear in the Bassus (in bb.3-10 and 25- 30).[30] After some anticipatory imitation in the three upper voices, it is again the Bassus that carries the chant in 'Salva nos' (edited in vol. ii, p.172), the Antiphon melody being laid out in long notes almost as a *cantus firmus*.[31] 'Da pacem' (edited as 'Da pacem II' in vol. ii, p.61), on the other hand, uses the opening of the popular Antiphon melody as a kind of free ostinato which though found mostly in the Cantus and Tenor does in fact appear in each voice at some point.[32]

Their unusual handling of pre-composed material differentiates all three pieces from other *cantus firmus* or paraphrase motets, as does the behaviour of the free voices, which are very close to those of the more obviously wordless pieces in style.[33] Thus despite their known textual associations, a non-verbal conception seems most probable and a classification among the 'songs without words' more useful if the above reservations are borne in mind.

The three-voiced 'O virgo' and 'Tristis es anima mea' are in the style of the Burgundian chanson, a type whose close connection with the Italian instrumental repertory has been firmly established.[34] The musical similarity of 'O virgo' (edited in vol. ii, p.149) to Tinctoris's 'O virgo miserere mei'[35] suggests that it was originally composed as a setting of the same text. However, since the words do not fit nearly as well here, and since the phrase structure does not seem to correspond to any *forme fixe*, it seems equally possible that 'O virgo' may have been a wordless piece from the start. This hypothesis is in fact supported by the decorative lines and details such as the Cantus octave leap in b.11 (unusual in chanson writing) as well as a typical partial *cantus firmus* in bb.29-33, so that a cautious non-verbal interpretation is again preferable to a definition as a motet.

That the music of 'Tristis es anima mea' (edited in vol. ii, p.191) was written to accommodate the form of a *rondeau cinquain* text is made abundantly clear by the its division into the appropriate number of phrases on either side of the *fermata* signs in all voices at b.25. The only unusual feature is the behaviour of the middle voice, which carries a threefold ostinato whose second statement is actually cleaved by the break in b.25. This is however less a contradiction of the form than an example of musical conceit, comparable to the use of chant material in motet-chansons such as Alexander Agricola's 'Belle sur toutes - Tota pulchra es'.[36] It has not proved possible to trace the origins of this melody as yet; certainly it seems to have nothing to do with the Responsory 'Tristis est anima mea',[37] which suggests that the name of the piece is not a misspelt incipit but a genuine title. Even if the piece were originally texted, then the *rondeau* form is an indication that it could not have been in Latin, so that it can hardly be considered as a motet.

Lastly, 'Venimus princeps' (edited in vol. ii, p.197) is exceptional among these pieces from BQ18 in making full and consistent use of all the stylistic traits associated with the contemporaneous motet, such as changes of meter, varied textures and chordal declamation, at the expense of any wordless features. In spite of this, it is still not possible to be certain that it was originally a genuine motet rather than an emulation of one. The title, for example, is not recognizable as part of any known text, though it may refer to a ceremony of some kind.[38] In addition there are musical details, such as the frequent repeated notes (as for example in the Cantus, bb.26-33), which make it hard to imagine exactly what kind of text would have inspired them. While the rhythms could have been changed as part of the adaption for instrumental performance, it should be noted that the latter passage is in fact yet another manifestation of the partial *cantus firmus* technique, providing a further subtle link with the non-verbal compositions that predominate in the manuscript.

The non-verbal style is not a unique property of the pieces with Latin incipits in BQ18, as is evinced by works such as Isaac's 'La mora' (f.72v.-73r.) or Josquin's 'La bernadina' (f.82v.-83r.), which have already been described elsewhere as 'almost certainly insrumental in conception and intent'.[39] The musical consistency of all these pieces makes a mockery of the process of dividing them up into motets, chansons or *frottole* on the strength of no more than the languages of their incipits. Therefore, the recognition of the 'song without words' as a genre distinct at least from the motet seems imperative if any sense is to be made out of the latter category. Certainly, the first ten pieces based on full or partial *cantus firmi* discussed above can be consigned to it without any doubt whatsoever, bearing as they do little relation to the motets considered in previous chapters. If 'O virgo' and 'Venimus princeps' are counted among the partial *cantus firmus* works and 'Nunc scio vere' and 'Salva nos' accepted as probably instrumental in origin, this only leaves 'Tristis es anima mea' which was plainly composed as a *rondeau* rather than a motet anyway. This means that the compositions that can be securely regarded as motets in BQ18 are merely those eight that can be identified from concordances; the others are all sufficiently different to be classed as a separate genre, albeit with reservations in a handful of cases.

Works of this type are not confined to sources compiled specifically for instrumental use like BQ18 and indeed it is not altogether surprising that a number can be detected among the 'motets' of such a catholic anthology as FP27. The scribe there was particularly scrupulous in his copying of Latin texts, to the extent of writing out the entire 'Ave Maria' five times on adjacent pages at the beginning of the manuscript, which makes it all the more surprising that in a total of fifteen other instances he was content to supply no more than an incipit. Eight of these have already been discussed as clearly belonging to one of the genres detailed in the present or previous chapters;[40] they show no signs of having been composed as 'songs without words' even if their lack of text suggests a instrumental function in this context. Similarly a ninth piece, 'Isachina Benedictus', can be identified as being derived from the 'Benedictus' section of a Mass[41] and so requires no further discussion here.

The remaining six, on the other hand, perfectly match the style of the BQ18 pieces. There are even three works with similarly pithy mottos as titles instead of incipits, one being 'Omnis laus in fine canitur' (edited in vol. ii, p.144), where the music is motivically insistent to the unusual extent of being completely monothematic throughout. The second is 'Non desina' (edited in vol. ii, p.130), a typically non- verbal piece whose name may derive from the almost obsessive use it makes of repetitive sequential writing. Lastly, the three-voiced 'Sine fraude' (edited in vol. ii, p.175) makes consistent use of these devices too, but is more remarkable for a partial *cantus firmus* at the end which is actually an ostinato on the notes *la, sol, la, mi* in the Cantus (see bb.44-56, with the motif anticipated in the preceding entry).

The title 'Alleluya', found at the head of two items (edited as nos. I and II in vol. ii, pp. 5 and 6), is hardly specific enough to be an actual textual incipit, but it might suggest that the music was intended to be vocalized to this word. Both works display all the hallmarks of the wordless style and could thus be viewed equally as 'songs without words' or as examples of the melismatic vocal pieces in the tradition of Isaac's 'Quant j'ay au cour' Benedictus which were composed in the same way.[42] One 'Domenicus' is credited as the author of the three-voiced 'Alleluya'; although it is not possible to identify him with any certainty, there are other circumstantially plausible references to musicians of that name, including two documentary accounts of a singer connected with the court of Mantua as well as the attribution of a *frottola* in a Sienese collection.[43] A version of the four-voiced 'Alleluya' is attributed to Isaac in *I-Fn* MS Banco Rari 229, where it carries no text whatsoever, thus strengthening the case for a wordless interpretation of the piece.[44]

The last of the apparently instrumental 'motets' in FP27, then, is the 'Ave Maria' on ff.5v.-7r. (edited as 'Ave Maria V' in vol. ii, p.22), attributed to an otherwise unknown 'Musipula'. The music is copied among the group of 'Ave Maria' *laude* at the beginning of the manuscript but is immediately distinguishable by its greater length and omission of the text, which was repeatedly copied in full in each of the other examples. Moreover, it is uniquely notable for its frequent reiterated motifs, which plainly owe little to the rhythms and phrasing of the Antiphon text and are typical of the wordless style. Nonetheless, the division into two *partes* with what look suspiciously like a distinct chordal phrase for 'Jesus' rounding off the *prima* and a separate 'amen' section at the end of the *secunda* suggest a connection with the form of the 'Ave Maria', while the irregularity, dogged rhythms and occasional *faux pas* in the part-writing are strongly reminiscent of the *lauda*. Therefore it is only possible to class the piece as non-verbal in conception rather than a *lauda* with reservations, although it is certainly unlike anything in the motet repertory and its copying without text implies an instrumental function in this source at least.

There is only one 'motet' among the more uniform contents of BQ19 whose text is incomplete, an anomaly which again coincides with a decidedly non-verbal style. The five-voiced 'Hec dies' (edited as 'Haec dies I' in vol. ii, p.81) looks is if it were first entered into the manuscript without any text at all. The first half (up to b.26) carries the words of the Gradual in all voices, haphazardly applied and with no attempt at underlaying the notes, to the extent that the final 'et laetemur' in the Bassus spills over into the second half. Otherwise the latter is untexted and although several continuations are possible, depending on whether the given two lines are construed as the opening of the Antiphon, Communion or Offertory, there is no indication as to which, if any, was intended. Moreover, the piece was copied as part of a small group of apparently instrumental works[45] which preceded the main body of the codex in its original form,[46] so that there are further external grounds for supposing that it was considered as separate from the motet collection.[47]

The music, while not exactly matching that of the BQ18 works in style, shares their combination of frequent cadences, harmonic bass lines, regular motivic work and decorative figuration as can be seen to particular advantage in the opening fourteen bars.[48] The subsequent concentration on brief syncopated ideas and repeated notes is also typically unsuited to any conceivable text (see, for example, the end of the first half), so that there is no doubt that the work is more closely related to the 'songs without words' in BQ18 than the other motets in BQ19.

The subject of instrumental ensemble music in the late fifteenth and early sixteenth centuries is one that has only just begun to receive the attention it deserves. The claim that the majority of textless works preserved in Italian sources from around that time were intended to be played rather than sung is not one that can be made lightly, which is why scholars have hitherto been understandably cautious in their assertion of it. Nevertheless, the survival of appropriate instruments, together with the evidence of documentary accounts and payments, bear witness to a flourishing instrumental tradition in late *quattrocento* Italy.[49] This testimony coincides with a substantial body of music copied without text, which simply could not have been performed except by instruments (or wordless vocalization), unless a text were supplied from elsewhere. The latter is highly improbable; the labour saved in copying a text is wholly insufficient to compensate for the inconvenience of performing from two books at once and besides, there is nothing to indicate the parallel existence of verse collections analogous to the multilingual musical *chansonniers* in Italy at this stage.[50] Nor is it likely that the words to a large body of songs in various foreign languages, which came and went with fashion, would have been committed to memory along with their underlay so that just a written record of the musical notes was additionally required to prepare a performance. Moreover, if texts were intended, then such rubrics or names as the pieces may have would be expected to clearly identify them in most cases, whereas many titles are self-sufficient 'mottos' without any possible continuation. To be sure, texts must occasionally have been omitted through carelessness or ignorance, but this would still not account for the copying of whole anthologies like BQ18 or the *Odhecaton* series with only an incipit to identify each piece.

With a few exceptions, therefore, the wordless pieces in Italian sources from the decades around 1500 would seem to have been intended for instrumental use. Some of them are plainly based on vocal models, but the majority lack any apparent antecedent and hence there is no reason to believe that they were not devised without text from the start. Although there is no question of the influence of instrumental technique or idioms, it is only to be expected that this music, which was not composed around verbal structures, should be markedly different from that of the motet, which was becoming increasingly characterized by an emphasis on textual expression and declamation.

Because elements of this wordless style are sometimes to be found in genuine *forme fixe* chansons, scholars have naturally been hesitant to isolate the textless examples of it as a separate genre. The obvious dissimilarity of such works to those in the contemporaneous motet tradition does on the other hand make the establishment of a categorical boundary between them a practical possibility. This is not merely important from the point of view of further refining the definition of the motet; it also provides a firm basis for the recognition of the 'songs without words' as yet another of the fundamental elements whose combinations and permutations underlie the seemingly inexhaustible variety of early renaissance musical style.

Notes

[1] The most immediately relevant of these are *KämperS*, *LittP*, *LittI*, *EdwardS* and *WeissB*, each of which provide evidence for both the nature of the sources and the instrumental ensembles; but see also *FullerB* and *BrownFC*, pp.140-2 and Pirrotta's comments regarding the *Odhecaton* trilogy in *Grove*, 'Italy' (ix, p.365), for further discussions.

[2] See *LittP*, p.480, and *LittI*, pp.118-19, and the use both there and in *KämperS* of the term 'instrumental chanson'.

[3] This category includes both through-composed works based on rhythmic adaptations of a given melody (sometimes treated in canon) and those that retain a *forme-fixe* structure through the literal use of one or more of the original lines; a distinction between these types, illustrated with examples of each, is made in *LittI*, p.118.

[4] See for example the anonymous 'La stangetta' or 'Omnis laus in fine

canitur' from FP27.

[5]All the relevant authorities are unanimous in their observation and interpretation of these characteristics; see *FullerB*, p.86, *LittP*, pp.480-1, *LittI*, p.118 and *BrownFC*, I, pp.140-2.

[6]See *EdwardS*, p.79.

[7]See *KämperS*, pp.66-73 and *LittI*, p.118.

[8]The arguments for this are most strongly expressed in *BrownFC*, p.142.

[9]Notably the 'Kyrie eleison', 'Sanctus' and 'Agnus Dei' movements of the Mass Ordinary; see *EdwardS*, pp.83-7.

[10]This point is argued more fully in *EdwardS*, p.81.

[11]See *HammCC*, i, p.72.

[12]See the inventory in *WeissB*, pp.69-70.

[13]Significantly, these form part of a group of sacred works described by Weiss as 'most often found textless in collections presumably prepared for instrumental purposes' (see *WeissB*, p.79).

[14]The original of this piece is a unique series of no less than ten movements, setting the successive verses of the complete sequence 'Benedicta semper sancta sit Trinitas' with its melody as a *cantus firmus* throughout. Only the first of these is contained in BQ18, which also omits the opening monophonic intonation on the word 'Benedicta', hence the misleading incipit 'Semper'. This curious composition is preserved entire solely in the 'Apel Codex' (Leipzig, Universitätsbibliothek MS 1494) where again only the opening fragment of the text was copied; the intention was presumably instrumental, as the musical style is almost definitively non- verbal by the criteria laid out above (see *GerberM*, ii, p.131).

[15]The piece is incomplete due to the loss of f.56. from the manuscript.

[16]This is another typical example of a misleading title; the text associated with this music actually begins 'Nam edunt de micis et castelli' (see *CattinL*, p.75). Cattin asserts both the titular nature of the incipit and the style of the music as 'built as a coordinate series of progressions disclosing an instrumental work' (*Idem*, p.xxxiii).

[17]As with 'Byblis' above, this incipit has nothing to do with the original text; the music corresponds to the section starting with 'Ad te clamamus' from Isaac's motet 'Salve regina'. An explanation of the change is postulated in *WeissB*, p.76.

[18]This work has already been considered in the present chapter on account of its appearance in Petrucci's *Libro primo* and its relationship to the various similar settings in FP27.

[19]Exactly the same music is preserved in FP27, ff.17v.-18r., without text except for the incipit 'Isachina Benedictus'. See *AMMM*, x, p.38, for the original Mass, where the 'Benedictus' is for three voices; the four-voiced version, which was evidently very popular in early sixteenth-century sources (see *BrownFC*, no.10, for full details) can be found transcribed in *GeerL*, no.8. It is also observed in *BrownFC* (p.266) that the music on f.32v.-33r. with the motet-like incipit 'Gaude virgo' is actually that of Isaac's four-voiced *rondeau*, 'Je ne me puis vivre' (published as no.129); for this reason the piece is excluded from the reckoning of numbers of motets both here and in *HammCC*.

[20]The 'Da pacem' on ff.30v.-31r. is also exceptional in being related to a distinct sub-genre of pieces based on this text and its associated melody discussed in chapter 5 (see p. 151, note 13).

[21]This example is exceptional in that the scalar motion is upward

rather than downward.

[22]This unusual technique can be found additionally in 'O virgo', bb.29-33 and 'Venimus princeps', bb.26-33, in exactly the same way. These pieces, though probably also instrumental, will be discussed separately below on account of certain other peculiarities of style. The almost certainly instrumental 'Sine fraude' from FP27 (to be discussed below) also belongs to this genre, even if its *cantus firmus* takes the form of an ostinato motif.

[23]Another example can be found in the 'Benedictus' of Isaac's 'Quant j'ay au cor' Mass (adapted as 'Absque verbis' in BQ18 as detailed above), bb.41-53. The use of the technique in such a principally melismatic text setting again indicates the close ties between this style and that of the 'songs without words' (see *EdwardS*, pp.83-7).

[24]See *LU*, pp.273-7.

[25]The other is the somewhat different 'Venimus princeps', to be discussed below.

[26]F. BEN TI VOL YA = *fa, re, mi, sol, la*; see *WeissB*, pp.71-2 and also pp.63-71 for the supporting circunstantial evidence.

[27]See *WeissB*, p.78.

[28]The Mazzola similarly used 'Deus fortitudo mea' as a motto and the musical connection lies in the solmization of their name as *fa, sol, la*, which three notes provide the entire motif of the *ostinato*; see *WeissB*, p.80, note 25.

[29]See Alessandro Coppini's contemporaneous motet 'Fiat pax in virtute tua' (preserved in the third Gaffurius codex and published in *D'AccFR*, ii, no. 31) for a comparably contrived *cantus firmus*.

[30]The words 'Nunc scio vere' would have to be supplied as an intonation, as the polyphonic paraphrase only starts on the second

phrase, 'quia misit Dominus Angelum suum'; see *GP*, f.130v., or *LU*, p.1518. This practice is already familiar from 'Semper' (see above) and the 'Stella caeli' in FP27 (see chapter 5, p.147 and vol. ii, p.181).

[31]See *LU*, p.271.

[32]The existence of a consistent genre of vocal 'Da pacem' motets was noted in chapter 5 (see p.151, note 13). However, while the present piece uses the same melody and to a certain extent imitative technique, the non-verbal style of the free voices and the irregular opening relate it much more closely to the 'songs withput words' from BQ18, distinguishing it as being a hybrid 'instrumental' version of a vocal type.

[33]It is possible to cite the motet 'Miserere mei, Domine', by Rufino Bartolucci da Assisi (*fl.* 1510-40), as another example of the *cantus firmus* being set in the Bassus; see *JepplS*, ii, p.107.

[34]See in particular *LittP*, *LittI*, and *EdwardS*.

[35]See *TinctO*, p.125.

[36]See *AgrO*, iv, no. 14.

[37]See *LU*, p.635.

[38]See *WeissB*, p.78.

[39]*Idem*, p.80.

[40]'Memento mei' and 'Miserere' are discussed as *laude* and the 'Dies irae' on ff. 23v.-24r. as a minor liturgical work in chapter 7; 'Adonai' and 'Felix namque' are considered as motets in chapter 4; while 'Ave maris stella', 'Regina caeli' and 'Veni creator spiritus' are grouped with the chant paraphrases in chapter 5.

[41]See the comments on 'Absque verbis' in note 19 above.

[42]The intimate relationship between these two genres has already been discussed above. The distinct sequential and plainly non-verbal 'Alleluia' section at the end of Brumel's 'Nativitas unde gaudia - Nativitas tua, Dei genetrix' is also of note in this context.

[43]See *JeppFR*, i, p.153 and ii, p.39.

[44]This version is essentially the same as that in FP27, apart from a few details; it is published in *HAM*, vol. i, no.88 (p.91), this edition itself being derived from that in *Wolf1*, Jg. xiv/I, p.119.

[45]These are generally considered as chansons, but their incomplete texting, restricted in most cases to no more than an incipit, suggest instrumental use. They include Moulu's 'J'ay' (ff. [4]v.-1r.), and the 'Fors seulement' compositions by Pipelare (ff. 1v.-2r.), Silva (ff. 2v.-3r.) and Anon. (ff. 3v.-4r.). Divitis's 'Fors seulement' (ff. 9v.- 11r.) is also virtually textless; it is published, along with the other 'Fors seulement' pieces, in *RRMMER*, xiv, where the case for instrumental use is advanced on stylistic as welll as textual grounds (see nos. 11, 17, 25 and 26).

[46]See *CrawCF* for an analysis of the construction of this manuscript.

[47]Another example of an apparently instrumental composition in an otherwise sacred context is Alessandro Coppini's textless motet in the third Gaffurius Codex (published in *D'AccFR*, ii, p.79). Although D'Accone argues the necessity of a text that has since been lost, the rigid ABABA form of the piece and its motivic patterns (such as at bb.44-8) at once distinguish it from Coppini's other motets and liken it to the 'songs without words' from BQ18.

[48]Significantly, a remarkably similar passage opens 'Probasti cor meum', one of the most characteristic 'songs without words' from BQ18 examined above.

[49]See for instance *FullerB*, p.93, *LittP*, p.480, or the latter part of

WeissB for examples of such accounts.

[50]Books of chanson verse seem first to have appeared in Paris at the start of the sixteenth century, but they were an exclusively French phenonemon; see the introduction to *JeffCV*, pp.11-22. For a list of early renaissance sources of Italian poetry, see *GallCI*, pp.91-3.

EPILOGUE

The motet is the most perennial category of polyphonic music, having served continuously from its first invocation to describe bitextual clausulae in the early thirteenth century right down to the present day. In the course of this long career, the term has embraced so many forms and styles that it has been inherited by the twentieth century shorn of all specific meaning, except as a casual designation of Latin sacred works unconnected with larger-scale forms such as the Mass or Magnificat. The generous cut of this definition reflects the displacement of the motet and indeed church music in general from the vanguard of musical evolution since the revolt against doctrinaire religion and establishment of the essentially secular 'classical' repertory in the eighteenth century.

The situation in the first decades of the sixteenth century was rather different. Motets were cultivated above all other polyphonic forms by the richest patrons and the most skilled composers. Though exclusively a written language, Latin was still in widespread use and indeed was only just coming to be supplanted by the various vernaculars in central Europe as the principal means of intellectual communication or formal ratification. Even if it was considered conservative in some quarters, it could hardly have had any of the connotations of archaism or exclusive religiosity that have grown up around it since the Reformation, as the numerous ceremonial or even amatory 'motets' from that time bear witness.

Without an inviolable alignment of sacred work with Latin and secular with a given vernacular, the decision as to which language to use in a musical setting would seem to be a matter of etiquette and context. There is, however, an equally important compositional consideration; while vernacular songs invariably set rigidly patterned verse, the Latin texts sanctioned by ecclesiastical tradition are more often than not free prose passages. Traditionally, while the line structure and overall form at least of secular poetry served also for its musical setting, no such restrictions applied to pieces based on Latin prose. The simple consequence was that if a composer wished to experiment with musical form he was effectively obliged to use a

237

Latin text as a vehicle for it regardless of any other considerations, a situation that only came to change with the later chansons of Josquin and Gombert.

In fact, it is possible to arrive at a positive definition of the motet along these lines, at least for the decades around 1500, as any through-composed vocal work with a deliberately contrived musical structure that may be related to but is not in fact prescribed by the form of its text. Clearly excluded from the category, therefore, are the line- by-line settings of the laude examined in chapter 7 (though the 'Ave Maria' pieces remain exceptional cases); the minor ritual works, whose syllabic writing is wholly dependent on the words; strophic or alternatim settings of hymns, the Lamentations or the Magnificat; and lastly the formulaic settings of forme fixe and frottola poetry alike. The remaining pieces, such as those characterized in chapters 4 to 6, tend naturally to be in Latin and predominantly sacred; but by not specifically disqualifying pieces for being in the wrong language it is possible to allow for works such as Josquin's 'Nymphes des bois', which have long been recognized as being closer to the style of the motet than the chanson.

This definition is not contradicted by that in Tinctoris's Terminorum musicae diffinitorium of ca.1495, where he states:

> Motetum est cantus mediocris, cui verba cuiusvis
> materiae sed frequentius divinae supponuntur.[1]

It is interesting to compare this with the entry under 'cantilena'. This is the only other comparable reference to a formal type in the Diffinitorium and since the wording is almost identical, it is most probable that the two were written in conjunction. Tinctoris maintains:

> Cantilena est cantus parvus, cui verba cuiuslibet
> materiae sed frequentius amatoriae supponuntur.[2]

In both descriptions he is careful to allow for texts of any sentiment before adding a subordinate qualification as to which is most common in each case, and he does not seem to discriminate on grounds of language. The only other distinction he makes is that of size, which when taken at face value is hardly a very useful means of distinguishing between types. However, implicit in the differentiation between 'mediocris' and 'parvus' are a number of other considerations, some of which can in fact be related to matters of musical structure. Since a good many forme fixe chansons are actually longer than the majority of single-movement motets when performed in their entirety, it is necessary to assume that Tinctoris had in mind their music as it stands notated on the page, which only achieves any length through its repeat scheme. This curious comparison of size can therefore be understood as embodying a distinction between the through- composition of the motet and the reiterative patterns of other forms.

If this is accepted, then Tinctoris's definition is in complete agreement with that based on musical structure proposed above, although it excludes the minor ritual works on account of their dimensions rather than their style. Whether or not he meant his definition of the term 'cantilena' to embrace Italian frottole and laude as well as French chansons, it certainly suits them; thus his two categories, together with the 'cantus magnus' of the Mass are sufficient for the description of all the types of music that would have been known to Tinctoris, except of course the instrumental works which he would presumably have considered as cantilenae on account of their derivation as a genre.

Although this structural definition of the motet is a positive one, it is by no means rigid, as the variety of forms encountered in the surviving music bears out. However, once the laude, minor ritual works and instrumental pieces have been set apart, parallels begin to emerge between the residual motet repertories of sources such as FP27 and BQ19 in spite of their initial diversity and few common

composers.   The works examined from both manuscripts can be
divided into strict cantus firmus settings, pieces where chant material
is paraphrased in more than one voice or free structures based on
contrasting textures in roughly equal proportions. The first of these
types is assured a certain universal homogeneity by the fixity of its
construction, but there is also a consistency to the second that can not
so easily be dismissed as the result of mere exigency, as was argued in
chapter 5. Even more striking is the way that the free pieces from both
sources obey similar conventions as to the procedures and techniques
employed at specific points in their overall design, to the extent that
nearly all of them can be analysed in terms of a common 'rhetorical'
model. To be sure, BQ19 differs in its preservation of a fair number
of more substantial motets, but it should be remembered that the
majority of these take whole psalms for their texts and thus represent a
type that was only beginning to establish itself in the years between its
compilation and that of FP27.   Also exceptional are the bipartite
pieces in BQ19 derived from the Canticum canticorum, but again their
close stylistic similarities both to each other and also to Weerbeke's
shorter settings in FP27, which are due partly to their peculiar textual
structures,[3] mean that they too can reasonably be segregated as
another internally consistent sub-species of the motet.

If these divisions are supplemented by specific genres such as
the 'Regina caeli' and 'Da pacem' settings as observed in chapter 5
(see notes 4 and 13 on pp. 142 and 151 respectively), the profile of
the motet seems not so much undisciplined as multi-faceted and an
accumulation of various overlapping traditions. It is the manifold
possibilities of interaction between these combined with the
idiosyncrasies of a given personal style that make grouping by text or
even composer so problematic. However, the identification of the
handful of different archetypes listed above enables the initial
complexity of the repertory to be broken down into specific
components, to yield a surprisingly clear picture of the models a
musician had before him if he chose to stray beyond the limits of a
purely verbal approach to form. Exceptional cases do of course exist,

for example Bruhier's ceremonial 'Vivite felices' which has a style all of its own, but even so the recognition of conventions elsewhere does at least provide a background against which its irregularities can be assessed. Besides, the present survey is principally confined to works preserved in only two sources from approximately the same time and place; there are surely other emulative traditions at work which can only be isolated by a much more general investigation of all manner of composers, regardless of stature or patronage.

This local repertory is however peculiarly significant as a mirror of the complex process of musical fermentation unique to northern Italy at the time. The invention and early commercial success of music printing, which are clear indications of a new social function for music as the recreation of an educated bourgeoisie, took place in Venice. In order to meet the demands of this market, popular but essentially charismatic types like the frottola and lauda came to be adapted not only to the rigours of mensural notation but also to the four-voiced format standardized in the earlier prints. Thus for the first time, these 'humanistic' forms were set before the same public as had traditionally sponsored the learned disciplines of the oltremontani as equal alternatives, a confluence of ideals that simply could not have occurred outside of the peninsula. Similarly, the evolution of imported forme fixe chansons into apparently instrumental pieces seems uniquely and necessarily to have taken place in Italy, being due in some measure to the redundancy of French texts for an audience steeped in its own literary traditions. The contemporaneous revival of ancient learning in general seems moreover to have relied on the northern Italian presses for its dissemination, as is demonstrated by the spread of classical rhetoric treatises discussed in chapter 3.

It is the combination of all these circumstances that lends the motet in Italy its own particular character in the years around 1500. As might be expected from the turmoil of influences that gave rise to it, it was a transitory form; the motet in the later sixteenth century owes more to a combination of the imitative style of Gombert with the spontaneous word-painting effects of the madrigalists than the carefully controlled formal balance of the music examined in chapter 4. It has been said of the instrumental ensemble repertory that it and the chanson 'appear to have died around 1500, presumably victims of a stylistic evolution that swept away many of the foundations on which they rested'.[4] Though to a lesser extent, this is also true of the motet types born of the same conditions; it would be unrealistic to claim that the compositions of Weerbeke or Sebastiano Festa were the predominant influences on the subsequent history of the form. Nevertheless, they are of no small value as works of art and their anticipation of some of the functions, ideology and even techniques of the 'serious' madrigal (particularly notable in the Canticum canticorum settings) are of crucial importance to the development of Italian music. Moreover, the significance of perceptibly incorporating radical and external ideas into the art of music should not be underrated, since it is one of the principal milestones in the transition from a consideration of composition as an impersonal medieval craft to its modern acceptance as a means of individual humanistic expression.

Notes

[1] See *ParrT*, p.42.

[2] *Idem*, p.12. There is also an entry under 'Missa' (see p.40), with a cross-reference under the synonym (as far as Tinctoris is concerned) 'Officium' (p.46), but this 'cantus magnus' is unambigously defined by its text.

[3] This point is discussed more fully with respect to 'Vulnerasti cor meum' in chapter 6 (see p.183).

[4] See *LittI*, p.127; these sentiments are echoed also in *EdwardS*, pp.91-2.

APPENDIX A: THE 'MOTETS' IN FP27

The present list of pieces is based on a reconciliation of the manuscript with *BecherC*, pp.118-22 and *JeppFR*, ii, pp.37- 42 and 124-5, and includes all those counted as motets and hymns in *HammCC*, i, p.232. This number has been preferred to the revised total of 40 motets, 7 hymns *et alia* in *HammCC*, iv, pp.375-6 as the reasoning behind the various reclassifications is not made explicit there, whereas such matters are discussed in some detail in chapters 7 and 8 of the present thesis. However, the total of 84 works given below differs from that of 86 in the original reckoning (i. e. *HammCC*, i, p.232, itself derived from *JeppFR*) due to the counting of the 'Tremens factus sum', 'Dies illa' and 'Requiem eternam' on ff.210v.-211r. as one piece (here called 'Dies illa'), for reasons discussed in chapter 7.

Composers' names have been standardized where possible, those not included in FP27 but traceable from concordances being given in brackets; for the attributions as found in the manuscript, see Appendix E. The titles of pieces, on the other hand, have been left in their original orthography. All compositions are for four voices unless otherwise indicated.

Ave Maria		Laurentius Bergomotius	ff. 1v.- 2r.
Ave Maria		J. Fogliano	ff. 2v.- 3r.
Ave Maria		Cara	ff. 3v.- 4r.
Qui seminant in lacrimis		Anon.	ff. 3v.- 4r.
Ave Maria		Anon.	ff. 4v.- 5r.
Vidimus enim stellam		Anon.	ff. 4v.- 5r.
Ave Maria		Musipula	ff. 5v.- 7r.
Ave Maria		Tromboncino	ff. 7v.- 8r.
Admirabile comertium		Anon.	ff. 8v.- 9r.
Amice ad quid ven	à3	A. Agricola	ff. 15v.- 16r.

Qui nos fecit	à2	Anon.	f. 17r.
Isachina		(Isaac)	ff. 17v.- 18r.
Benedictus			
Benedicamus domino		Anon.	f. 18v.
Benedicamus domino	à3	Anon.	f. 18v.
Benedicamus domino		Anon.	f. 18v.
Benedicamus domino	à3	Anon.	f. 19r.
Benedicamus domino	à3	Anon.	f. 19r.
Ave Maria	à2	Anon.	f. 19v.
Lauda Syon	à3	Anon.	f. 20v.
Dies ire		Anon.	ff. 23v.- 24r.
Altera autem die		Anon.	ff. 25v.- 26r.
Utile conscilium		Anon.	ff. 27v.- 28r.
Cum autem venissem	à3	(J. de Quadris)	f. 28v.
Christi corpus ave	à3	Anon.	f. 29r.
Gaude virgo		Anon.	ff. 29v.- 30r.
Da pacem		Anon.	ff. 31v.- 32r.
Mater digna Dei		(Weerbeke)	ff. 39v.- 40r.
In te domine speravi		Josquin	ff. 42v.- 43r.
Ave maris stella	à3	Anon.	f. 46v.
Aures ad nostras	à3	Anon.	f. 47r.
Miserere		Anon.	ff. 48v.- 49r.
O gloriosa domina	à3	Anon.	f. 52r.
Omnis laus in fine canitur		Anon.	ff. 52v.- 53r.
O gloriosa regina mundi	à3	(J. Touront)	ff. 53v.- 54r.
Verbum caro	à3	Anon.	f. 56v.

Memento mei	à3	Anon.	f. 57r.
Si dedero	à3	A. Agricola	ff. 57v.- 58r.
Surge propera		Jo. de Pinarol	ff. 58v.- 59r.
O pulcherima mulierum		Weerbeke	ff. 59v.- 60r.
Regina celi letare		Brumel	ff. 61v.- 63r.
O quam glorifica	à3	A. Agricola	ff. 63v.- 64r.
Virgo Maria		Weerbeke	ff. 66v.- 67r.
Christi mater ave		(Weerbeke)	ff. 67v.- 68r.
Stella celi		Anon.	ff. 69v.- 70r.
Adonai		Weerbeke	ff. 70v.- 71r.
Tristitia		Renaldo	ff. 71v.- 72r.
Quemadmodum desiderat	à3	Anon.	f. 73r.
Veni creator spiritus	à3	Anon.	ff. 73v.- 74r.
Lucis creator optime	à3	Anon.	ff. 75v.- 76r.
Regina celi	à3	Compère	f. 77r.
Tu solus qui facis		Josquin	ff. 79v.- 80r.
Verbum caro panem verum		Anon.	ff. 81v.- 82r.
Incipit oratio Jeremie	à3	Anon.	ff. 82v.- 84r.
O Domine yhesu christe		(Brumel)	ff. 86v.- 87r.
O Domine yhesu christe		Anon.	ff. 87v.- 88r.
Nunc dimittis	à3	Anon.	f. 88v.
Regina celi	à3	Ant. Peragulfus Lucensis	ff. 94v.- 95r.
Propter gravamen		Compère	ff. 95v.- 97r.
Ave stella matutina		Weerbeke	ff. 99v.-100r.

Ibo mihi ad montem		(Weerbeke)	ff.100v.-101r.
Mater patris	à3	Brumel	ff.101v.-102r.
Ave Maria		Anon.	ff.102v.-103r.
Sancta Maria		Anon.	f.102v.
Sancta Maria	à3	Anon.	f.103r.
Dies illa	à2	Anon.	f.103v.
Verbum caro	à3	Anon.	f.104r.
Alleluya	à3	Domenicus	f.105r.
Alleluya		(Isaac)	ff.105v.-106r.
Tenebre facte sunt		Anon.	ff.107v.-108r.
Ave sanctissima Maria		Anon.	ff.108v.-109r.
Verbum caro	à3	Anon.	f.109v.
Verbum caro	à2	Anon.	f.110r.
Felix namque		Anon.	ff.130v.-132r.
Lucis creator optime	à3	Anon.	ff.132v.-133r.
Non desina		Anon.	ff.139v.-140r.
Sine fraude	à3	Anon.	ff.142v.-143r.
Ave gratia plena		Anon.	ff.143v.-144r.
Ave Maria		Anon.	ff.146v.-147r.
Incipit oratio Jeremie		Anon.	ff.147v.-149r.
Rex autem david		Anon.	ff.149v.-150r.
[R]equiem eternam		Anon.	ff.209v.-210r.
Dies illa	à2	Anon.	ff.210v.-211r.
Dies ire	à2	Anon.	ff.210v.-211r.
Dies ire		Anon.	ff.212v.-213r.

APPENDIX B: THE 'MOTETS' IN BQ18

A detailed inventory of the entire manuscript can be found in WeissB, pp.69-71. The total of 26 works listed below corresponds to the number of motets given in HammCC, i, p.72 rather than the revised figure of 17 in HammCC, iv, p.276. The larger figure is preferred as it includes all those pieces with Latin incipits without taking into account the reclassifications made on the basis of WeissB, whose stylistic conclusions differ in certain details from those reached in the present thesis (see chapter 8).

There are no composer attributions in BQ18, so that those supplied below are all from concordances. Their names have therefore been standardized, although the titles of pieces have been left in their original orthography. All compositions are for four voices unless otherwise indicated. For full critical notes and details of modern editions, see Appendix E.

Ave Maria	(Tromboncino)	ff. 19v.- 20r.
Salva nos	Anon.	ff. 20v.- 21r.
Ave regina celorum	Anon.	ff. 21v.- 22r.
Noe, noe	(Brumel)	ff. 22v.- 23r.
Venimus princeps	Anon.	ff. 23v.- 24r.
In te domine sperabo	Anon.	ff. 24v.- 25r.
Surge	Anon.	ff. 29v.- 30r.
Da pacem	Anon.	ff. 30v.- 31r.
Deus fortitudo mea	Anon.	ff. 31v.- 32r.
Semper	(G. F.)	ff. 38v.- 39r.
Spes mea	Anon.	ff. 41v.- 42r.
Probasti cor meum deus	Anon.	ff. 43v.- 44r.
Adiuva me deus	Anon.	ff. 44v.- 45r.
Nu[n]c scio vere	Anon.	ff. 50v.- 51r.
De ramo in ramo	Anon.	ff. 53v.- 54r.
Bonus et misereator dominus	Anon.	ff. 54v.- 55r.
Alma redemptoris[1]	(Josquin)	ff. 55v.- 57r.
Absque verbis	(Isaac)	ff. 63v - 64r.

Tristis es anima mea	à3	Anon.	ff. 66v.- 67r.
Sy dedero	à3	(A. Agricola)	ff. 70v.- 71r.
Mater patris	à3	(Brumel)	ff. 75v.- 76r.
Byblis	à3	Anon.	ff. 77v.- 78r.
Thysis		(Isaac)	ff. 79v.- 80r.
Speciosa		Anon.	ff. 83v.- 84r.
Parce domine		(Obrecht)	ff. 84v.- 85r.
O virgo	à3	Anon.	ff. 92v.- 93r.

Notes

[1]This motet is incomplete because f.56 is missing from the manuscript.

APPENDIX C: THE 'MOTETS' IN BQ19

The present total of 76 motets and 2 motet-chansons (the latter pair distinguished below by asterisks) differs from both that of 75 motets and 2 motet-chansons given in HammCC, i, p.73, and that of 77 motets and 2 motet-chansons given in HammCC, iv, p.277, an anomaly that it has so far proved impossible to resolve.

Composers' names have been standardized where appropriate, those not included in BQ19 but traceable from concordances being given in brackets; for the attributions as found in the manuscript, see Appendix E. The titles of pieces, on the other hand, have been left in their original orthography. All compositions are for four voices unless otherwise indicated.

Angele dei		Sebastiano Festa	ff.[1]v.-[2]r.[1]
Moriens lux	à5	Mouton	ff.[3]v.-[4]r.
Nobis sancte spiritus		Alex. Agricola	ff. 4v.- 5r.
Hec dies	à5	Anon.	ff. 5v.- 6r.
Corde et animo		Mouton	ff. 6v.- 7r.
Paradisi portas aperuit		Renaldo	ff. 7v.- 8r.
Peccantem me quotidie		Hutinet	ff. 8v.- 9r.
Regem archangelorum		Costanzo Festa	ff. 11v.- 12r.
Emendemus in melius		Richafort	ff. 12v.- 15r.
Noe noe		Jacquet of Mantua	ff. 15v.- 17r.
O vos qui transitis		Jacquet of Mantua	ff. 17v.- 21v.
Veni sancte spiritus		Jacquet of Mantua	ff. 21v.- 22r.
Salva nos	à6	Mouton	ff. 22v.- 23r.
Illuminavit eum		Renaldo	ff. 23v.- 25r.
Hec dies		Renaldo	ff. 25v.- 26r.
Ecclesiam tuam deus		Jacquet of Mantua	ff. 26v.- 28r.

Vox de celis intonuit		Jhan of Ferrara	ff. 28v.- 30r.
Regina celi	à5	Renaldo	ff. 30v.- 32r.
Sufficiebat nobis	à5	Jacquet of Mantua	ff. 33v.- 36r.
O Jesu Christe		Renaldo	ff. 36v.- 37r.
O Jesu Christe		Jacquet of Mantua	ff. 37v.- 38r.
Maria ergo		Symon Ferrariensis	ff. 38v.- 41r.
O pulcherima virgo		Costanzo Festa	ff. 41v.- 43r.
Ave Maria...virgo serena	à5	Mouton	ff. 43v.- 44r.
In illo tempore loquente Jesu ad turbas		Silva	ff. 44v.- 45r.
O Domine Jesu Christe		Renaldo	ff. 45v.- 46r.
Hodie salvator mundi		Anon.[2]	ff. 46v.- 48r.
Vivite felices		Bruhier	ff. 48v.- 50r.
Ave sanctissima Maria		Renaldo	ff. 50v.- 52r.
Helisabeth beatissima		Costanzo Festa	ff. 52v.- 53r.
Hec est illa		Sebastiano Festa	ff. 53v.- 54r.
Da pacem		Anon.	ff. 54v.- 55r.
Circumdederunt me		Remi	ff. 55v.- 56r.
Dum complerentur		Lhéritier	ff. 57v.- 61r.
In illo tempore postquam consumati sunt		Sebastiano Festa	ff. 62v.- 63r.
In illo tempore Maria Magdalena		Mouton	ff. 63v.- 66r.
O sacrum convivium	à5	Jhan of Ferrara	ff. 66v.- 67r.
Vox in rama		(Sermisy)	ff. 67v.- 69r.

Puer natus est nobis		Mouton	ff. 69v.- 73r.
Congratulamini		Richafort	ff. 73v.- 75r.
Simile est regnum		Carpentras	ff. 75v.- 76r.
Quis dabit oculis meis		Costanzo Festa	ff. 76v.- 78r.
Peccata mea	à5	Mouton	ff. 78v.- 79r.
Quam pulcra es		Moulu[3]	ff. 79v.- 81r.
Per lignum salvi facti sumus	à5	Mouton	ff. 81v.- 82r.
Sufficiebat* [on 'Mon souvenir']		Richafort	ff. 82v.- 83r.
Per lignum crucis	à5	Divitis	ff. 83v.- 84r.
In convertendo		Lupus	ff. 84v.- 86r.
Benedicta mater matris		Anon.	ff. 86v.- 87r.
Vulnerasti cor meum		Anon.	ff. 87v.- 89r.
Ave fuit prima salus		Mouton	ff. 89v.- 91r.
Salve regina Barbara		Moulu	ff. 91v.- 93r.
O Domine Jesu Christe		Brumel	ff. 93v.- 94r.
Rosa novum dans odorem		Brumel	ff. 94v.- 98r.
In illo tempore		Moulu[4]	ff. 98v.-100r.
Ecce tu pulcra es amica mea		Josquin	ff.100v.-101r.
Stetit Jesus [in fact the secunda pars of Mouton's 'Confitemini'; see ff.185v.-186r.]		Mouton	ff.101v.-102r.
Lectio actuum [= In diebus illis]		Mouton	ff.102v.-106r.
Ave mater matris dei* [on 'Fortuna desperata']	à5	Jacquet of Mantua	ff.106v.-107r.
Ave Maria		Mouton	ff.107v.-109r.
O gemma clarissa Caterina		Willaert	ff.109v.-110r.

O dulcis amica dei	à5	Moulu	ff.110v.-111r.
Judica me deus		Silva	ff.111v.-113r.
Hodie complecti sunt		Anon.	ff.113v.-114r.
Dominus regit me		Willaert	ff.114v.-116r.
Quia devotis laudibus		Willaert	ff.116v.-117r.
In nomine Jesu		Lupus	ff.117v.-119r.
De profundis		Jacopo Fogliano	ff.119v.-122r.
Beati omnes		Jacopo Fogliano	ff.122v.-124r.
Regem regum dominum		Costanzo Festa	ff.124v.-127r.
Miserere...infirmus	à6	Lupus	ff.127v.-128r.
Nisi quia		Symon Ferrariensis	ff.128v.-130r.
Miserere...tribulor	à5	Lupus	ff.130v.-131r.
Confitemini [see ff.101v.-102r. for the secunda pars, 'Stetit Jesus']		Mouton	ff.185v.-186r.
Nigra sum		Lupus[5]	ff.186v.-188r.
O magnum misterium		Jhan of Ferrara	ff.188v.-190r.
O rex gentium		Anon.	ff.201v.-202r.
Beata apolonia		Anon.	ff.202v.-203r.
O dulcis (incomplete) [T: 'Cela sans plus']		Anon.	f.203v.

APPENDIX D: MOTETS CONSIDERED IN THIS THESIS

This appendix includes all those works from FP27, BQ18 and BQ19 discussed in chapters 4-8, which are listed in alphabetical order. Spellings of both titles and composers have been standardized. All compositions are for four voices unless otherwise indicated. For full critical notes and details of modern editions, see Appendix E.

Absque verbis [identical to 'Isachina Benedictus' below]		(Isaac)	FP27	ff. 63v - 64r.
Adiuva me deus		Anon.	BQ18	ff. 44v.- 45r.
Adonai		Weerbeke	FP27	ff. 70v.- 71r.
Alleluya I	à3	Domenicus	FP27	f.105r.
Alleluya II		(Isaac)	FP27	ff.105v.-106r.
Altera autem die		Anon.	FP27	ff. 25v.- 26r.
Angele dei		Sebastiano Festa	BQ19	ff.[1]v.-[2]r.
Aures ad nostras	à3	Anon.	FP27	f. 47r.
Ave gratia plena		Anon.	FP27	ff.143v.-144r.
Ave Maria I		Laurentius Bergomotius	FP27	ff. 1v.- 2r.
Ave Maria II		J. Fogliano	FP27	ff. 2v.- 3r.
Ave Maria III		Cara	FP27	ff. 3v.- 4r.
Ave Maria IV		Anon.	FP27	ff. 4v.- 5r.
Ave Maria V		Musipula	FP27	ff. 5v.- 7r.
Ave Maria VI [also in BQ18, ff.19v.-20r., at a pitch a fourth lower]		Tromboncino	FP27	ff. 7v.- 8r.
Ave Maria VII	à2	Anon.	FP27	f. 19v.
Ave Maria VIII		Anon.	FP27	ff.146v.-147r.

Ave maris stella	à3	Anon.	FP27	f. 46v.
Ave regina caelorum		Anon.	BQ18	ff. 21v.- 22r.
Ave sanctissima Maria I		Anon.	FP27	ff.108v.-109r.
Ave sanctissima Maria II		Renaldo	BQ19	ff. 50v.- 52r.
Ave stella matutina		Weerbeke	FP27	ff. 99v.-100r.
Beata Apollonia		Anon.	BQ19	ff.202v.-203r.
Beati omnes		Jacopo Fogliano	BQ19	ff.122v.-124r.
Benedicamus domino I		Anon.	FP27	f. 18v.
Benedicamus domino II	à3	Anon.	FP27	f. 18v.
Benedicamus domino III		Anon.	FP27	f. 18v.
Benedicamus domino IV	à3	Anon.	FP27	f. 19r.
Benedicamus domino V	à3	Anon.	FP27	f. 19r.
Benedicta mater matris		Anon.	BQ19	ff. 86v.- 87r.
Bonus et misereator dominus		Anon.	BQ18	ff. 54v.- 55r.
Christi corpus ave	à3	Anon.	FP27	f. 29r.
Christi mater ave		(Weerbeke)	FP27	ff. 67v.- 68r.
Circumdederunt me		Remi	BQ19	ff. 55v.- 56r.
Cum autem venissem	à3	(J. de Quadris)	FP27	f. 28v.
Da pacem I		Anon.	FP27	ff. 31v.- 32r.
Da pacem II		Anon.	BQ18	ff. 30v.- 31r.
Da pacem III		Anon.	BQ19	ff. 54v.- 55r.

De profundis	Jacopo Fogliano	BQ19	ff.119v.-122r.
De ramo in ramo	Anon.	BQ18	ff. 53v.- 54r.
Deus fortitudo mea	Anon.	BQ18	ff. 31v.- 32r.
Dies illa I à2	Anon.	FP27	f.103v.
Dies illa II[6] à2	Anon.	FP27	ff.210v.-211r.
Dies irae I	Anon.	FP27	ff. 23v.- 24r.
Dies irae II à2	Anon.	FP27	ff.210v.-211r.
Dies irae III	Anon.	FP27	ff.212v.-213r.
Felix namque	Anon.	FP27	ff.130v.-132r.
Gaude virgo	(Issac)	BQ19	ff. 32v.- 32r.
Gaude virgo, mater Christi	Anon.	FP27	ff. 29v.- 30r.
Haec dies I à5	Anon.	BQ19	ff. 5v.- 6r.
Haec dies II	Renaldo	BQ19	ff. 25v.- 26r.
Haec est illa	Sebastiano Festa	BQ19	ff. 53v.- 54r.
Hodie complecti sunt	Anon.	BQ19	ff.113v.-114r.
Ibo mihi ad montem	(Weerbeke)	FP27	ff.100v.-101r.
Illuminavit eum	Renaldo	BQ19	ff. 23v.- 25r.
Incipit oratio à3 Jeremiae I	Anon.	FP27	ff. 82v.- 84r.
Incipit oratio Jeremiae II	Anon.	FP27	ff.147v.-149r.
In convertendo	Lupus	BQ19	ff. 84v.- 86r.
In illo tempore	Sebastiano Festa	BQ19	ff. 62v.- 63r.
In nomine Jesu	Lupus	BQ19	ff.117v.-119r.
In te domine sperabo	Anon.	BQ18	ff. 24v.- 25r.

Isachina Benedictus [identical to 'Absque verbis' above]		(Isaac)	FP27	ff. 17v.- 18r.
Lauda Syon	à3	Anon.	FP27	f. 20v.
Lucis creator optime I	à3	Anon.	FP27	ff. 75v.- 76r.
Lucis creator optime II	à3	Anon.	FP27	ff.132v.-133r.
Maria ergo		Symon Ferrariensis	BQ19	ff. 38v.- 41r.
Mater digna Dei		(Weerbeke)	FP27	ff. 39v.- 40r.
Memento mei	à3	Anon.	FP27	f. 57r.
Miserere		Anon.	FP27	ff. 48v.- 49r.
Miserere...infirmus	à6	Lupus	BQ19	ff.127v.-128r.
Miserere...tribulor	à5	Lupus	BQ19	ff.130v.-131r.
Nigra sum		Lupus	BQ19	ff.186v.-188r.
Nisi quia		Symon Ferrariensis	BQ19	ff.128v.-130r.
Non desina		Anon.	FP27	ff.139v.-140r.
Nunc dimittis	à3	Anon.	FP27	f. 88v.
Nu[n]c scio vere		Anon.	BQ18	ff. 50v.- 51r.
O admirabile commertium		Anon.	FP27	ff. 8v.- 9r.
O Domine Jesu Christe I		Anon.	FP27	ff. 87v.- 88r.
O Domine Jesu Christe II		Renaldo	BQ19	ff. 45v.- 46r.
O gloriosa domina	à3	Anon.	FP27	f. 52r.
O gloriosa regina mundi	à3	(J. Touront)	FP27	ff. 53v.- 54r.
O Jesu Christe		Renaldo	BQ19	ff. 36v.- 37r.
O pulcherima mulierum		Weerbeke	FP27	ff. 59v.- 60r.

O rex gentium		Anon.	BQ19	ff.201v.-202r.
O virgo	à3	Anon.	FP27	ff. 92v.- 93r.
Omnis laus in fine canitur		Anon.	FP27	ff. 52v.- 53r.
Paradisi portas aperuit		Renaldo	BQ19	ff. 7v.- 8r.
Peccantem me quotidie		Hutinet	BQ19	ff. 8v.- 9r.
Per lignum crucis	à5	Divitis	BQ19	ff. 83v.- 84r.
Probasti cor meum deus		Anon.	BQ18	ff. 43v.- 44r.
Quemadmodum desiderat	à3	Anon.	FP27	f. 73r.
Qui nos fecit	à2	Anon.	FP27	f. 17r.
Qui seminant in lacrimis		Anon.	FP27	ff. 3v.- 4r.
Regina caeli I	à3	Ant. Peragulfus Lucensis	FP27	ff. 94v.- 95r.
Regina caeli II	à5	Renaldo	BQ19	ff. 30v.- 32r.
[R]equiem eternam		Anon.	FP27	ff.209v.-210r.
Rex autem david		Anon.	FP27	ff.149v.-150r.
Salva nos		Anon.	BQ18	ff. 20v.- 21r.
Sancta Maria I		Anon.	FP27	f.102v.
Sancta Maria II	à3	Anon.	FP27	f.103r.
Sine fraude	à3	Anon.	FP27	ff.142v.-143r.
Speciosa		Anon.	BQ18	ff. 83v.- 84r.
Spes mea		Anon.	BQ18	ff. 41v.- 42r.
Stella caeli		Anon.	FP27	ff. 69v.- 70r.
Surge		Anon.	BQ18	ff. 29v.- 30r.
Surge propera		Jo. de Pinarol	FP27	ff. 58v.- 59r.
Tenebrae facte sunt		Anon.	FP27	ff.107v.-108r.
Tristis es anima mea	à3	Anon.	FP27	ff. 66v.- 67r.
Tristitia		Renaldo	FP27	ff. 71v.- 72r.

Utile conscilium		Anon.	FP27	ff. 27v.- 28r.
Veni creator spiritus	à3	Anon.	FP27	ff. 73v.- 74r.
Venimus princeps		Anon.	BQ18	ff. 23v.- 24r.
Verbum caro I	à3	Anon.	FP27	f. 56v.
Verbum caro II	à3	Anon.	FP27	f.104r.
Verbum caro III	à3	Anon.	FP27	f.109v.
Verbum caro IV	à2	Anon.	FP27	f.110r.
Verbum caro panem verum		Anon.	FP27	ff. 81v.- 82r.
Vidimus enim stellam		Anon.	FP27	ff. 4v.- 5r.
Virgo Maria		Weerbeke	FP27	ff. 66v.- 67r.
Vivite felices		Bruhier	BQ19	ff. 48v.- 50r.
Virgo gloriosa		Sebastiano Festa	BQ20	no.8
Vulnerasti cor meum		Anon.	BQ19	ff. 87v.- 89r.

Notes

[1]The original foliation does not begin until the sixth folio of the manuscript as it stands today; the preceding five folios, which contain the *tabula* and the montage of the chained stag as well as these two motets, are thus identified by numbers in brackets here. For a discussion and diagram of the physical construction of these opening pages, see *CrawCF*, pp.107-8.

[2]Att. elsewhere to Mouton and Lhéritier.

[3]Att. Mouton in *1519*[2] and Josquin in *1537*[1].

[4]Att. Mouton in *1537*[1].

[5]Att. Conseil in *1539[10]*.

[6]'Dies illa II' includes the 'Tremens factus sum', 'Dies illa' and 'Requiem aeternam' on ff.210v.-211r., which are listed as three seperate pieces in *BecherC*: see chapter 7 for details of the reasons behind this.

APPENDIX E: CRITICAL COMMENTARY TO THE MOTETS DISCUSSED IN THIS THESIS

As with appendix D, all those works from FP27, BQ18 and BQ19 discussed in chapters 4-8 are listed in alphabetical order. Original spellings of both titles and composers have been retained. Critical notes on texts and concordances are generally not given for pieces that have been re-edited and printed in modern times and for which reference can be made directly to an existing publication, unless the latter is considered to be inadequate, inaccessible or out of date. Where a liturgical *cantus firmus* can be identified, a reference has been given to the *AP* as the most accessible contemporaneous source of chant material, as well as the relevant modern liturgical book. Any variants from the musical texts as they stand in FP27, BQ18, BQ19 and in one case BQ20 listed here are editorial, as the transcriptions have been prepared from these sources alone, without collation, unless there is any specific indication to the contrary.

Absque verbis (4v.)

Source:	BQ18, ff. 63v.- 64r., anon.
Composer:	Heinrich Isaac.
Text:	incipit in Cantus only, which literally translated means 'without words'; thus the music is presumably intended to be instrumental here, although it is in fact derived from the Benedictus section of a Mass (see notes below).
Edition:	*GeerL*, no. 8; see also *BrownFC*, no. 10, and pp.210-11 for details of concordances.
Notes:	This piece is a four-voiced version of the three-voiced Benedictus section of Isaac's 'Quant j'ay au cour' Mass (see *AMMM*, x, p.66). It is also musically identical to the 'Isachina Benedictus' in FP27 (see below). For further comment, see p.219.

Adiuva me deus (4v.)

Source:	BQ18, ff. 44v.- 45r., anon.

Text: incipit in Cantus only; probably an instrumental piece.
Edition: vol. ii, p.1.
Notes: for further comment, see p.220.
                    Altus, b.48: MS has *A* instead of *G*.
                    Bassus, b.5: MS has *F*, quarter note, instead of *G*, quarter note.

Adonai (4v.)
Source: FP27, ff. 70v.- 71r., 'Gaspar' [= Gaspar van Weerbeke].
Concordances: *1501*², ff. 15v.- 16r., 'Gaspar'.
                    CH-SGs MS 463 (incomplete), no. 104, 'Gaspar'.
                    CH-SGs MS 530, ff. 83v.- 84r., 'Gaspar'.
Text: incipits in Cantus and Altus only in FP27 (though the full text is supplied in *1501*²); unidentified though related to the Antiphon for the Saturday before the fourth Sunday of September (*LU*, p.993).
Edition: vol. ii, p.3.
Notes: for analytical comment, see p.82. Text in brackets taken from *1501*².
                    Cantus, b.56: clef changes to C_2 before the *D*.

Alleluya I (3v.)
Source: FP27, f. 105r., 'Domenicus'.
Text: incipits in all three voices.
Edition: vol. ii, p.5.
Notes: for further comment, see p.226.
                    Cantus, b.22: MS has *G* instead of *F*.

Alleluya II (4v.)
Source: FP27, ff.105v.-106r., anon.
Concordance: *I-Fn* MS Banco Rari 229, att. to Heinrich Isaac.
Composer: Heinrich Isaac.
Text: incipits in Cantus, Tenor and Bassus only.

| Edition: | vol. ii, p.6. For the version in *I-Fn* MS Banco Rari 229 (differing in several details), see *HAM*, vol. i, no. 88 (p.91), this edition itself being derived from that in *WolfI*, Jg. xiv/1, p.119. |
| Notes: | for further comment, see p.226. |

Altera autem die (4v.)

Source:	FP27, ff. 25v.- 26r., anon.
Text:	given in Cantus only; Matt. 27: 62-66.
Edition:	vol. ii, p.8.
Notes:	for further comment, see p.204.
	Altus, b.33: MS omits *fermata* sign.

Angele Dei (4v.)

Source:	BQ19, ff. [1]v.- [2]r., 'Seb. Festa'.
Edition:	*JeppIS*, ii, p.184.
Notes:	facsimiles in *LowMC*, ii, p.55 and *MGG*, iv, p.102; for analytical comment, see p.112.

Aures ad nostras (3v.)

Source:	FP27, f. 47r., anon.
Text:	none; the title of the hymn is written above the Cantus.
Edition:	vol. ii, p.13.
Notes:	The Cantus and Tenor freely paraphrase the traditional melody as given in *StäbH*, pp.383 and 414; for analytical comment, see p.154.

Ave gratia plena (4v.)

Source:	FP27, ff. 143v.- 144r., anon.
Text:	Marian Antiphon (*LU*, p.1861) with the omission of the second word 'Maria'.
Edition:	vol. ii, p.14.
Notes:	for analytical comment, see p.203.
	Bassus, b.21: MS omits one *F*.

Ave Maria I (4v.)

Source:	FP27, ff. 1v.- 2r., 'Laurentius Bergomotius mut.' [= mutinensis].
Text:	Antiphon (*LU*, p.1861). Full text in Cantus only, with incipit in Bassus; other voices textless.
Edition:	vol. ii, p.16; see also *JeppL*, no. 95.
Notes:	for analytical comment, see p.199.
	Bassus, bb.4-5: *sic* (possibly *F-E-flat* was intended instead of *D-C*); b.32: MS has *semibrevis* instead of *brevis*.

Ave Maria II (4v.)

Source:	FP27, ff. 2v.- 3r., 'Jacobus Foglianus mut.' [= mutinensis].
Text:	Antiphon (*LU*, p.1861). Full text in Cantus only, with incipit in Bassus; other voices textless.
Edition:	vol. ii, p.17; see also *JeppL*, no. 96.
Notes:	for analytical comment, see p.198.
	Tenor, b.1: MS omits time signature.

Ave Maria III (4v.)

Source:	FP27, ff. 3v.- 4r., 'Marcetus' [= Cara].
Text:	Antiphon (*LU*, p.1861), in Cantus only.
Edition:	vol. ii, p.19; see also *JeppL*, no. 48.
Notes:	for analytical comment, see p.196.

Ave Maria IV (4v.)

Source:	FP27, ff. 4v.- 5r., anon., also ff. 102v.- 103r., anon.
Text:	Antiphon (*LU*, p.1861), given in Cantus only on ff. 4v.- 5r. and in Cantus, Tenor and Bassus only on ff. 102v.- 103r.
Edition:	vol. ii, p.21.
Notes:	for analytical comment, see p.197.

The given version is from ff. 4v.- 5r. That on
ff.102v.- 103r. differs in the following details:
Cantus, b.23: *A* and *G* in ligature.
Altus, b.10: *A* and *D* in ligature.
Tenor, b.23: one whole note instead of two halves.
Bassus, b.23: *F* and *C* in ligature.

Ave Maria V (4v.)

Source:	FP27, ff. 5v.- 7r., 'Musipula'.
Text:	incipit of Antiphon (*LU*, p.1861) given in Cantus only.
Edition:	vol. ii, p.22; see also *JeppL*, no. 97.
Notes:	probably an instrumental piece; for analytical comment, see p.226.

Cantus, bb.67-8: MS has *F-E-D-C-G* instead of *C-F-E-D-A*.
Altus, b.6: MS has *A* instead of first *G*; b.32: MS has *minima* instead of *semibrevis* rest; bb.58-9: MS has *B-C-D* instead of *A-B-C*.

Ave Maria VI (4v.)

Sources:	FP27, ff. 7v.- 8r., 'B. T.' [= Tromboncino].
	BQ18, ff. 19v.- 20r., anon.
Text:	Antiphon (*LU*, p.1861); given in all voices, though that in Bassus stops after 'tecum'.
Edition:	vol. ii, p.25: see also *JeppL*, no 40.
Notes:	the BQ18 version is at a pitch a fourth lower than that in FP27; for analytical comment, see p.195 (for further comment, see also p.219).

Cantus, bb.51-3: notated as a *brevis* in MS.
Altus, b.50: clef changes to C_4 before second note;
b.51: MS has a *fermata* sign on this note; b.53: MS has a *longa* instead of a *brevis*.
Tenor, b.29: MS has *A* instead of *G*; bb.52-3: MS repeats this *longa*.

Bassus, b.33: clef changes to F_4.

Ave Maria VII (2v.)

Source:	FP27, f. 19v., anon.
Text:	possibly opening of Antiphon (*LU*, p.1861); incipits only given in both voices.
Edition:	vol. ii, p.28.
Notes:	for further comment, see p.206.
	Both voices, b.11: MS has *semibrevis* instead of *brevis*.

Ave Maria VIII (4v.)

Source:	FP27, ff. 146v.- 147r., anon.
Text:	Antiphon (*LU*, p.1861); full text in Cantus only, with incipits in other three voices.
Edition:	vol. ii, p.29; see also *JeppL*, no. 34.
Notes:	for analytical comment, see p.196.
	Altus, b.59: MS omits *fermata* sign.
	Tenor, b.4: MS has *longa* instead of *brevis*; b.30: MS has *A* instead of *G*.

Ave maris stella (3v.)

Source:	FP27, f. 46v., anon.
Text:	incipit in Cantus only; hymn (*LU*, p.1259).
Edition:	vol. ii, p.31.
Notes:	Cantus paraphrases a form of the traditional melody similar to that used by Willaert (see *WillO*, iii, p.107 and *LU*, p.1259); for analytical comment, see p.155.
	Altus, bb.11-14: MS has only a *brevis* rest between the *D* in b.11 and the *G* in b.14; the passage in brackets is therefore editorial.

Ave regina celorum (4v.)

Source:	BQ18, ff. 21v.- 22r., anon.

Text:	incipit in Cantus only; probably an instrumental piece.
Edition:	vol. ii, p.32.
Notes:	see p.220.
	Tenor, b.47: MS has *B* instead of first *C*.

Ave sanctissima Maria I (4v.)

Source:	FP27, ff. 108v.- 109r., anon.
Text:	unidentified.
Edition:	vol. ii, p.34.
Notes:	for analytical comment, see p.201.
	Altus, b.18: MS has *G* instead of *A*.
	Bassus, b.64: MS has *G* instead of second *F*.

Ave sanctissima Maria II (4v.)

Source:	BQ19, ff. 50v.- 52r., '*Re* - naldo'.
Text:	unidentified.
Edition:	vol. ii, p.37.
Notes:	attribution given as a partial rebus. Also published in *MaldTM*, xii, p.4, with an erroneous attribution to 'Renaldus van Melle'; for analytical comment, see p.60.

Ave stella matutina (4v.)

Source:	FP27, ff. 99v.- 100r., 'Gaspar' [= Gaspar van Weerbeke].
Concordances:	*1502[1]*, ff. 51v.- 52r., 'Gaspar'.
	I-Mcap(d) Librone 1, ff. 116v.- 117r., 'Gaspar'.
Text:	Sequence for the presentation of the Virgin: see *ChevRH*, no. 2135, and *MoneH*, vol. ii, p.321.
Edition:	vol. ii, p.40: see also *AMMM*, xi, p.8.
Notes:	the present edition is based on that in *AMMM*, xi, p.8; for analytical comment, see p.81.

Beata Apolonia (3v.)

Source: BQ19, ff. 202v. - 203r., anon.
Text: unidentified prayer to Saint Apollonia.
Edition: vol. ii, p.43.
Notes: for analytical comment see p.126.

Beati omnes (4v.)
Source: BQ19, ff. 122v.- 124r., 'Ja. fol.' [= Jacopo
                   Fogliano].
Edition: *JepplS*, i, p.70.
Notes: for analytical comment, see p.171.

Benedicamus Domino I (4v.)
Source: FP27, f. 18v., anon.
Text: Office dismissal (*LU*, p.124-6).
Edition: vol. ii, p.46.
Notes: for further comment, see p.207.
                   Tenor, Bassus, b.10: MS omits *fermata* signs.

Benedicamus Domino II (3v.)
Source: FP27, f. 18v., anon.
Text: Office dismissal (*LU*, p.124-6).
Edition: vol. ii, p.46.
Notes: for further comment, see p.207.
                   Bassus, b.10: MS omits *fermata* sign.

Benedicamus Domino III (3v.)
Source: FP27, f. 19r., anon.
Text: Office dismissal (*LU*, p.124-6).
Edition: vol. ii, p.47.
Notes: Uses traditional fifth-tone melody in the Cantus (see
                   LU, p.124); for further comment, see p.207.
                   All voices, b.13: MS has a sign indicating that both
                   halves of the piece are to be repeated; the structure
                   given has been derived from the plainsong.
                   Tenor, b.13: MS omits *fermata* sign.

Benedicamus Domino IV (3v.)

Source:	FP27, f. 19r., anon.
Text:	given fully in Cantus only; Office dismissal (*LU*, p.124- 6).
Edition:	vol. ii, p.47.
Notes:	for further comment, see p.207.

Benedicamus Domino V (4v.)

Source:	FP27, f. 18v., anon.
Text:	Office dismissal (*LU*, p.124-6).
Edition:	vol. ii, p.48.
Notes:	Uses traditional sixth-tone melody in the Tenor (see *LU*, p.125); for further comment, see p.207.
	Tenor, Bassus, b.20: MS omits *fermata* signs.

Benedicta mater matris (4v.)

Source:	BQ19, ff. 86v.- 87r., anon.
Text:	unidentified.
Edition:	vol. ii, p.49.
Notes:	for analytical comment, see p.119.
	Cantus, bb.24-5; bracketed text is editorial.

Bonus et misereator dominus (5v.)

Source:	BQ18, ff. 54v.- 55r., anon.
Text:	incipit in Cantus only; probably an instrumental piece.
Edition:	vol. ii, p.51.
Notes:	based on a regular abstract *cantus firmus*; for further comment, see p.221.

Christi corpus ave (3v.)

Source:	FP27, f. 29r.
Text:	Corpus Christi Sequence (*MoneH*, i, p.281).
Edition:	vol. ii, p.54.

Notes: for further comment, see p.203.

Christi mater ave (4v.)
Source: FP27, ff. 67v.- 68r., anon.
Concordances: *1502¹*, ff. 50v.- 51r., 'Gaspar'.
                       I-Mcap(d) Librone 1, ff. 114v.- 115r., 'Gaspar'.
Composer: Gaspar van Weerbeke.
Edition: vol. ii, p.56; see also *AMMM*, xi, p.1.
Text: unidentified Marian prayer.
Notes: the present edition is based on that in *AMMM* xi,
                       p.1; for analytical comment, see p.80.

Circumdederunt me (4v.)
Source: BQ19, ff. 55v.- 56r., *'Re - mi'*.
Text: Psalm 94, vv. 1-4, with opening of the Introit for
                       Septuagesima Sunday (see *LU*, p.497) used as a
                       refrain at the beginning, middle and end.
Edition: vol. ii, p.58.
Notes: Attribution given as a rebus; for analytical comment,
                       see p.98.
                       Altus, b.39: MS has *F* instead of *G*; bb.60-2:
                       bracketed text is editorial.
                       Tenor, b.29: MS has 'dominus' instead of 'eius'.

Cum autem venissem (3v.)
Source: FP27, f. 28v., anon.
Composer: Johannes de Quadris.
Edition: *AMP*, xiv, p.467 (including extensive notes and a
                       full list of concordances on p.156); see also *DamilL*,
                       p.79, and *CattinPA*, pp.5-6, for editions or partial
                       editions of other versions of the piece.
Notes: for further comment, see p.202.

Da pacem I (4v.)
Source: FP27, ff. 31v.- 32r., anon.

Edition: *GreyL*, app., no. 4 (see also p.73).
Notes: for analytical comment, see p.151.

Da pacem II (4v.)
Source: BQ18, ff. 30v.- 31r., anon.
Text: incipit in Cantus only; probably an instrumental piece.
Edition: vol. ii, p.61.
Notes: based on a free *ostinato* derived from the opening of the 'Da pacem' Antiphon melody as in *AP*, f.138v., or *LU*, p.1867; for analytical comment, see p.222. Tenor: MS omits mensuration sign.

Da pacem III (4v.)
Source: BQ19, ff. 54v.- 55r., anon.
Text: Antiphon (*LU*, p.1867).
Edition: vol. ii, p.64.
Notes: Based on a canonic *cantus firmus* itself derived from the Antiphon melody as in *AP*, f.138v., or *LU*, p.1867; for analytical comment, see p.150.
Cantus, b.29: MS has *E* instead of *F*.
Altus, b.12: MS has *D* instead of *C*; bb.46-8: bracketed text is editorial.
Bassus, b.24: clef changes to C_4.

De profundis (4v.)
Source: BQ19, ff. 119v.- 122r., 'Ja. fol.' [= Jacopo Fogliano].
Edition: *JeppIS*, i, p.77.
Notes: for analytical comment, see p.173.

De ramo in ramo (4v.)
Source: BQ18, ff. 53v.- 54r., anon.
Text: incipit in Cantus only; probably an instrumental piece.

Edition: vol. ii, p.66.
Notes: facsimile in *JeppFR*, ii, p.ix. Based on a
                            proportionally accelerated Tenor *ostinato*,
                            apparently abstract or freely composed; for further
                            comment, see p.221.

Deus fortitudo mea (4v.)
Source: BQ18, ff. 31v.- 32r., anon.
Text: incipit in Cantus only; probably an instrumental
                            piece.
Edition: vol. ii, p.68.
Notes: based on a regular abstract *cantus firmus*. Incipit
                            was a motto of the Este family; for analytical
                            comment, see p.221. Cantus, b.21: MS has a
                            presumably cautionary *diesis* sign above the first *F*;
                            b.41: MS has *D* instead of *E*.

Dies illa I (2v.)
Source: FP27, f.103v., anon.
Text: the three verses of the Requiem Responsory 'Libera
                            me Domine' (*LU*, p.1767).
Edition: vol. ii, p.70.
Notes: for further comment, see p.205.
                            Both voices, bb.26 and 51: MS has single vertical
                            line.

Dies illa II (2v.)
Source: FP27, ff. 210v.- 211r., anon.
Text: the three verses of the Requiem Responsory 'Libera
                            me Domine' (*LU*, p.1767).
Edition: vol. ii, p.72.
Notes: this piece includes the 'Tremens factus sum', 'Dies
                            illa' and 'Requiem aeternam' on ff. 210v.- 211r.,
                            which are listed as three seperate pieces in *BecherC*,
                            for reasons given on p205.. They are actually

written in the order 'Tremens factus sum' - 'Dies
illa' - 'Requiem aeternam' on ff. 210v.- 211r.
Bassus I, bb.3, 7, 11, 27, 29, 31, 36, 45, 50: MS
has final note written as a *semibrevis* with a *fermata*
sign; b.57: MS notates *A* as a dotted *semibrevis*.
Bassus II, bb.3, 29, 31, 36, 45, 50: MS has final
note written as a *semibrevis* with a *fermata* sign.
Both voices, b.64: MS has single vertical line.

Dies ire I (4v.)

Source:	FP27, ff. 23v.- 24r., anon.
Text:	none except for the above incipit in the Cantus; from the Requiem Sequence, v.1 (*LU*, p.1810).
Edition:	vol. ii, p.74.
Notes:	based on the traditional melody (see *LU*, p.1810); for further comment, see p.206.
	Tenor, bb.14-15: MS has descending *C-B-A-G-F* instead of *E- D-C-B-A*.

Dies ire II (2v.)

Source:	FP27, ff. 210v.- 211r., anon.
Text:	Requiem Sequence, v.1 (*LU*, p.1810).
Edition:	vol. ii, p.75.
Notes:	for further comment, see p.205.
	Bassus II: MS omits mensuration sign.

Dies ire III (4v.)

Source:	FP27, ff. 212v.- 213r.
Text:	given in Altus, Tenor and Bassus only; Requiem Sequence, v.1, with the incipits to vv. 7 and 13 also given in the Tenor and Bassus (*LU*, pp.1810-12).
Edition:	vol. ii, p.75.
Notes:	based on the traditional melody as in *LU*, p.1810; for further comment, see p.206.
	Cantus, b.20: MS omits *fermata* sign.

Tenor, b.5: MS has *G* instead of *A*.

Felix namque (4v.)
Source: FP27, ff. 130v.- 132r., anon.
Text: incipits in Cantus and Bassus only; no known
                     continuations fit the music satisfactorily.
Edition: vol. ii, p.76.
Notes: the MS supplies an alternative Bassus part, identical
                     to the original except that the rests are filled in with
                     decorative passage-work, which has been transcribed
                     below the main body of the piece where appropriate.
                     The passage at bb.16-26 is marked 'loco istarum
                     pausarum' and is written in the Bassus clef above the
                     Tenor part on f.130v, while the remainder is written
                     immediately after the Bassus on f.132r. The words
                     'prima pars' and 'secunda pars' are found at the
                     heads of ff.130v. and 131v. respectively
                     (corresponding to bb.1 and 51 in the present edition)
                     despite the lack of any clear discontinuity; for
                     analytical comment see p.122.
                     Tenor, b.62: MS has *F* instead of *E*.

Gaude virgo (4v.)
Source: BQ18, ff. 32v.- 33r., anon.
Composer: Heinrich Isaac.
Text: incipit in Cantus only.
Edition: *BrownFC*, no.129 ('Je ne me puis vivre').
Notes: despite the Latin incipit, the music is actually that of
                     Isaac's four-voiced *rondeau* 'Je ne me puis vivre';
                     for this reason the piece has not been considered in
                     the discussion of the 'motets' from BQ18 in chapter
                     8 (see p.219, note 19).

Gaude virgo, mater Christi (4v.)
Source: FP27, ff. 29v.- 30r., anon.

Text:	Marian Sequence, v.1 (see *DufayO*, v, pp.ix and 1)
Edition:	vol. ii, p.80.
Notes:	for further comment, see p.206.

Hec dies I (5v.)

Source:	BQ19, ff. 5v.- 6r., anon.
Text:	given for *prima pars* only; Easter Gradual (*LU*, p.778; see also *AP*. f.56v.).
Edition:	vol. ii, p.81.
Notes:	edited in *MaldTM*, iii, p.25, where it is attributed to A. Agricola (presumably on account of the clear attribution of his 'Nobis sancte spiritus' on the previous folio of the manuscript). It is also 'corrected', resulting in a different reading which among other things eliminates the Tenor bottom *E* at the opening of the second part (b.29) which renders the original C_3 clef redundant, hence its change to C_2; for further comment, see p.227.
	Cantus, b.37: MS has *C* and *B*, *fusae* and *C*, *minima*, instead of even *semiminimae*.
	Altus I, bb.23-6: MS has *D-E* in ascending ligature *sine proprietate et cum perfectione*.

Hec dies II (4v.)

Source:	BQ19, ff. 25v.- 26r., 'Renaldo'.
Text:	Easter Gradual (*LU*, p.778; see also *AP*, f.56v.).
Edition:	vol. ii, p.83.
Notes:	the opening point of imitation seems to be derived from the Gradual melody (see *AP*, f.56v., or *LU*, p.778), but otherwise the motet is freely composed. Also published in *MaldTM*, xi, p.43, with an erroneous attribution to 'Renaldus van Melle'; for analytical comment, see p.94.

Hec est illa (4v.)

Source:	BQ19, ff. 53v.- 54r., 'Sebastiano Festa'.
Concordance:	*I-ModE* MS L.11.8, anon.
Text:	unidentified Marian Sequence, similar to one set by Carpentras (see *CarpO*, iv, pp.xvi and 26).
Edition:	vol. ii, p.85.
Notes:	for analytical comment, see p.109.
	Tenor, bb.36-8: MS omits 'super omnis', repeating 'gratiosa' instead.

Hodie complecti sunt (4v.)

Source:	BQ19, ff. 113v.- 114r., anon.
Text:	Antiphon for Pentecost (*LU*, p.886; see also *AP* f.122r.).
Edition:	vol. ii, p.87.
Notes:	for analytical comment, see p.101.
	Altus, b.4: natural indicated by *diesis* sign.

Ibo mihi (4v.)

Source:	FP27, ff. 100v.- 101r., anon.
Concordance:	1502[1], ff. 37v.- 38r., 'Gaspar'.
Composer:	Gaspar van Weerbeke.
Text:	Canticum Canticorum 4:7-8, though substantially altered.
Edition:	vol. ii, p.90.
Notes:	for analytical comment, see p.77.
	Bassus, b.48: MS has dotted *semibrevis F* as first note, instead of *semibrevis* plus *minima* rest.

Illuminavit eum (4v.)

Source:	BQ19, ff. 23v.- 25r., 'Renaldo'.
Text:	opening undientified; after 'Oremus' the collect for the feast of St. James (*LU*, p.1570).
Edition:	vol. ii, p.92.
Notes:	for analytical comment, see p.89.

Incipit oratio I (3v.)

Source:	FP27, ff. 82v.- 84r., anon.
Text:	Lamentations 5:1-8, i.e. lesson three for Holy Saturday (*LU*, p.758).
Edition:	vol. ii, p.95.
Notes:	for further comment, see p.204.

MS has no mensuration signs in any voice. Double barlines indicate single strokes in the MS, preceding which the final notes are all *longae*, as are those at bb.20 (except for that in the Cantus, which is notated as a *brevis*), 120 and 137; these have been transcribed variously to suit the modern barring procedure.

Tenor, b.55: MS omits *fermata* sign; b.88: MS has *semibrevis* instead of *brevis*; b.95: MS omits barline.

Bassus, b.42: MS has *semibrevis* instead of *brevis*; b.98: MS has *E* instead of *F*; b.105: MS has *D* instead of *E*; b.149: MS notates *G* as a *semibrevis* instead of a *minima*.

Incipit oratio II (4v.)

Source:	FP27, ff. 147v.- 149r., anon.
Text:	Lamentations 5:1-4, i.e. lesson three for Holy Saturday (*LU*, p.758).
Edition:	vol. ii, p.99.
Notes:	for further comment, see p.205.

Double barlines indicate single strokes in the MS, preceding which the final notes are all *longae*; these have been transcribed variously to suit the modern barring procedure.

Altus, b.29: MS has *F* instead of *G*.

Tenor, b.17: MS omits barline.

Bassus, b.17: MS omits barline; b.48: MS notates *D* as a *minima* instead of a *semibrevis*; b.53: MS notates *A* as a *minima* instead of a *semibrevis*.

In convertendo (4v.)
Source: BQ19, ff. 84v.- 86r., 'Lupus'.
Edition: *SmijT*, ix, p.37.
Notes: for analytical comment, see p.144.

In illo tempore (4v.)
Source: BQ19, ff. 62v.- 63r., 'S. Festa'.
Concordances: *1521⁵*, att. Sebastiano Festa.
                   H-Bn MS OS 23, no. 4, att. Costanzo Festa.
                   no. 109, att. Sebastiano Festa.
Edition: vol. ii, p.102.
Notes: for analytical comment, see p.107.

In nomine Jesu (4v.)
Source: BQ19, ff. 117v.- 119r., 'Lupus'.
Text: a combination of an Introit (*LU*, p.446) and Gradual
                   (*LU*, p.669; see also *AP*, f.9r.).
Edition: vol. ii, p.104.
Notes: for analytical comment, see p.177.
                   The double barline at b.95 is indicated by a double
                   stroke in the Altus, and a single in the Cantus and
                   Tenor; it is not indicated in the Bassus.
                   Cantus, b.127: MS sets the word 'tue' under the *G*
                   as well as to the next phrase.
                   Altus, b.138: clef changes to C_4.
                   Tenor, b.83: clef changes to C_3.
                   Bassus, b.71: clef changes to F_3; b.143: clef
                   changes to F_4.

In te domine sperabo (4v.)
Source: BQ18, ff. 24v.- 25r., anon.
Text: incipit in Cantus only; probably an instrumental
                   piece.

Edition: vol. ii, p.109.
Notes: for further comment, see p.220.

Isachina benedictus (4v.)
Source: FP27, ff. 17v.- 18r., anon.
Composer: Heinrich Isaac.
Edition and notes: see 'Absque verbis' above.

Lauda Syon (3v.)
Source: FP27, f. 20v., anon.
Text: incipits in Cantus and Bassus only; Corpus Christi
                      Sequence (*LU*, p.945).
Edition: vol. ii, p.112.
Notes: for further comment, see p.206.

Lucis creator optime I (3v.)
Source: FP27, ff. 75v.- 76r.
Text: Incipit in Cantus only; Vespers Hymn (*LU*, p.256).
Edition: vol. ii, p.112.
Notes: paraphrases the traditional melody in the Cantus and
                      Tenor as in *LU*, p.256; for analytical comment, see
                      p.153.
                      Tenor, b.29: MS has *A* instead of *B*.
                      Bassus, b.39: Bassus has *C* instead of *D*.

Lucis creator optime II (3v.)
Source: FP27, ff. 132v.- 133r., anon.
Text: Vespers Hymn (*LU*, p.256).
Edition: vol. ii, p.114.
Notes: paraphrases the traditional melody in the Cantus and
                      Tenor as in *LU*, p.256; for analytical comment, see
                      p.154.
                      Bassus, b.9: MS has *A* instead of *G*.

Maria ergo (4v.)

Source: BQ19, ff. 38v.- 41r., 'Symo Ferrar.' [= Symon
                Ferrariensis].
Edition: *JeppIS*, ii, p.141.
Notes: the edition in *JeppIS* contains an error of
                transcription, in that the Tenor and Bassus entries in
                his b.73 should come in under the Cantus and Altus
                at the beginning of b.71. Although this means that
                Jeppesen's version of the motet is two bars longer
                than it should be, his bar numberings have been
                retained for ease of reference. For analytical
                comment, see p.167.

Mater digna dei (4v.)
Source: FP27, ff. 39v.- 40r., anon.
Concordances: 1502^1, ff. 54v.- 55r., 'Gaspar'.
                I-Mcap(d) Librone 1, ff. 115v.- 116r., 'Gaspar'.
                I-Pc MS A17, f. 156r., anon.
                I-VEcap MS 758, ff. 19v.- 20r., anon.
                Cape Town, MS Grey 3.b.12, ff. 107v. - 108r.,
                anon.
Composer: Gaspar van Weerbeke.
Text: Marian Hymn; see *ChevRH*, vol. ii, no. 11335.
                Full text in Cantus only, with incipit in Altus; other
                voices textless.
Edition: vol. ii, p.115; see also *AMMM*, xi, p.4.
Notes: for analytical comment, see p.76.

Memento mei (3v.)
Source: FP27, f. 57r., anon.
Edition: *LuisiL*, p.76.
Notes: for further comment, see p.202.

Miserere (4v.)
Source: FP27, ff. 48v.- 49r., anon.
Edition: *GreyL*, p.xxx.

Notes: for further comment, see p.202.

Miserere...infirmus (6v.)
Source: BQ19, ff. 127v.- 128r., 'Lupus'.
Text: Psalm 6, v.3.
Edition: vol. ii, p.118.
Notes: for analytical comment, see p.115.
                      Cantus I, b.35: MS has only one *semibrevis A*.
                      Altus II, b.33: clef changes to C_4.

Miserere...tribulor (5v.)
Source: BQ19, ff. 130v.- 131r., 'Lupus'.
Text: unidentifed penitential prayer.
Edition: vol. ii, p.122.
Notes: also published in *MaldTM*, xx, p.25; for analytical
                      comment, see p.117.
                      Cantus, b.71: MS omits *fermata* sign.
                      Cantus and Altus II, b.33 (consecutive fifths): *sic*.
                      Tenor, b.68: MS has only three *minimae* (on *A*).

Nigra sum (4v.) Source: BQ19, ff. 186v.- 188r., 'Lupus'.
Concordance: 1539^{10}, att. 'Consilium'.
Text: Canticum Canticorum 1:4, 5, 9, 14-15; 2:1-3, 5.
Edition: vol. ii, p.125.
Notes: for analytical comment, see p.175.

Nisi quia (4v.)
Source: BQ19, ff. 128v.- 130r., 'Symo Ferrar.' [= Symon
                      Ferrariensis].
Edition: *JeppIS*, ii, p.149.
Notes: for analytical comment, see p.163.

Non desina (4v.)
Source: FP27, ff. 139v.- 140r., anon.
Text: incipits in Cantus and Tenor only; probably an

instrumental piece.

Edition: vol. ii, p.130.

Notes: for further comment, see p.225.

Cantus, b.20: MS omits all three notes.

Bassus: MS omits mensuration sign; b.49: MS has *G* instead of *A*; b.56: MS has an extra *C*, *semiminima*, after the *B*.

Nunc dimittis (3v.)

Source: FP27, f. 88r., anon.

Text: Compline Canticle (*LU*, p.271).

Edition: vol. ii, p.132.

Notes: carries the rubric '3ij toni'; the tone is paraphrased in the Cantus (for further comment see p.155).

MS notates all final notes before double barlines as *longae*; the plainsong is omitted and is here supplied from *LU*, p.271.

Nu[n]c scio vere (4v.)

Source: BQ18, ff. 50v.- 51r., anon.

Text: incipit in Cantus only; probably an instrumental piece.

Edition: vol. ii, p.135.

Notes: loosely based on the 'Nunc scio vere' Introit melody (see *GP*, f.130v., or *LU*, p.1518); for further comment, see p.222.

Bassus, b.33: MS has *E* instead of second *F*.

O admirabile comertium (4v.)

Source: FP27, ff. 8v.- 9r., anon.

Text: Antiphon for the feast of the Circumcision (*LU*, p.442). The last 12 bars are left untexted in the source.

Edition: vol. ii, p.137.

Notes: for analytical comment, see p.97.

Tenor, b.49: MS omits *fermata* sign.
Bassus, b.32: MS has *C* instead of *B-flat*.

O Domine Jesu Christe I (4v.)

Source:	FP27, ff. 86v.- 87r., anon.
Text:	one of a series of prayers alleged to grant indulgences; see *BrumelO*, v, p.xxxix.
Edition:	vol. ii, p.139.
Notes:	for analytical comment, see p.201.
	All voices, b.56: MS has single barline.
	Cantus, b.56: clef changes to G_2.
	Tenor, bb.37-9: MS notates first, third and fourth *A*s as dotted *semibreves*.

O Domine Jesu Christe II (4v.)

Source:	BQ19, ff. 45v.- 46r., '*Re* - naldo'.
Text:	one of a series of prayers alleged to grant indulgences; Renaldo's text a possibly incomplete or corrupt variant of that set by Josquin in the second part of his own 'O Domine Jesu Christe' (*JosqM*, II, pp.35-40); see *BrumelO*, v, p.xxxix.
Edition:	vol. ii, p.141.
Notes:	attribution given as a partial rebus. Also published in *MaldTM*, xii, p.3, with an erroneous attribution to 'Renaldus van Melle'; for analytical comment, see p.92.

O gloriosa domina (3v.)

Source:	FP27, f. 52r., anon.
Text:	given fully in Cantus only; Marian hymn (*StàbH*, p.356).
Edition:	vol. ii, p.142.
Notes:	for further comment, see p.206.
	MS writes out the same music twice to accomodate the given text.

O gloriosa regina mundi (3v.)
Source: FP27, ff.53v.- 54r., anon.
Composer: Jo. Touront.
Edition: *RRMMER*, ix/x, p.176.
Notes: for analytical comment, see p.128.

O Jesu Christe (4v.)
Source: BQ19, ff. 36v.- 37r., '*Re* - naldo'.
Text: unidentified penitential prayer.
Edition: vol. ii, p.142.
Notes: attribution given as a partial rebus. Also published
                    in *MaldTM*, i, p.25, with an erroneous attribution to
                    Renaut de Melle; for analytical comment, see p.93.

Omnis laus in fine canitur (4v.)
Source: FP27, ff. 52v.- 53r., anon.
Text: title only, inscribed over the Cantus on f. 52v.;
                    probably an instrumental piece.
Edition: vol. ii, p.144.
Notes: for further comment, see p.225.

O pulcherima mulierum (4v.)
Source: FP27, ff. 59v.- 60r., 'Gaspar' [= Gaspar van
                    Weerbeke].
Concordance: *1502^1*, ff. 40v.- 41r., 'Gaspar'.
Text: full text in Cantus and Tenor only; Canticum
                    Canticorum 2:10, 14; 5:9, 17 (with alterations).
Edition: vol. ii, p.145.
Notes: for analytical comment, see p.78.
                    Altus, bb.20-1: MS has *D-E-F* instead of *E-F-G*;
                    b.24: clef changes to C_3.

O rex gentium (4v.)
Source: BQ19, ff. 201v.- 202r., anon.

Text:	unidentified; drawn from two Antiphons for the Saturday in Ember Week of Advent (see 'O oriens' and 'O rex gentium', *LU*, p.342) and the Advent Reponsory 'Veni ad liberandum' (*LU*, p.238).
Edition:	vol. ii, p.147.
Notes:	for analytical comment, see p.120.

O virgo (3v.)

Source:	BQ18, ff. 92v.- 93r., anon.
Text:	incipits in all three voices; probably an instrumental piece.
Edition:	vol. ii, p.149.
Notes:	for further comment, see p.223.
	Bassus, b.6: MS notates triplets simply as three *fusae*; b.19: MS notates last *D* as a *semibrevis* and the following *B-flat* (in b.20) as a *minima*.

Paradisi portas aperuit (4v.)

Source:	BQ19, ff. 7v.- 8r., 'Renaldo'.
Concordance:	*I-VEcap* MS 760, att. 'Lupus'.
Text:	Antiphon; unidentified, though similar to 'Paradisi portas aperuit' in *LA*, p.129.
Edition:	vol. ii, p.150.
Notes:	for analytical comment, see p.90.
	Altus, b.31: MS has *B-flat* instead of *A*.

Peccantem me quotidie (4v.)

Source:	BQ19, ff. 8v.- 9r., 'Hutinet' [= Barra].
Text:	Requiem Responsory (*LU*, p.1797).
Edition:	vol. ii, p.152.
Notes:	also published in *MaldTM*, xx, p.13; for analytical comment, see p.103.
	Altus, bb.30-2: MS has *E-D-C-A-B-C-D-E* instead of *C-F-E-C- D-E-F-G*.

Per lignum crucis (5v.)

Source:	BQ19, ff. 83v.- 84r., 'Divitis'.
Edition:	*LowMC*, iii, p.188.
Notes:	for analytical comment, see p.148.

Probasti cor meum deus (4v.)

Source:	BQ18, ff. 43v.- 44r., anon.
Text:	incipit in Cantus only; probably an instrumental piece.
Edition:	vol. ii, p.155.
Notes:	based on an irregular but unidentifiable *cantus firmus*; for further comment, see p.222.
	Altus, bb.69-72: MS omits this entire passage, which is thus conjectural.
	Bassus, b.76: MS omits first *C* and *G*, which are thus conjectural.

Quemadmodum desiderat (3v.)

Source:	FP27, f.73r.
Text:	Psalm 41, v.1; see also Gradual for June 4 (*LU* 1478).
Edition:	vol. ii, p.157.
Notes:	For analytical comment, see p.129.
	Cantus, b.12: MS has *E* instead of *D*.

Qui nos fecit (2v.)

Source:	FP27, f. 17r., anon.
Concordances:	see *CorsiPP* for a list of sources.
Text:	in upper voice only: Benedicamus Domino trope for the feast of the Assumption.
Edition:	vol. ii, p.158.
Notes:	for further comment, see p.206.

Qui seminant in lacrimis (4v.)

Source:	FP27, ff. 3v.- 4r., anon.

Text: Tract (*LU*, p.1164).
Edition: vol. ii, p.159.
Notes: for analytical comment, see p.125.
                    Altus, b.11: MS has *B-A* instead of *C-B*.

Regina celi I (3v.)

Source: FP27, ff. 94v.- 95r., 'Ant. perg. Luc.' [= Ant. Peragulfus Lucensis].
Text: incipit in Cantus only; Compline Antiphon (*LU*, p.275).
Edition: vol. ii, p.160.
Notes: based freely on the Antiphon melody as in *AP*, f.62v. (see also *LU*, p.275); for analytical comment, see p.152.
                    Middle voice, b.12: MS has *G* instead of *A*.

Regina celi II (5v.)

Source: BQ19, ff. 30v.- 32r., '*Re* - naldo'.
Text: Compline Antiphon (*LU*, p.275), with the Litany 'Sancta Maria, ora pro nobis' in the Cantus.
Edition: vol. ii, p.163.
Notes: attribution given as a partial rebus. Lower voices parapharase the Antiphon melody (see *AP*, f.62v., or *LU*, p.275), while the upper is based on a variant of the traditional tone (see *LU*, p.836); published in *MaldTM*, xi, p.40, with an erroneous attribution to 'Renaldus van Melle'; for analytical comment, see p.142.

Requiem eternam (4v.)

Source: FP27, ff. 209v.- 210r., anon.
Text: Requiem Introit (*LU*, p. 1807).
Edition: vol. ii, p.167.
Notes: the Introit melody is used as a Tenor *cantus firmus*; for further comment, see p.204.

Cantus and Altus, b.31: MS omits *fermata* sign.
Tenor, b.31: MS leaves the 'Te decet' intonation
until the very end of the part, after 'omnis caro
veniet'; b.43: MS has *F* instead of *G*.
Bassus, bb.43-4: MS has one *C*, *semibrevis*, not
two.

Rex autem David (4v.)
Source: FP27, ff. 149v.- 150r., anon.
Text: given fully in Cantus only; derived from 2 Samuel
                 18:33 and similar to an Antiphon text (*WA*, p.165).
Edition: vol. ii, p.169.
Notes: for further comment, see p.203.
                 Cantus, bb.54-9: notated as a *brevis* with a *fermata*
                 sign; b.60: MS omits *fermata* sign.
                 Tenor, bb.5-6: MS has *A-G-F-G-A-G* instead of *B-
                 A-G-A-B-G*; bb.49-50: MS omits this phrase and
                 rest, which are thus conjectural.
                 Bassus, bb.7, 25 and 42: MS has a *longa* instead of
                 a *brevis*.

Salva nos (4v.)
Source: BQ18, ff. 20v.- 21r., anon.
Text: incipit in Cantus only; probably an instrumental
                 piece.
Edition: vol. ii, p.172.
Notes: based on a version of the Antiphon melody (*LU*,
                 p.271), which is carried in the Bassus; for further
                 comment, see p.222.
                 Altus, final note: MS has *C* instead of *E*.
                 Bassus, b.56: MS has *E*, *brevis*, instead of *G*,
                 followed by the final *E*, *longa*.

Sancta Maria I (4v.)
Source: FP27, f.102v., anon.

Text:	given fully in Bassus only; Litany (*LU*, p. 836).
Edition:	vol. ii, p.174.
Notes:	carries the rubric 'Litenie'; for further comment, see p.207.
	Mensuration sign in Cantus only.

Sancta Maria II (3v.)

Source:	FP27, f.103r., anon.
Text:	Litany (*LU*, p. 836).
Edition:	vol. ii, p.174.
Notes:	for further comment, see p.207.
	MS omits any mensuration sign.
	Bassus, final note: MS repeats low *A* instead of *D*.

Sine fraude (3v.)

Source:	FP27, ff. 142v.- 143r., anon.
Text:	incipits in all three voices; probably an instrumental piece.
Edition:	vol. ii, p.175.
Notes:	for further comment, see p.225.
	Cantus, b.50: MS has *D-C* instead of *E-D*.
	Tenor, b.51: MS notates *B* as a *minima* instead of a *semibrevis*.
	Bassus, opening: MS notates only 6 *breves* and a *semibrevis* rest instead of 7 *breves*; bb.47-9: MS omits the notes from the *A* in b.47 to the *D* in b.49, which are thus conjectural.

Speciosa (4v.)

Source:	BQ18, ff. 83v.- 84r., anon.
Text:	incipits in all four voices; probably an instrumental piece.
Edition:	vol. ii, p.176.
Notes:	for further comment, see p.220.
	Altus, b.41: MS omits these two notes, which are

thus conjectural.

Spes mea (4v.)

Source:	BQ18, ff. 41v.- 42r., anon.
Text:	incipits in all four voices; probably an instrumental piece.
Edition:	vol. ii, p.179.
Notes:	based on a proportionally accelerated *ostinato*; for further comment, see. p.221.
	Bassus, b.31: MS has *G* instead of first *A*.

Stella celi estirpavit (4v.)

Source:	FP27, ff. 69v.- 70r., anon.
Concordance:	*1502¹*, ff. 40v.- 41r., anon.
Text:	in Cantus only; hymn (*DrevesH*, xxxi, p.210, vv. 1-2). Bracketed text in other voices and amendments to that of the Cantus derived from *1502¹*.
Edition:	vol. ii, p.181.
Notes:	based on Tenor *cantus firmus* with Cantus intonation; for further comment see p.147.

Surge (4v.)

Source:	BQ18, ff. 29v.- 30r., anon.
Text:	incipit in Cantus only; probably an instrumental piece.
Edition:	vol. ii, p.183.
Notes:	for further comment, see p.220.
	Tenor, b.53: MS has *A* instead of *B-flat*.

Surge propera (4v.)

Source:	FP27, ff. 58v.- 59r., 'Jo. de Pinarol'.
Concordance:	*1502¹*, ff. 6v.- 7r., 'Jo. de Pinarol'.
Text:	Canticum Canticorum 2:13-14.
Edition:	vol. ii, p.186.
Notes:	for analytical comment, see p.104.

Tenebrae (4v.)
Source: FP27, ff. 107v.- 108r., anon.
Text: Good Friday Responsory (*LU*, p.703).
Edition: vol. ii, p.189.
Notes: for analytical comment, see p.123.
Cantus and Tenor, b.55: MS omits *fermata* sign.
All voices, bb.7-8 and 23-4: *sic*.

Tristis es anima mea (3v.)
Source: BQ18, ff. 66v.- 67r., anon.
Text: incipit in all three voices; probably an instrumental piece.
Edition: vol. ii, p.191.
Notes: apparently originated as a *rondeau*; for analytical comment, see p.223.
Cantus, b.32: MS has *E* instead of *D*.
Bassus, b.38: MS has *C* instead of *B-flat*.

Tristitia (4v.)
Source: FP27, ff. 71v.- 72r., 'Renaldo'.
Text: Easter Responsory (*LR*, p.165).
Edition: vol. ii, p.192.
Notes: for analytical comment, see p.96.
Bassus, bb.33-4: MS omits *G* and *D*, which are thus conjectural.

Utile conscilium (4v.)
Source: FP27, ff. 27v.- 28r., anon.
Text: incipit in all four voices.
Edition: vol. ii, p.195.
Notes: for further comment, see p.202.
Altus, b.5: MS has *A* instead of *G*.

Veni creator spiritus (3v.)

Source:	FP27, ff. 73v.- 74r., anon.
Text:	incipit in Cantus only; Vespers hymn (*LU*, p.885).
Edition:	vol. ii, p.196.
Notes:	Cantus and Tenor paraphrase traditional melody as in *LU*, p.885; for analytical comment, see p.154.

Venimus princeps (4v.)

Source:	BQ18, ff. 23v.- 24r., anon.
Text:	incipit in Cantus only; probably an instrumental piece.
Edition:	vol. ii, p.197.
Notes:	incipit could be ceremonial in origin; for further comment, see p.224.

Verbum caro I (3v.)

Source:	FP27, f. 56r., anon.
Edition:	*LuisiL*, p.201 (see also p.lxxx).
Notes:	almost identical to 'Verbum caro III' (FP27, f. 109v., anon.); their differences are discussed in *LuisiL*, p.lxxx. For analytical comment, see p.201.

Verbum caro II (3v.)

Source:	FP27, f. 104r., anon.
Edition:	*LuisiL*, p.200 (see also p. lxxx).
Notes:	for analytical comment, see p.201.

Verbum caro III (3v.)

Source:	FP27, f. 109v., anon.
Edition:	*LuisiL*, p.201 (see also p.lxxx).
Notes:	see 'Verbum caro I' above.

Verbum caro IV (2v.)

Source:	FP27, f. 110r., anon.
Edition:	*LuisiL*, p.202 (see also p.lxxx).
Notes:	for analytical comment, see p.201.

Verbum caro panem verum (4v.)

Source: FP27, ff. 81v.- 82r., anon.

Text: v.4 of the hymn 'Pange lingua' (*LU*, p.950).

Edition: vol. ii, p.200.

Notes: based on the traditional melody as in *LU*, p.950; for analytical comment, see p.146.
Altus, b.26: clef changes to C_3 after *E*.
Tenor, b.37: MS has *semibrevis* instead of *brevis*; b.40: MS has *D* instead of *C*.
Bassus, b.25: MS omits *F*, which is thus conjectural.

Vidimus enim stellam (4v.)

Source: FP27, ff. 4v.- 5r., anon.

Text: Communion for Epiphany (*LU*, p.462); also used as an Alleluia verse for Epiphany (*LU*, p.460).

Edition: vol. ii, p.202.

Notes: for analytical comment, see p125..

Virgo gloriosa Christi (4v.)

Source: BQ20, no. 8., 'Sebastiano Festa'.

Text: unidentified.

Edition: vol. ii, p.204.

Notes: for analytical comment, see p.114.

Virgo Maria, non est tibi similis (4v.)

Source: FP27, ff. 66v. - 67r., 'Gaspar' [= Gaspar van Weerbeke].

Concordances: *1502[1]*, ff. 21v. - 22r., 'Gaspar'.
CH-SGs MS 530, f. 89v., 'Gaspar'.

Text: Antiphon for the Nativity of the Virgin (*PM*, p.186).

Edition: vol. ii, p.210; see also *AmbrosG*, v, p.183.

Notes: the present edition is based on that in *AmbrosG*, v, p.183; for analytical comment, see p.79.

Vivite felices (4v.)
Source: BQ19, ff. 48v.- 49r., 'Bruhier'.
Edition: *DunnVS*, no. 2.
Notes: for analytical comment, see p.180.

Vulnerasti cor meum (4v.)
Source: BQ19, ff. 87v.- 88r., anon.
Text: free pastiche of Canticum Canticorum verses,
                 drawing on (in order) 4:9-10, 5:1, 6:3, 4:8 and 2:10
                 as well as including certain similar but unidentifiable
                 passages.
Edition: vol. ii, p.212.
Notes: for analytical comment, see p.183.

APPENDIX F: MOTETS CONSIDERED IN CHAPTER 4

Works are listed in the order of their individual discussion in chapter 4, where they are grouped primarily by composer. Certain of the anonymous pieces (and also those whose author is known solely from the one attribution) are discussed alongside those of the given composers on account of shared musical characteristics; the remainder are considered separately, as are the three-voiced works. Spellings of titles and composers' names have been standardized; all pieces are for four voices unless otherwise marked. For full critical notes and details of modern editions, see Appendix E.

Weerbeke

Mater digna Dei	pp. 95 - 97.
Ibo mihi	pp. 97 - 99.
O pulcherrima mulierum	pp. 99 - 100.
Virgo Maria	pp.100 - 101.
Christi mater ave	pp.101 - 103.
Ave stella matutina	pp.103 - 104.
Adonai	pp.104 - 106.

Renaldo

Ave sanctissima II[1]	pp. 79 - 83.
Illuminavit eum	pp.116 - 118.
Paradisi portas	pp.118 - 120.
O Domine Jesu Christe II	pp.120 - 122.

Lupus

Miserere...infirmus	à6		pp.156 - 160.
Miserere...tribulor	à5		pp.160 - 162.
Benedicta mater matris		(Anon.)	pp.162 - 164.
O rex gentium		(Anon.)	pp.164 - 166.

Other anonymous motets

Felix namque	pp.166 - 169.
Tenebrae	pp.169 - 170.
Qui seminant in lachrimis	pp.170 - 171.
Vidimus enim stellam	pp.171 - 172.

Motets for three voices

Beata Apollonia	(Anon.)	pp.172 - 176.
O gloriosa regina	(Jo. Touront)	pp.176 - 177.
Quemadmodum desiderat	(Anon.)	pp.177 - 178.

---

[1]Actually discussed at the end of chapter 3.

APPENDIX G: MOTETS CONSIDERED IN CHAPTER 5

Works are given in the order of their individual discussion in chapter 5, where they are grouped by composer or shared musical characteristics as appropriate. Spellings of titles and composers' names have been standardized; all pieces are for four voices unless otherwise marked. For full critical notes and details of modern editions, see Appendix E.

Imitative paraphrase compositions:

Regina caeli II	à5	Renaldo	pp.182 - 185.
In convertendo		Lupus	pp.185 - 188.
Verbum caro, panem verum		Anon.	pp.188 - 189.

Cantus firmus compositions:

Stella caeli extirpavit		Anon.	pp.190 - 191.
Per lignum crucis	à5	Divitis	pp.192 - 194.
Da pacem III		Anon.	pp.194 - 196.
Da pacem I		Anon.	pp.196 - 198.
Regina caeli I	à3	Ant. Peragulfus Lucensis	pp.198 - 199.

Strophic chant settings:

Lucis creator I	à3	Anon.	p. 200.
Lucis creator II	à3	Anon.	pp.200 - 201.
Veni creator spiritus	à3	Anon.	p. 201.

Aures ad nostras	à3	Anon.	pp.201 - 202.
Ave maris stella	à3	Anon.	p. 202.
Nunc dimittis	à3	Anon.	pp.202 - 203.

APPENDIX H: MOTETS CONSIDERED IN CHAPTER 6

Works are given in the order of their individual discussion in chapter 6, where they are grouped by composer or shared musical characteristics as appropriate. Spellings of titles and composers' names have been standardized; all compositions are for four voices unless otherwise marked. For full critical notes and details of modern editions, see Appendix E.

Nisi quia	Symon Ferrariensis	pp.209 - 214.
Maria ergo	Symon Ferrariensis	pp.214 - 218.
Beati omnes	Jacopo Fogliano	pp.220 - 223.
De profundis	Jacopo Fogliano	pp.223 - 226.
Nigra sum	Lupus	pp.226 - 229.
In nomine Jesu	Lupus	pp.229 - 233.
Vivite felices	Bruhier	pp.234 - 237.
Vulnerasti cor meum	Anon.	pp.237 - 241.

APPENDIX I: MOTETS CONSIDERED IN CHAPTER 7

Works are given in the order of their individual discussion in chapter 7, where in the absence of any common composer attributions they are grouped according to such consistencies of musical style as are discernible. Spellings of titles and composers' names have been standardized; all compositions are for four voices unless otherwise marked. For full critical notes and details of modern editions, see Appendix E.

Ave Maria settings:[1]

Ave Maria VI	Tromboncino	pp.250 - 251.
Ave Maria III	Cara	pp.251 - 252.
Ave Maria VIII	Anon.	pp.252 - 253.
Ave Maria IV	Anon.	p. 253.
Ave Maria II	J. Fogliano	pp.254 - 255.
Ave Maria I	Laurentius Bergomotius mut.	pp.255 - 256.

Other laude:

Ave sanctissima I		Anon.	pp.258 - 259.
O Domine Jesu		Anon.	pp.258 - 259.
Verbum caro I	à3	Anon.	pp.260 - 261.
Verbum caro III	à3	Anon.	pp.260 - 261.
Verbum caro IV	à2	Anon.	pp.260 - 261.
Verbum caro II	à3	Anon.	p. 261.
Cum autem	à3	J. de Quadris	pp.261 - 262.

Memento mei	à3	Anon.	p. 262.
Miserere		Anon.	p. 262.
Utile conscilium		Anon.	pp.262 - 263.
Ave gratia plena		Anon.	p. 263.
Rex autem David		Anon.	p. 263.
Christi corpus	à3	Anon.	p. 264.

Minor ritual works:

Altera autem die		Anon.	p. 265.
Requiem aeternam		Anon.	p. 265.
Incipit oratio I	à3	Anon.	pp.265 - 266.
Incipit oratio II		Anon.	p. 266.
Dies illa I	à2	Anon.	pp.267 - 268.
Dies illa II^2	à2	Anon.	pp.267 - 268.
Dies irae II	à2	Anon.	p. 268.
Dies irae I		Anon.	pp.268 - 269.
Dies irae III		Anon.	pp.268 - 269.
Gaude virgo, mater Christi		Anon.	pp.269 - 270.
Lauda Syon	à3	Anon.	pp.269 - 270.
O gloriosa	à3	Anon.	pp.269 - 270.
Ave Maria VII	à2	Anon.	p. 270.
Qui nos fecit	à2	Anon.	p. 270.
Benedicamus III	à3	Anon.	pp.270 - 271.

Benedicamus V		Anon.	pp.270 - 271.
Benedicamus I		Anon.	pp.270 - 271.
Benedicamus II	à3	Anon.	pp.270 - 271.
Benedicamus IV	à3	Anon.	pp.270 - 271.
Sancta Maria I		Anon.	p. 271.
Sancta Maria II	à3	Anon.	p. 271.

Notes

[1]In addition to and after these works from FP27, three more comparable 'Ave Maria' settings from Petrucci's two prints of 1508 are discussed. Those from the *Libro secondo* are by Tromboncino (*JeppL* no. 47) and Anon. (*JeppL* no. 46), while that from the *Libro primo* is by Innocentus Dammonis (*JeppL*, no. 67).

[2]'Dies illa II' includes the 'Tremens factus sum', 'Dies illa' and 'Requiem aeternam' on ff.210v.-211r., which are listed as three seperate pieces in *BecherC*; see chapter 7 for details of the reasons behind this.

APPENDIX J: WORKS CONSIDERED IN CHAPTER 8

Works are given in the order of their individual discussion in chapter 8, where in the absence of any common composer attributions they are grouped by such shared musical characteristics as are discernible. All compositions are for four voices unless otherwise marked. Because the majority only carry an incipit that is often unconnected with any known text, it is given in full and the original orthography has been retained. For full critical notes and details of modern editions, see Appendix E.

Works from BQ18

Ave Maria VI	(Tromboncino)	pp.278 - 279.
Absque verbis	(Isaac)	p. 279.
Gaude virgo	(Isaac)	p. 279.
Adiuva me deus	Anon.	p. 280.
In te domine sperabo	Anon.	p. 280.
Speciosa	Anon.	pp.280 - 281.
Ave regina celorum	Anon.	pp.280 - 281.
Surge	Anon.	pp.280 - 282.
Spes mea	Anon.	p. 282.
Deus fortitudo mea	Anon.	pp.282 - 283.
De ramo in ramo	Anon.	p. 283.
Bonus et misereator à5 dominus	Anon.	p. 283.
Probasti cor meum deus	Anon.	pp.283 - 284.
Nu[n]c scio vere	Anon.	pp.284 - 285.
Salva nos	Anon.	pp.284 - 285.

Da pacem II		Anon.	pp.284 - 285.
O virgo	à3	Anon.	pp.285 - 286.
Tristis es anima mea	à3	Anon.	pp.285 - 287.
Venimus princeps		Anon.	p. 287.

Works from FP27

Isachina Benedictus		(Isaac)	p. 289.
Omnis laus in fine canitur		Anon.	pp.289 - 290.
Non desina		Anon.	p. 290.
Sine fraude	à3	Anon.	p. 290.
Alleluya I	à3	Domenicus	pp.290 - 291.
Alleluya II		(Isaac)	pp.290 - 291.
Ave Maria V		Musipula	pp.291 - 292.

Works from BQ19

| Hec dies I | à5 | Anon. | pp.292 - 293. |

ABBREVIATIONS

In addition to the codes used in the bibliography for literature published in book form, the following abbreviations are also used to refer to periodical publications and modern printed editions of music issued as parts of series.

AcM	*Acta Musicologica.*
AMMM	Migliavacca, L., et al. (eds.): *Archivium musices metropolitanum* mediolanense, 16 vols. to date (Milan, 1958-).
AnMC	*Analecta Musicologica*, Veröffentlichungen der Musikabteilung des Deutschen historischen Instituts in Rom (Cologne, 1963-).
AnnM	*Annales musicologiques.*
CHM	*Colllectanea historiae musicae* (in series Biblioteca historiae musicae cultores) (Florence, 1953-).
CMM	*Corpus Mensurabilis Musicae.*
DTO	*Denkmäler der Tonkunst in Osterreich.*
JAMS	*Journal of the American Musicological Society.*
EDM	*Das Erbe deutscher Musik.*
IMa	*Instituta et monumenta.*
MD	*Musica Disciplina.*
ML	*Music and Letters.*
MQ	*The Musical Quarterly.*
MSD	*Musicological Studies and Documents*, ed. A. Carapetyan (Rome, 1951-).
NA	*Note d'archivio per la storia musicale.*
PAMS	*Papers of the American Musicological Society.*
PRMA	*Proceedings of the Royal Musical Association.*

Quad.	*Quadrivium.*
RBM	*Revue belge de musicologie.*
RIM	*Rivista italiana di musicologia.*
RISM	Lesure, F. (ed.): *Répertoire Internationale des Sources Musicales. Receuils Imprimés XVIe - XVIIe Siècles* (Munich - Duisberg, 1960).
RN	*Renaissance News.*
RRMMER	*Recent Researches in the Music of the Middle Ages and Early Renaissance* (A-R Editions, Madison, Wisconsin, 1975-).
TVNM	*Tijdschrift van de Vereniging voor Nederlandse musiekgeschiedenis.*
UVNM	*Uitgaven der Vereniging voor Nederlandse musiekgeschiedenis.*

BIBLIOGRAPHY

1. PRIMARY SOURCES, MUSICAL

A. MANUSCRIPTS

Bergamo, Biblioteca Civica, MS 1208 D.

Bologna, Civico Museo Bibliografico Musicale, MS Q18 [BQ18].

Bologna, Civico Museo Bibliografico Musicale, MS Q19, 'Rusconi Codex' [BQ19].

Bologna, Civico Museo Bibliografico Musicale, MS Q20.

Bologna, Civico Museo Bibliografico Musicale, MS Q23.

Bologna, Civico Museo Bibliografico Musicale, MS Q27.

Budapest, Orszagos Széchényi Könyvtar (National Széchényi Library), MS Bartfa 23.

Cape Town, South African Public Library, MS Grey 3.b.12.

Florence, Biblioteca Mazionale Centrale, MS Banco Rari 229 (olim Magliabechi XIX. 59).

Florence, Biblioteca Nazionale Centrale, MS Panciatichi 27 [FP27].

London, Royal College of Music, MS 2037 (olim Sacred Harmonic Society S. H. 1743).

Milan, Archivio del Duomo, Libroni 1-4, 'Gaffurius Codices'.

Milan, Biblioteca Ambrosiana, MS Trotti 519.

Modena, Duomo, Biblioteca e Archivio Capitolare, MS Mus. IV.

Modena, Duomo, Biblioteca e Archivio Capitolare, MS Mus. XI.

Paris, Bibliothèque Nationale, MS Rés. Vm^7 676.

Perugia, Biblioteca Communale Augusta, MS 431 (G.20).

Vatican City, Biblioteca Apostolica Vaticana, MS Cappella Giulia XII 27, 'Medici Codex'.

Vatican City, Biblioteca Apostolica Vaticana, MS Cappella Sistina 18.

Vatican City, Biblioteca Apostolica Vaticana, Chigiana, MS C. VIII. 234, 'Chigi Codex'.

Treviso, Biblioteca Capitolare del Duomo, MS 36.

Verona, Biblioteca Capitolare, MS DCCLX.

Washington, Library of Congress, Music Library MS 171 J6.

B. PRINTS

1501	*Harmonice Musices Odhecaton A* (Venice, O. Petrucci, 1501).
1502[1]	*Motetti A. numero trentatre. A* (Venice, O. Petrucci, 1502).
1502[2]	*Canti B. numero cinquanta B* (Venice, O. Petrucci, 1502).
1503[1]	*Motetti De passione De cruce De sacramento De beata virgine et huius modi* (Venice, O. Petrucci, 1503).
1504[1]	*Motetti C* (Venice, O. Petrucci, 1504).
1504[3]	*Canti C. N⁰ cento cinquanta* (Venice, O. Petrucci, 1504).
1504[4]	*Frottole libro primo* (Venice, O. Petrucci, 1504).
1505[5]	*Strambotti, ode, frottole, sonetti. Et modo de cantar versi latini e capituli. Libro quarto* (Venice, O. Petrucci, 1505).
1506[1]	*Lamentationem Jeremie prophete liber primus* (Venice, O. Petrucci, 1506).

1507⁵   *Intabolatura de lauto libro primo* [Francesco Spinacino] (Venice, O. Petrucci, 1507).

1508¹   *Motetti a cinque libro primo* (Venice, O. Petrucci, 1508).

1508   *Laude libro primo* (Venice, O. Petrucci, 1508) [not cited in *RISM*].

1508³   *Laude libro secondo* (Venice, O. Petrucci, 1508).

1509³   *Tenori e contrabassi intabolati...Libro primo. Francisci Bossinensis Opus* (Venice, O. Petrucci, 1509).

1519²   *Motetti de la corona. Libro tertio* (Venice, O. Petrucci, 1519).

1521⁵   *Motetti libro quarto* (Venice, A. Antico, 1521).

1526⁶   *Canzoni frottole et capitoli...Libro primo. De la croce* (Rome, G. Pasoti and V. Dorico, 1526).

1532⁹   *Secundus liber cum quinque vocibus. Motetti del fiore* (Lyons, J. Moderne, 1532).

1537¹   *Novum et insignum opus musicum, sex, quinque et quatuor vocum,...* (Nuremberg, H. Grapheus (Formschneider), 1537).

1539¹⁰   *Tertius liber cum quatuor vocibus. Motetti del fiore* (Lyons, J. Moderne, 1539).

1563⁶   *Libro primo delle laudi spirituali...Raccolte dal. R. P. Fra serafino Razzi fiorentino* (Venice, F. Rampazetto, 1563).

1563   Giovanni Animuccia: *Il primo libro delle laudi* (Rome, V. Dorico, 1563) [not cited in *RISM*].

1564   Giulio Schiavetto: *Motetti a cinque et a sei voci*
                (Venice, G. Scotto, 1564) [not cited in *RISM*].

2. OTHER PRIMARY SOURCES

A. MANUSCRIPTS

Dressler, Gallus: *Praeceptae musicae poeticae* (1563; modern edition in *EngelD*).

Burchardus, Joannes (Bishop of Civiltà Castellana and Orte): *Diaries, 1483-1506* (see *BurchD*).

B. PRINTS

Aaron, Pietro: *Trattato della natura e cognizione di tutti gli toni di canto figurato* (Venice, 1525). Chapters 1-7 trans. in *StrunkSR*, pp.205-18.

Antiphonale Pataviense (Vienna, 1519). For facsimile edition see *AP*.

Burmeister, Joachim: *Musica Poetica* (Rostock, 1606). The book is an expanded version of the *Musica autoschediastike* (Rostock, 1601). Facsimile edition by M. Ruhnke (*Documenta musicologica*, Reihe 1, no. 10: Kassel and Basel, 1955).

Cortesius, Paulus (Bishop of Urbino): *[De cardinalatu]* (Castro Cortesio, Symeon Nicolai Nardi Senensis alias Rufus Calchographus, 1510).

Graduale Pataviense (Vienna, 1511). For facsimile edition, see *GP*.

Lacepiera [Lemovicensis], Petrus: *Libro del occhio morale et spirituale* (Venice, 1496). Actually a translation of Lacepiera's fourteenth-century Latin work *Liber de oculo morali*, itself printed in Venice in 1496.

Lanfranco, Giovanni Maria: *Scintille di musica* (Brescia, 1533; trans. in *LeeL* below).

Maffeus, Celsus: *De sensibilibus deliciis paradisi* (Verona, Luca Antonius, 1504).

Monaldi, Michele: *Irene, overo Della Bellezza* (Venice, 1599).

Rimbertinus, Bartholomeus: *De deliciis sensibilibus paradisi* (Venice, Lazarus de Soardis, 1498).

Tinctoris, Johannes: *Terminorum Musicae Diffinitorium* (Treviso, Geradus de Lisa, 1495; trans. and ed., with facsimile and Latin text, in *ParrT* below).

Vanneo, Stephano: *Recanetum de Musica aurea a magistro S. Vanneo Recinensi...* (Rome, V. Dorico, 1533). Facsimile edition by S. Clercx (Kassel, 1969).

Zacconi, Lodovico: *Prattica di musica seconda parte...* (Venice, A. Vincenti, 1622).

Zarlino, Gioseffo: *Le Istitutioni harmoniche* (Venice, 1558). Reduced photographic reprint of the 1573 edition issued by Gregg Press (Ridgewood, 1966); see also *ZarlinC* below.

3. SECONDARY SOURCES

AgricO   Lerner, E. R. (ed.): *Alexandri Agricolae Opera Omnia*, CMM 22, i-v (American Institute of Musicology, 1966).

AldA   Aldrich, P.: 'An Approach to the Analysis of Renaissance Music, *MR*, xxx (1969), 1-26.

AllenP   Allen, W.: *Philosophies of Music History* (California, 1939).

AM   *Antiphonale monasticum pro diurnis horis...* (Paris, Tournai, Rome; Desclée No. 818; 1934).

AmbrosG   Ambros, A. W.: *Geschichte der Musik* (Breslau, 1862-8: rev.2/1893 by O.Kade/R1968).

AMMM   Migliavacca, L., *et al.* (eds.): *Archivium musices metropolitanum mediolanense*, 16 vols. to date (Milan, 1958-).

AMP   Feicht, H. (ed.): *Antiquitates musicae in Polonia* (Polish Scientific Publications, Warsaw, 1963-).

AP   Schlager, Karlheinz (ed.): *Antiphonale Pataviense (Vienna, 1519). Facsimile herausgegeben von Karlheinz Schlager*, EDM 88 (Kassel, 1985).

ApelGC   Apel, W.: *Gregorian Chant* (London, 1958).

      N   Apel, W.: *The Notation of Polyphonic Music 900-1600* (Cambridge, Massachusetts, 1953).

AR   *Antiphonale sacrosanctae Romanae ecclesiae...* (Paris, Tournai, Rome; Desclée No. 820; 1949).

AtchW   Atcherson, W.: 'Theory Accomodates Practice: Confinalis Theory in Renaissance Treatises', *JAMS*, xiii (1970), 326-30.

AtlA — Atlas, A. W.: 'Alexander Agricola and Ferrante I of Naples' *JAMS*, xxx (1977), 313.

N — Atlas, A. W.: *Music at the Aragonese Court of Naples* (Cambridge, 1985).

NP — Atlas, A. W.: 'On the Neapolitan Provenance of the Manuscript Perugia, Biblioteca Comunale Augusta, 431 (G 20)', *MD*, xxxi (1977), 45-105.

QD — Atlas, A. W.: 'A Note on Isaac's *Quis dabit capiti meo aquam*', *JAMS*, xxvii (1974), 103-10.

BarbFG — Barblan, G.: 'Franchino Gaffurio musico-umanista', *Musicisti lombardi ed emiliani*, Chigiana, xv (1958), 41.

M — Barblan, G.: 'La vita musicale nella prima metà nel Cinquecento', *Storia di Milano*, ix (Milan, 1961), 853.

S — Barblan, G.: 'Vita musicale alla corte Sforzesca', *Storia di Milano*, ix (Milan, 1961), 787.

BarbirO — Meier, B. (ed.): *Jacobi Barbireau Opera Omnia*, CMM 7, i-ii (American Institute of Musicology, 1954-7).

BasCA — Bas, G.: *Manuale di canto ambrosiano* (Turin, 1929).

BassoR — Basso, A.: 'Repertorio generale dei *Monumenta Musicae*, delle antologie, raccolte e pubblicazioni di musica antica sino a 1970', *RIM*, vi (1971), 3.

BaxPE — Baxandall, M.: *Painting and Experience in Fifteenth-Century Italy* (Oxford, 1972).

BecherA   Becherini, B.: 'Autori minori nel codice
                    fiorentino Magl. xix 176' *RBM*, iv (1950), 19-
                    31.

        C   Becherini, B.: *Catalogo dei manoscritti musicali
                    della Biblioteca Nazionale di Firenze* (Kassel,
                    1959).

        I   Becherini, B.: 'Isacco Argiropulo ed Henricus
                    Isaac', *RBM*, xvii (1963), 11.

        M   Becherini, B.: 'Musica italiana a Firenze nel
                    cinquecento', *RBM*, viii (1954), 109-21.

BeckF   Beck, J.: 'Formalism and Virtuosity: Franco-
                    Burgundian Poetry, Music and Visual Art, 1470-
                    1520, *Critical Enquiry*, x (1984), 644-67.

BenoitJ   Benoit-Castelli, G.: 'L'Ave Maria de Josquin des
                    Prez et la séquence "Ave Maria...virgo serena"',
                    Etudes grégoriennes, i (1954), 187.

BentDF   Bent, M.: 'Diatonic Ficta', *Early Music History*,
                    iv (1984), 1.

        F   Bent, M.: 'Musica Recta and Musica Ficta', *MD*,
                    xxvi, (1972), 73.

BernB   Bernstein, L.: 'The Bibliography of Music in C.
                    Gesner's *Pandectae* (1548)', *AcM*, xlv (1973),
                    119.

        C   Bernstein, L.: *'La Courone et fleur des chansons
                    a troys*: The French Chanson in Italy between
                    Petrucci and Gardane', *JAMS*, xxvi (1973), 1.

BerzB   Berz, E.-L.: 'Bibliographie der Aufsätze zur
                    Musik in aussermusikalischen italianischen
                    Zeitschriften II', *AnMc*, ii (1965), 144 (see also
                    KastB).

BessBU — Besseler, H.: 'MS Bologna Biblioteca Universitaria 2216', *MD*, vi (1952), 39.

N — Besseler, H.: 'Das Neue in der Musik des 15. Jahrhunderts', *AcM*, xxvi (1954), 75.

BlackCP — Blackburn, B.: 'On Compositional Process in the Fifteenth Century', *JAMS*, xl (1987), 210.

LH — Blackburn, B.: 'Johannes Lupi and Lupus Hellinck: a Double Portrait', *MQ*, lix (1973), 547.

T — Blackburn, B.: *Music for Treviso Cathedral in the Late Sixteenth Century: a Reconstruction of the Lost Manuscripts 29 and 30* (London, 1987).

VM — Blackburn, B.: 'A Study of the Musical Veneration of Mary', *MQ*, liii (1967), 53.

BökerV — Böker-Heil, N.: *Die Motetten von Philippe Verdelot* (Frankfurt am Main, 1967).

BollAS — Bollandus, with Henschenius, eds.: *Acta Sanctorum*, 58 vols. (Antwerp, 1643-1867). See British Library 1980 catalogue, 'Bollandus' (xxxvi, 363-4) for further details.

BollinLM — Bollini, A.: 'L'attività liutistica a Milano dal 1450 al 1550: nuovi documenti', *RIM*, xxi (1986), 31.

BondFG — Bondioli, P.: 'Per la biografia di F. Gaffurio da Lodi', *CHM*, i (1953), 19.

BoorO — Boorman, S.: 'The "First" Edition of the Odhecaton A', *JAMS*, xxx (1977), 183-207.

P — Boorman, S. (ed.): *Studies in the Performance of Late Medieval Music* (Cambridge, 1983).

BorrenA

Borren, C. van der: 'Actions et réactions de la polyphonie neerlandaise et de la polyphonie italienne aux environs de 1500', *RBM*, xxi (1967), 36.

C

Borren, C. van der: 'Considerations sur la conjunction de la polyphonie italienne et de la polyphonie du nord pendant la première moitié du quinzième siècle', *RBM*, xxi (1967), 45.

E

Borren, C. van der: *Etudes sur le quinzième siècle musical* (Antwerp, 1941).

T

Borren, C. van der: 'Johannes Tinctoris', *RBM*, xxi (1967), 10.

BorsiP

Borsi, F.: 'Note sulle proporzioni musicali nell'architectura del rinascimento', *Quaderni della RaM*, iv (1968), 85.

BragMU

Bragard, A.-M.: 'Les musiciens ultramontains des chapelles du pape Médicis Léon X (1513-1521)', *Bulletin de l'Institut historique belge de Rome*, fasc. 1 (1980), 187.

BrassO

Mixter, K. E. (ed.): *Johannis Brassart Opera Omnia*, CMM 35, i-ii (American Institute of Musicology, 1965- 71).

BridgMI

Bridgman, N.: 'Un manuscrit italien du debut du seizième siècle à la Bibliothèque Nationale (Département de la musique, Rés. Vm^7 676)', *AnnM*, i (1953), 177 and iv (1956), 259.

MM

Bridgman, N.: 'Un manuscrit milanais (Biblioteca Nazionale cod. AD xiv.49)', *RIM*, i (1966), 237.

BrownIE   Brown, C. M.: *Isabella d'Este and Lorenzo de Pavia*, Travaux d'Humanisme et Renaissance, CLXXXIX (Geneva, 1982).

BrownF   Brown, H. M.: 'A Cook's Tour of Ferrara in 1529', *RIM*, x (1975), 216-41.

FC   Brown, H. M. (ed.): *A Florentine Chansonnier from the Time of Lorenzo the Magnificent. Florence Biblioteca Nazionale Centrale MS Banco Rari 229.* Vol. vii of *Monuments of Renaissance Music* (Chicago, 1983).

MR   Brown, H. M.: *Music in the Renaissance* (New Jersey, 1976).

TI   Brown, H. M.: 'Theories of Imitation in the Renaissance', *JAMS*, xxxv (1982), 1.

BrumelW   Hudson, B. (ed.): *Antoine Brumel: Collected Works*, CMM 5, i-v (American Institute of Musicology, 1969- 72).

BuelR   Buelow, G. J.: 'Music, Rhetoric and the Concept of the Affections: a Selective Bibliography', *Music Library Notes*, xxxi (1973), 250.

BujicR   Bujic, B.: 'A Rondellus from Dalmatia', *Arti Musices*, Special Issue, ii (Zagreb, 1979), 91-102.

BukofC   Bukofzer, M.: 'Changing Aspects of Medieval and Renaissance Music', *MQ* xliv (1958), 1.

BuningO   Buning-Jurgens, J.: 'More about Jacob Obrecht's *Parce Domine*', *TVNM*, xxi/3 (1970), 167.

BurchD — Thuasne, L. (ed.): *Johannis Burchardi...Diarium, sive rerum urbanarum commentarii, 1483-1506. Texte latine publié intégralement pour la première fois....* 3 vols. (Paris, 1883-5).

BurckKR — Burckhardt, J.: *Die Kultur der Renaissance* (Basel, 1860; Eng. trans. in numerous edns., incl. London, 1944; Oxford, 1945; New York, 1958).

CaretFG — Caretta, A. (with Cremascoli, L. and Salamina, L.): *Franchino Gaffurio* (Lodi, 1951).

CarpO — Seay, A. (ed.): *Eliziari Geneti (Carpentras) Opera Omnia*, CMM 58, i-v (American Institute of Musicology, 1972-3).

CarpenRU — Carpenter, N.: *Music in the Medieval and Renaissance Universities* (Oklahoma, 1958).

CartaM — Carta, F.: *Codici corali e libri a stampa miniati della Biblioteca Nazionale di Milano* (Rome 1891).

CasimP — Casimiri, R.: 'Musica e musicisti nella cattedrale di Padova nei secoli xiv, xv e xvi' *NA*, xviii (1941), 1 and xix (1942), 49.

CattinB — Cattin, G.: 'Canti polifonici del repertorio benedettino in uno sconosciuto *Liber quadragesimalis* e in altre fonte italiane dei secoli xv e xvi inc.', *Benedictina*, xix (1972), 445.

CC — Cattin, G.: 'Musiche per le laude di Castellano Castellani', *RIM*, xii (1977), 183.

L	Cattin, G.: 'Contribuiti alla storia della lauda spirituale', *Quad*, ii (1958), 45.
NF	Cattin, G.: 'Nuova fonte italiana della polifonia intorno al 1500 (MS Cape Town, Grey 3.b.12)', *AcM*, xlv (1973), 165.
PA	Cattin, G.: 'Le composizioni musicali del MS. Pavia Aldini 361', *L'ars nova italiana del Trecento II* (Certaldo, 1968), 1.
Q	Cattin, G.: 'Il Presbyter Johannes de Quadris', *Quad*, x (1969), 5 and Tav.i-iv.
TF	Cattin, G.: 'Canti, canzoni a ballo e danze nelle Maccheonee di Teofilo Folengo', *RIM*, x (1975), 180.
CaveCT	Cave, T.: *The Cornucopian Text* (Oxford, 1979).
CesariM	Cesari,G.: *La cappella musicale del Duomo di Milano* (Milan, 1956).
S	Cesari, G.: *Musica e musicisti alla corte Sforzesca* (Milan, 1923).
ChapFC	Chapman, C.: 'Printed Collections of Polyphony Owned by Ferdinand Columbus' *JAMS*, xxi (1968), 34.
ChevRH	Chevalier, U.: *Repertorium Hymnologicum*, 6 vols. (Louvain, 1892-1920).
ChiesaM	Chiesa, R.: 'Machiavelli e la musica', *RIM*, iv (1969), 3.
CiceroDI	Hubbell, H. M. (ed.): *Cicero. De Inventione* (Loeb, London, 1949).

O Orelli, I. C., and Baiter, I. G. (eds.): *M. Tullii Ciceronis opera quae supersunt omnia.* 8 vols. (Turin, 1833-91).

RH Caplan, H. (ed.): *Cicero. Rhetorica ad Herrenium* (Loeb, London, 1954).

CiconO Bent, M., with Hallmark, A. (eds.): *The Works of Johannes Ciconia,* Polyphonic Music of the Fourteenth Century, 24 (Editions de l'Oiseau Lyre, Monaco, 1985).

ClerxAC Clerx-Lejeune, S.: 'Ancora su Johannes Ciconia (1335- 1411', *NRMI,* xi (1977), 573.

C Clerx, S.: *Johannes Ciconia: un musicien liegeois et son temps* (Brussels, 1960).

FJ Clerx-Lejeune, S.: 'Fortuna Josquini: un ritratto di Josquin', *NRMI,* iv (1972), 315.

ColsonQ Colson, F.: 'Knowledge and Use of Quintilian after 1416', in *M. Fabii Quintiliani Institutionis Oratoriae Liber 1* (Cambridge, 1924), lxiv-lxxviii.

CompO Finscher, L. (ed.): *Loyset Compère Opera Omnia,* CMM 15, i-v (American Institute of Musicology, 1958-).

CorsiPP Corsi, C., and Petrobelli, P. (eds.): *Le polifonie primitive in Friuli e in Europa,* Atti del congresso internazionale Cividale del Friuli, 22-24 agosto 1980 (Rome, 1989).

CrawCF Crawford, D.: 'A Review of Costanzo Festa's Biography', *JAMS,* xxviii (1975), 102-11.

CM   Crawford, D.: *Sixteenth-Century Choirbooks in the Archivio Capitolare at Casale Monferrato*, Renaissance Manuscript Studies 2 (American Institute of Musicology, 1975).

M   Crawford, D.: Review of *NoblitMM, Current Musicology*, x (1975), 102.

CrockD   Crocker, R.: 'Discant, Counterpoint, Harmony', *JAMS*, xv (1962), 1.

CrollGW   Croll, G.: 'The Life and Works of Gaspar van Weerbeke', *MD*, vi (1952), 67-81.

T   Croll, G.: 'Zu Tromboncinos *Lamentationes Jeremiae*', *CHM*, ii (1957), 111.

CrossCP   Cross, R.: 'The Chansons of Matthaeus Pipelare', *MQ*, lv (1969), 500.

LP   Cross, R.: 'The Life and Works of Mattheus Pipelare', *MD*, xvii (1963), 97.

CummF   Cummings, A.: 'A Florentine Sacred Repertory from the Medici Restoration', *AcM*, lv (1983), 267.

M   Cummings, A.: 'Towards an Interpretation of the Sixteenth-century Motet', *JAMS*, xxxiv (1981), 43.

CurtMN   Curtis, A. (ed.): *Exempla Musica Neerlandica* (Amsterdam, 1964).

CuylCC   Cuyler, L.: 'The Sequences of Isaac's *Choralis Constantinus*', *JAMS*, iii (1950), 3.

D'AccBP   D'Accone, F.: 'Bernardo Pisano: an Introduction to his Life and Works', *MD*, xvii (1963), 115.

CB   D'Accone, F.: 'Alessandro Coppini and
        Bartolomeo degli Organi: Two Florentine
        Composers of the Renaissance', *AnMc*, iv
        (1967), 38.

F   D'Accone, F.: 'The Musical Chapels at the
        Florentine Cathedral and Baptistry in the First
        Half of the Sixteenth Century', *JAMS*, xxiv
        (1971), 1.

FR   D'Accone, F. (ed.): *Music of the Florentine
        Renaissance*, CMM 32, i-xi (American Institute
        of Musicology, 1967-).

I   D'Accone, F.: 'Heinrich Isaac in Florence: New
        and Unpublished Documents', *MQ*, xlix (1963),
        464.

J   D'Accone, F.: 'The Performance of Sacred Music
        in Italy in Josquin's Time, 1475-1525', *Josquin
        des Prez: New York 1971*, 601.

L   D'Accone, F.: 'Alcune note sulle compagnie
        fiorentine dei laudesi nel '500', *RIM*, x (1975),
        86.

N   D'Accone, F.: 'Some Neglected Composers in
        the Florentine Chapels, 1475-1525', *Viator*, i
        (1970), 263.

SG   D'Accone, F.: 'The Singers of San Giovanni in
        Florence in the Late Fifteenth Century', *JAMS*,
        xiv (1961), 307.

T   D'Accone, F.: 'Transitional Forms and Text
        Settings in an Early Sixteenth-century Florentine
        Manuscript', in *Words and Music: the Scholar's
        View* (Cambridge, Mass., 1972).

D'AlGL   D'Alessi, G.: *Il tipopgrafico fiammingo Gerado di Lisa cantore e maestro di cappella nella Cattedrale di Treviso* (Vedelago, 1925).

M   D'Alessi, G.: 'I manoscritti musicali del secolo seidicesimo del Duomo di Treviso', *AcM*, iii (1931), 148.

T   D'Alessi, G.: *La cappella musicale del Duomo di Treviso*, (Vedelago, 1954).

DamilL   Damiliano, P.: 'Fonti musicali della lauda polifonica intorno alla metà del secolo XV', *CHM*, iii (1963), 59.

DanT   Daniel, H.: *Thesaurus Hymnologicus*, 5 vols. (Halle and Leipzig, 1841-56).

DartIM   Dart, T. (ed.): *Music of the Later Fifteenth Century*, Invitation to Medieval Music 2 (London, 1969).

DavisR   Davison, N.: 'The Motets of Pierre de la Rue', *MQ*, xlviii (1962), 19.

DeanC   Dean, J. J.: 'The Occasion of Compère's *Sola Caret Monstris*: A Case Study in Historical Interpretation', *MD*, xl (1986), 99-133.

DegradD   Degrada, F.: 'Dante e la musica del '500', *Chigiana*, xxii (1965), 257.

DiserFB   Disertori, B. (ed.): *Le frottole per canto e liuto intabulate da Franciscus Bossinensis* (Istituzioni e monumenti dell'arte musicale italiana vol.3, nuova serie: Milan, 1964).

DrevesH   Dreves, G. (ed): *Analecta Hymnica Medii Aevi*, 55 vols. (Leipzig, 1886-1922).

DufayO   Van, G. der, and Besseler, H. (eds.): *Guillaume Dufay: Opera Omnia*, CMM 1, i-vi (Americam Institute of Musicology, 1948-66).

DunnS   Dunning, A.: *Die Staatsmotette 1480-1555* (Utrecht, 1970).

VS   Dunning, A. (ed.): *Vier Staatsmotetten des 16. Jahrhunderts...zu vier bis acht Stimmen*, Das Chorwerk 120 (Wolfenbüttel, 1977).

EdwardS   Edwards, W.: 'Songs Without Words by Josquin and his Contemporaries', *Music in Medieval and Early Modern Europe*, ed. I. Fenlon (Cambridge, 1981), 79-92.

EinsF   Einstein, A.: 'Eine unbekannte Ausgabe eines Frottolen-Druckes', *AcM*, viii (1936), 154.

M   Einstein, A.: *The Italian Madrigal* (Princeton, 1949).

EldersG   Elders, W.: 'Josquin's *Gaudeamus* Mass', *Studi Musicali*, xiv (1985), 221.

PJ   Elders, W.: 'Plainchant in the Motets, Hymns and Magnificat of Josquin des Prez', *Josquin des Prez: New York 1971*, 523.

S   Elders, W.: 'Das Symbol in der Musik von Josquin des Prez', *AcM*, xli (1969), 164.

Z   Elders, W.: 'Zusammenhänge zwischen den Motetten *Ave nobilissima creatura* und *Huc me sydereo* von Josquin des Prez', *TVNM*, xxii/1 (1971), 67.

EngelD   Engelke, B.: 'Einige Bemerkungen zu Dresslers "Praecepta musicae poeticae"', *Geschichtsblätter für Stadt und Land Magdeburg*, xlix-l (1914-15), 395.

FabbriV   Fabbri, P.: 'Vita musicale nel Cinquecento ravennate: qualche integrazioni', *RIM*, xiii (1978), 30.

FalckCT   Falck, R.: 'Theory Accomodates Practice: Confinalis Theory in Renaissance Music Treatises', *JAMS*, xxiii (1970), 326.

FallowC   Fallows, D.: 'Ciconia padre e figlio', *RIM*, xi (1976), 171.

D   Fallows, D.: *Dufay* (London, 1982).

PE   Fallows, D.: 'The Performing ensembles in Josquin's Sacred Music', *TVNM*, xxxv (1985), 32.

S   Fallows, D.: 'Specific Information on the Ensembles for Composed Polyphony, 1400-74', *Studies in the Performance of Late Medieval Music*, ed. S. Boorman (Cambridge, 1983), 109.

FenlonM   Fenlon, I.: *Music and Patronage in Sixteenth-Century Mantua*, 2 vols. (Cambridge, 1980-2).

FestaO   Main, A., and Seay, A. (eds.): *Costanzo Festa Opera Omnia*, CMM 25 (American Institute of Musicology, 1962-).

FiedHF   Fiedler, E.: 'Heinrich Finck, Gaspar van Weerbeke und die Göttin Venus', *Renaissance-Studien: Helmuth Osthoff zum 80. Geburstag*, ed. L. Finscher (Tutzing, 1979), 29.

FinschCF	Finscher, L.: 'Zur Cantus-Firmus-Behandlung in der Psalm-Motette der Josquinzeit', *Hans Albrecht in memoriam* (Kassel, 1962), 53.
HR	Finscher, L.: 'Historical Reconstruction vs. Structural Interpretation in the Performance of Josquin's Motets', *Josquin Des Prez: New York, 1971*, 627.
LC	Finscher, L.: *Loyset Compère (c. 1450-1518): Life and Works*, MSD, xii (1964).
N	Finscher, L.: 'Die nationalen Komponenten in der Musik der ersten Hälfte des 16. Jahrhunderts', *IMSCR*, ix (Salzburg, 1964), i, 37.
FischO	Fischer, K. von: 'Organal and Chordal Style in Renaissance Sacred Music: New and Little-Known Sources', *Aspects of Medieval and Renaissance Music: a Birthday Offering to Gustave Reese* (New York, 1966), 173.
FlorenM	Florentiis, G. de: 'Storia della cappella musicale dalle origini al 1714', *Sei secoli di musica nel Duomo di Milano* (Milan, 1986), 41.
FratiB	Frati, L.: 'Per la storia della musica in Bologna dal secolo XV a XVI', *RMI*, xxiv (1917), 449.
FrereAS	Frere, W. H.: *Antiphonale Sarisburiense*, 3 vols. (London, 1901-25/R1967).
FullerB	Fuller, S.: 'Additional Notes on the 15th-Century Chansonnier Bologna Q16', *MD*, xxiii (1969), 81.

GallCI   Gallico, C.: 'Per la compilazione di un inventario di poesia e musica italiana del primo rinascimento', *RIM*, i (1966), 88.

OP   Gallico, C.: 'Dal laboratorio di Ottavanio Petrucci: immagine, trasmissione e cultura della musica', *RIM*, xvii (1982), 187.

UR   Gallico, C.: *L'età dell'umanismo e del rinascimento* (Turin, 1978).

GalloCP   Gallo, A.: 'Cantus planus binatim. Polifonia primitiva in fonti tardive', *Quadrivium*, vii (1966), 79-89.

GamerB   Gamer, C.: 'Busnois, Brahms and the Syntax of Temporal Proportions', *A Festschrift for Albert Seay: Essays by his Friends and Colleagues*, ed. M. Grace (Colorado Springs, 1982), 201-15.

GasparC   Gaspari, G.: *Catalogo della biblioteca musicale G. B. Martini a Bologna*, 5 vols. (Bologna, 1890-1905/R 1961).

GeerL   Geering, A., with Trümpy, H., (eds.): *Das Liederbuch des Johannes Heer von Glarus*, Schweizerische Musikdenkmäler, vol. 5 (Basel, 1967).

GerberM   Gerber, R. (ed.): *Der Mensuralkodex des Nikolaus Apel*, 2 vols. Das Erbe deutscher Musik, 32-3 (Kassel, 1956-60).

GhisiCC   Ghisi, F.: *I canti carnascialeschi nelle fonti musicali del XV e XVI secolo* (Florence, 1937).

SL   Ghisi, F.: 'Strambotti e laude nel travestimento spirituale della poesia musicale del Cinquecento', *CHM*, i (1953), 45.

GP   Väterlein, C. (ed.): *Graduale Pataviense (1511)*.
                Facsimile herausgegeben von C. Väterlein, EDM
                87 (Kassel, 1981).

GR   *Graduale sacrosanctae Romanae ecclesiae...*
                (Paris, Tournai, Rome; Desclée No. 696; 1952).

GraftH   Grafton, A., with Jardine, L.: *From Humanism
                to the Humanities: Education and the Liberal Arts
                in Fifteenth- and Sixteenth-Century Europe*
                (London, 1987).

GreyL   Cattin, G. (ed.): *Italian 'Laude' and Latin Unica
                in MS Cape Town Grey 3. b. 12*, CMM 76
                (American Institute of Musicology, 1977).

Grove   Sadie, S. (ed.): *The New Grove Dictionary of
                Music and Musicians*, 20 vols. (London, 1980).

GuerB   Guerrini, P.: 'Gli organi e gli organisti delle
                cattedrali di Brescia', *NA*, xvi (1939), 205.

         O   Guerrini, P.: 'L'organaro bresciano G. B.
                Fachetti e l'organo di Merlin Cocaio', *NA*, xix
                (1942), 136.

HaarG   Haar, J.: 'On Musical Games of the Sixteenth
                Century', *JAMS*, xv (1962), 22.

         IP   Haar, J.: *Essays on Italian Poetry and Music in
                the Renaissance, 1350-1600* (Berkeley, 1986).

         MC   Haar, J.: 'A Sixteenth-Century Attempt at Music
                Criticism', *JAMS*, xxxvi (1983), 191.

         MH   Haar, J.: 'Music History and Cultural History',
                Journal of Musicology, i (1982), 5.

         P   Haar, J.: 'A Study of Literary and Musical
                Parody', *MD*, xx (1966), 95.

HaberlSC   Haberl, F. X.: *Die Römische 'Schola Cantorum'*
                  und die päpstlichen Kapellsänger bis zur Mitte
                  des 16. Jahrhunderts, Bausteine für
                  Musikgeschichte, iii (Leipzig, 1888).

HalpMM   Halpern Ward, L.: 'The *Motetti Missales*
                  Repertory Reconsidered', *JAMS*, xxxix (1986),
                  491-523.

HAM   Davison, A. T. and Apel, W. (eds.): *Historical*
                  Anthology of Music (rev. ed., Cambridge, Mass.,
                  1949).

HammCC   Hamm, C. and Kellman, H. (eds.): *Census*
                  Catalogue of Manuscript Sources of Polyphonic
                  Music, 1400-1530, Compiled by the University of
                  Illinois Musicological Archives for Renaissance
                  Manuscript Studies, 5 vols. Renaissance
                  Manuscript Studies, 1 (Neuhausen - Stuttgart,
                  1979-88).

HarasI   Haraszti, E.: 'La technique des improvisateurs de
                  langue vulgaire et de latin au quattrocento', *RBM*,
                  ix (1955), 12-29.

HarranCS   Harran, D.: 'New Evidence for Musica Ficta: the
                  Cautionary Sign', *JAMS*, xxix (1976), 77.

M   Harran, D.: 'More Evidence for Cautionary
                  Signs', *JAMS*, xxxi (1978), 490.

U   Harran, D.: 'New Light on Text Underlay Prior
                  to Zarlino', *AcM*, xlv (1973), 24-56.

HewB   Hewitt, H. (ed.): *Ottaviano Petrucci: Canti B*,
                  vol. ii of *Monuments of Renaissance Music*
                  (Chicago and London, 1967).

O   Hewitt, H. (with I. Pope, eds.): *Harmonice*
             Musices Odhecaton A (Cambridge, Mass., 1942).

HirschB   Hirsch, H.: 'Biblographie der Aufsätze zur Musik
             in aussermusikalischen italienischen Zeitschriften
             III', *AnMc*, iii (1966), 122 (see also *KastB*).

HoraceC   Bennet, C. (ed.): *Horace. Carmina* (Loeb,
             London, 1978).

HudsonB   Hudson, B.: 'Antoine Brumel's *Nativitas unde*
             gaudia', *MQ*, lix (1973), 519.

IGC   Bryden, J. R., and Hughes, D. G. (eds.): *An*
             Index of Gregorian Chant (Harvard Univ. Pr.,
             Cambridge, Mass., 1969).

JeffCV   Jeffery, B.: *Chanson Verse of the Early*
             Renaissance (London, 1981).

JeppBR   Jeppesen, K.: 'The MS Florence BNC Banco Rari
             230: an Attempt at Diplomatic Reconstruction',
             Aspects of Medieval and Renaissance Music: a
             Birthday Offering to Gustave Reese (New York,
             1966, 2/1978), 440.

FR   Jeppesen, K.: *La Frottola*, 3 vols. (Copenhagen,
             1968- 70).

G   Jeppesen, K.: 'Die 3 Gafurius-Kodizes der
             Fabbrica del Duomo, Milano', *AcM*, iii (1931),
             14.

GA   Jeppesen, K.: 'A Forgotten Master of the Early
             Sixteenth Century: Gaspar de Albertis', *MQ*, xliv
             (1958), 311.

IS   Jeppesen, K. (ed.): *Italia Sacra Musica*, 3 vols.
             (Copenhagen, 1962).

K   Jeppesen, K.: 'Eine musiktheoretische Korrespondenz des früheren 16. Jahrhundert', *AcM*, xiii (1941), 3.

L   Jeppesen, K.: *Die mehrstimmige italienische Lauda um 1500* (Leipzig, 1935/R 1971).

JosephP   Josephson, N. S. (ed.): *Early Sixteenth-Century Sacred Music from the Papal Chapel*, CMM 95, i-ii (American Institute of Musicology, 1982).

JosqM   Smijers, A., *et al.* (eds.): *Werken van Josquin Desprez: Motetten Bundel I-XXV* (Amsterdam, 1922-64).

JuddAM   Judd, C. Collins: 'Some Problems of Pre-Baroque Analysis: an Examination of Josquin's *Ave Maria...virgo serena*', *Music Analysis*, iv (1985), 201.

JustI   Just, M.: 'Heinrich Isaacs Motetten in italienischen Quellen', *AnMc*, i (1963), 1.

KämperS   Kämper, D.: *Studien zur instrumentalen Ensemblemusik des 16. Jahrhunderts in Italien*, Analecta Musicologica, 10 (Cologne, 1970).

KanazV   Kanazawa, M.: 'Two Vesper Repertories from Verona, *ca.* 1500', *RIM*, x (1975), 155.

KastB   Kast, P.: 'Bibliographie der Aufsatze zur Musik in aussermusikalischen italienischen Zeitschriften I', *AnMc* i (1963), 90 (see also *BerzB*, *HirschB* and *WitzB*).

KellC   Kellman, H.: 'The Origins of the Chigi Codex: The Date, Provenance and Original Ownership of Rome, Biblioteca Vaticana, Chigiana, C.VIII. 234', *JAMS*, xi (1958), 6.

KennCR   Kennedy, G.: *Classical Rhetoric and its Christian and Secular Traditions* (Univ. of N. Carolina Press, 1980).

KirkCT   Kirkendale, W.: 'Circulatio Tradition, *Maria Lactans*, and Josquin as a Musical Orator', *AcM*, lvi (1984), 69.

R   Kirkendale, W.: 'Ciceronians versus Aristotelians on the Ricercar as Exordium, from Bembo to Bach', *JAMS*, xxxii (1979), 1.

KirschTA   Kirsch, W.: 'Zur Funktion der tripeltaktigen Abschnitte in den Motetten des Josquin-Zeitalters', *Renaissance-Studien: Helmuth Osthoff zum 80. Geburtstag*, ed. L. Finscher (Tutzing, 1979), 145.

KrisML   Kristeller, P. O,: 'Music and Learning in the Early Renaissance', *MD*, i (1947), 255.

R   Kristeller, P. O.: *Renaissance Thought and its Sources*, ed. M. Mooney (New York, 1979).

RT   Kristeller, P. O.: *Papers on Humanism and the Arts*. (Vol. 2 of *Renaissance Thought*; New York, 1965).

LA   *Antiphonaire monastique; XIIe siècle: Codex 601 de la Bibliothèque Capitulaire de Lucques*, Paléographie musicale, IX (Tournai, 1906).

LeeL   Lee, B.: *Giovanni Maria Lanfranco's 'Scintille di musica' and its Relation to 16th-Century Music Theory* (diss., Cornell U., 1961).

LeechM   Leech-Wilkinson, D.: 'Machaut's *Rose, Lis* and the Problem of Early Music Analysis', *Music Analysis*, iii (1984), 9-28.

LenC   Lenaerts, R.: 'Contribution à l'histoire de la musique belge de la Renaissance', *RBM*, ix (1955), 103.

LernerMI   Lerner, E.: 'Some Motet Interpolations in the Catholic Mass', *JAMS*, xiv (1961), 24.

PM   Lerner, E.: 'Polyphonic Magnificats in 15th-Century Italy', *MQ*, l (1964), 44.

LippM   Lippman, E.: 'The Place of Music in the System of Liberal Arts', *Aspects of Medieval and Renaissance Music: A Birthday Offeering to Gustave Reese*, ed. J. LaRue and others (New York, 1966, 2/1978), 545.

LittI   Litterick L.: 'On Instrumental Ensemble Music in the Late Fifteenth Century', *Music in Medieval and Early Modern Europe*, ed. I. Fenlon (Cambridge, 1981), 117- 30.

P   Litterick, L.: 'Performing Franco-Netherlandish Secular Music of the Late Fifteenth Century', *Early Music*, viii (1980), 474-85.

LiuzziL   Liuzzi, F.: *La lauda e i primordi della melodia italiana* (Rome, 1934).

LockF   Lockwood, L.: *Music in Renaissance Ferrara 1400-1505* (Oxford, 1984).

IT   Lockwood, L.: 'Pietrobono and the Instrumental Tradition in Ferrara in the Fifteenth Century', *RIM*, x (1975), 115-33.

MM   Lockwood, L.: 'Jean Mouton and Jean Michel: New Evidence on French Music and Musicians in Italy, 1505-20', *JAMS*, xxxii (1979), 191.

P   Lockwood, L.: 'On "Parody" as a Term and
Concept in 16th-Century Music', *Aspects of
Medieval and Renaissance Music: A Birthday
Offering to Gustave Reese*, ed. J. LaRue and
others (New York, 1966, 2/1978), 560.

LowAS   Lowinsky, E. E.: 'Ascanio Sforza's Life: A Key
to Josquin's Biography and an Aid to the
Chronology of his Works', *Josquin des Prez:
New York 1971*, 31.

C   Lowinsky, E. E.: 'Canon Technique and
Simultaneous Conception in Fifteenth-Century
Music: A Comparison of North and South',
*Essays on the Music of J. S. Bach and Other
Divers Subjects: A Tribute to Gerhard Herz*, ed.
R. Weaver (Louisville, 1981), 181.

CR   Lowinsky, E. E.: 'Music in the Culture of the
Renaissance', *Journal of the History of Ideas*, xv
(1954), 509: repr. in *Renaissance Essays*, ed. P.
O. Kristeller and P. Weiner (New York, 1968),
iii and v.

J   Lowinsky, E. E. (ed.): *Josquin des Prez* (New
York, 1971).

HM   Lowinsky, E. E.: 'Humanism in the Music of the
Renaissance' *Medieval and Renaissance Studies*,
ix, ed. F. Tiro (Durham, N. C., 1982), 87-220.

MC   Lowinsky, E. E.: *The Medici Codex of 1518: A
Choirbook of Motets Dedicated to Lorenzo De'
Medici Duke of Urbino*. Vols. iii-v of
Monuments of Renaissance Music (Chicago,
1968), cited by these volume numbers.

MH   Lowinsky, E. E.: 'Music History and its Relationship to the History of Ideas', *Music Journal*, 1946, Nov.- Dec.

MR   Lowinsky, E. E.: 'Music of the Renaissance as Viewed by Renaissance Musicians', *The Renaissance Image of Man and the World*, ed. B. O'Kelly (Columbus, Ohio, 1966), 129.

LR   *Liber reponsorialis pro festis I. classis...* (Solesmes, 1895).

LU   *The Liber Usualis with Introduction and Rubrics in English* (Tournai, New York; Desclée No. 801; 1963).

LuisiL   Luisi, F.: *Laudario giustinianeo*, 2 vols (Venice, 1983). All citations refer to vol. ii.

MV   Luisi, F.: *La musica vocale nel Rinascimento* (Turin, 1977).

MacClM   MacClintock, C.: 'Molinet, Music, and Medieval Rhetoric', *MD*, xiii (1959), 109.

MacQuN   MacQueen, J.: *Numerology. Theory and Outline of a Literary Mode* (Edinburgh, 1985).

McGeeAB   McGee, T.: '"*Alla Battaglia*": Music and Ceremony in Fifteenth-Century Florence', *JAMS*, xxxvi (1983), 288.

MacePB   Mace, D.: 'Pietro Bembo and the Literary Origins of the Italian Madrigal', *MQ*, lv (1969), 65.

MaceyS   Macey, P.: 'Savoranola and the Sixteenth-Century Motet', *JAMS*, xxxvi (1983), 422.

MaldTM   Maldeghem, R. van (ed.): *Trésor Musical:*
                 Collection Authentique de Musique Sacrée et
                 Profane des Anciens Maîtres Belges. Musique
                 religieuse. 29 vols. (Brussels, 1865-93/R1965).

ManMC   Maniates, M.: 'Mannerist Composition in
                 Franco- Flemish Polyphony, 1450-1530', *MQ*,
                 lii (1966), 17.

MM   Maniates, M.: 'Musical Mannerism: Effeteness
                 or Virility?', *MQ*, lvii (1971), 270.

MarCS   Marbach, C.: *Carmina Scriptuarum* (Hildesheim,
                 1963: a reprint of the 1907 edn.).

MarixB   Marix, J.: *Les musiciens de la cour de Bourgogne*
                 au XVe siècle (1420-1467) (Paris, 1937).

MassenL   Massenkeil, G. (ed.): *Mehrstimmige*
                 Lamentationen aus der ersten Hälfte des 16.
                 Jahrhunderts. Musikalische Denkmäler der
                 Akademie der Wissenschaften und der Literatur
                 in Mainz, 6 (Mainz, 1965).

MattR   Mattfeld, J.: 'Some Relationships between Texts
                 and Cantus Firmi in the Liturgical Motets of
                 Josquin des Pres', *JAMS*, xiv (1961), 159.

MenghS   Menghini, M. (ed.): *Le rima de Serafino de'*
                 Cimelli dall'Aquila (Bologna, 1894).

MeyerL   Meyer-Baer, K.: *Liturgical Music Incunabula*
                 (London, 1962).

MGG   Blume, F. (ed.): *Die Musik in Geschichte und*
                 Gegenwart, 17 vols. (Kassel, 1949-51).

MillerE   Miller, C.: 'Erasmus on Music', *MQ*, lii (1966),
                 332.

G   Miller, C.: 'Gaffurius' *Practica Musicae*: Origin
           and Contents', *MD*, xxii (1968), 105.

H   Miller, C. (trans. and ed.): *Franchinus Gaffurius
           De Harmonia Musicorum Instrumentorum Opus*,
           MSD, xxxiii (American Institute of Musicology,
           1977).

PM   Miller, C. (trans. and ed.): *Franchinus Gaffurius
           Practica Musicae*, MSD, xx (American Institute
           of Musicology, 1968).

MiyazO   Miyazaki, H.: 'New Light on Ockeghem's *Missa
           "Mi-Mi"'*, *Early Music*, xiii (1985), 367-75.

MoneH   Mone, F.: *Hymni latini medii aevi*, 3 vols.
           (Freiberg, 1853-5).

MonfC   Monfasani, J. (ed.): *Collectanea Trapezuntiana,
           Texts, Documents and Bibliographies* (Medieval
           and Renaissance Texts and Studies, vol. 25;
           Renaissance Society of America, Renaissance
           Texts Series, vol. 8; Binghampton, 1984).

MontF   Monterosso, R., with Cattin, G. (eds.): *Le
           frottole nell'edizione di Ottaviano Petrucci, Tomo
           1: Lib. I, II e III*, IMa, First ser., i (Cremona,
           1954).

MorinF   Morin, C.: 'La frottola e l'armonia verticale nel
           Quattrocento', *Quad*, xv (1974), 147.

MottaS   Motta, E.: 'Musici alle corte degli Sforza',
           Archivio storico lombardo, xiv (1877), 29-64,
           278-340 and 514- 61; pubd. seperately (Geneva,
           1977).

NobleF   Noble, J.: 'The Function of Josquin's Motets',
           TVNM, xxxii (1985), 9.

NoblitMM   Noblitt, T.: 'The Ambrosian "Motetti missales"
                  Repertory', *MD*, xxii (1968), 77.

O   Noblitt, T.: 'Obrecht's *Missa Sine nomine* and its
                  Model', *MQ*, lxviii (1982), 102.

NowacP   Nowacki, E.: 'The Latin Psalm Motet 1500-
                  1535', *Renaissance-Studien: Helmuth Osthoff
                  zum 80. Geburtstag*, ed. L. Finscher (Tutzing,
                  1979), 159.

NugentD   Nugent, W. A.: *The Life and Works of Antonius
                  Divitis* (Unpub. Ph.D Diss., North Texas State
                  Univ., 1970).

ObrO   Smijers, A., and Crevel, M. van der (eds.):
                  Jacobus Obrecht, Opera omnia, editio altera
                  (UVNM, Amsterdam, 1953-).

OckO   Plamenac, D. (ed.): *Johannes Ockeghem:
                  Collected Works* (American Musicological
                  Society, 1947-).

O'MallPB   O'Malley, J.: *Praise and Blame in Renaissance
                  Rome: Rhetoric, Doctrine and Reform in the
                  Sacred Orators of the Papal Court c.1450-1521*
                  (Durham, N. Carolina, 1971).

OsthofJ   Osthoff, H.: *Josquin Desprez*. 2 vols. (Tutzing,
                  1962-5).

PalH   Palisca, C.: *Humanism in Italian Renaissance
                  Musical Thought* (New Haven, 1985).

UO   Palisca, C.: 'Ut Oratorica Musica: The Rhetorical
                  Basis of Musical Mannerism', *The Meaning of
                  Mannerism*, ed. F. Robinson and S. Nichols, Jr.
                  (New England Renaissance Society, Hanover,
                  New Hampshire, 1972), 37.

ParrN

Parrish, C.: *The Notation of Medieval Music* (London, 1958).

T

Parrish, C. (trans. and ed.): *Johannes Tinctoris. Dictionary of Musical Terms (Terminorum Musicae Diffinitorium)* (London, 1963).

PaschEC

Paschini, P. (ed.): *Enciclopedia Cattolica*, xii vols. (Vatican City, 1948-54).

PeliP

Pelicelli, N.: 'Musicisti in Parma nei secoli XV-XVI', *NA*, viii (1931), 132, 196, 278; ix (1932), 41, 112. All references are to vol. viii.

PèrG

Pèrcopo, E. (ed.): *Le rime di Benedetto Gareth detto il Chariteo* (Naples, 1892).

PerkJ

Perkins, L.: 'Mode and Structure in the Masses of Josquin', *JAMS*, xxvi (1973), 189.

R

Perkins, L.: Review of *LowMC*, *MQ*, lv (1969), 255.

PevF

Peverada, E.: 'Vita musicale nelle cattedrale di Ferrara nel Quattrocento. Note e Documenti', *RIM*, xv (1980), 3.

PipeO

Cross, R. (ed.): *Matthaeus Pipelare Opera Omnia*, CMM 34, i-iii (American Institute of Musicology, 1966-7).

PirrCT

Pirrotta, N.: 'Music and Cultural Tendencies in Fifteenth-Century Italy', *JAMS*, xix (1966), 127.

MC

Pirrotta, N.: *Music and Culture in Italy from the Middle Ages to the Baroque: A Collection of Essays* (Cambridge, Mass., 1984).

PM   Pirrotta, N. (with E. Povoledo): *Music and Theatre from Poliziano to Monteverdi* (Cambridge, 1982).

PM   *Processionale monasticum ad usum congregationis Gallicae* (Solesmes, 1893).

PMFC   Schrade, L., with others (eds.): *Polyphonic Music of the Fourteenth Century* (Monaco, 1956-).

PopeM   Pope, I. (with Kanazawa, M., eds.): *The Musical Manuscript Montecassino 871: A Neopolitan Repertory of Sacred and Secular Music of the Late Fifteenth Century* (Oxford, 1978).

PowellF   Powell, N.: 'Fibonacci and the Golden Mean: Rabbits, Rumbas and Rondeaux', *Journal of Music Theory*, xiii (1979), 227.

PowersT   Powers, H.: 'Tonal Types and Modal Categories in Renaissance Polyphony', *JAMS*, xxxiv (1981), 428.

PrizerC   Prizer, W. F.: *Courtly Pastimes: The Frottole of Marchetto Cara*, Studies in Musicology, 33 (Ann Arbor, 1980).

    CF   Prizer, W. F. (ed.): *Canzoni, frottole et capitoli... libro primo della croce* (New Haven, A-R Editions, 1978).

    F   Prizer, W. F.: 'The Frottola and the Unwritten Tradition', *Studi musicali*, xv (1986), 3.

    L   Prizer, W. F.: 'Lutenists at the Court of Mantua in the Late Fifteenth and Early Sixteenth Centuries', *Journal of the Lute Society of America*, xiii (1980), 1.

M   Prizer, W. F.: 'La cappella di Francesco Gonzaga
                 e la musica sacra a Mantova nel primo
                 Cinquecento', *Mantova e i Gonzaga nella civiltà
                 del Rinascimento* (Mantua, 1973).

P   Prizer, W. F.: 'Isabella d'Este and Lucrezia
                 Borgia as Patrons of Music: The Frottola at
                 Mantua and Ferrara', *JAMS*, xxxviii (1985), 1.

QuerP   Quereau, Q.: 'Sixteenth-Century Parody: An
                 Approach to Analysis', *JAMS*, xxxi (1978), 407.

RandelT   Randel, D.: 'Emerging Triadic Tonality in the
                 Fifteenth Century', *MQ*, lvii (1971), 73.

RastN   Rastall, R.: *The Notation of Western Music*
                 (London, 1983).

ReeseMR   Reese, G.: *Music in the Renaissance* (New York,
                 1954).

PM   Reese, G.: 'The Polyphonic Magnificat of the
                 Renaissance as a Design in Tonal Centres',
                 JAMS, xiii (1960), 68.

RegisO   Lindenburg, C. W. H. (ed.): *Johannis Regis
                 Opera Omnia*, CMM 9, i-ii (American Institute
                 of Musicology, 1956).

ReynCP   Reynolds, C.: 'Musical Evidence of
                 Compositional Planning in the Renaissance:
                 Josquin's *Plus nulz regretz*', *JAMS*, xl (1987),
                 53.

RifkinSC   Rifkin, J.: 'Scribal Concordances for some
                 Renaissance Manuscripts in Florentine Libraries',
                 JAMS, xxvi (1973), 305.

RISM   Lesure, F. (ed.): *Répertoire Internationale des Sources Musicales. Receuils Imprimés XVIe - XVIIe Siècles* (Munich - Duisburg, 1960).

RossTC   Ross, D.: 'Toward a Theory of Tonal Coherence: The Motets of Obrecht', *MQ*, lxvii (1981), 143.

RRMMER   *Recent Researches in the Music of the Middle Ages and Early Renaissance* (A-R Editions, Madison, Wisconsin, 1975-).

RubsJ   Rubsamen, W.: 'The Justiniane or Viniziane of the 15th Century', *AcM*, xxix (1957), 172.

SF   Rubsamen, W.: 'Sebastiano Festa and the Early Madrigal', *GfMKB* (Kassel, 1962), 122.

U   Rubsamen, W.: 'Unifying Techniques in Selected Masses of Josquin and La Rue: A Comparison', *Josquin des Prez: New York 1971*, 369.

SaccR   Sacchetti-Sassetti, A.: 'La cappella musicale del Duomo di Rieti', *NA*, xvii (1940), 89, 121.

SalmonF   Salmons, J. (ed.): *The Renaissance in Ferrara* (Univ. of Wales Pr., 1984).

SalopO   Salop, A.: 'Jacob Obrecht and the Early Development of Harmonic Polyphony', *JAMS*, xvii (1964), 288.

SandGS   Sandresky, M.: 'The Golden Section in Three Byzantine Motets of Dufay', *Journal of Music Theory*, xxv (1981), 291.

P   Sandresky, M.: 'The Continuing Concept of the Platonic-Pythagorean System and its Application to the Analysis of Fifteenth-Century Music', *Music Theory Spectrum*, i (1979), 107.

SartBP   Sartori, C.: *Bibliografia delle opere stampate da Ottaviano Petrucci* (Florence, 1948).

C   Sartori, C.: *La cappella musicale del Duomo di Milano,catalogo delle musiche dal archivio* (Milan, 1957).

J   Sartori, C.: 'Josquin des Pres cantore del Duomo di Milano', *AnnM*, iv (1956), 55.

M   Sartori, C.: 'La musica nel Duomo e alla corte sino alla seconda metà del Cinquecento', *Storia di Milano*, ix (Milan, 1961), 723.

NP   Sartori, C.: 'Nove conclusive aggiunte alla "Bibliografia del Petrucci"', *CHM*, i (1953), 175.

QC   Sartori, C.: 'Il quarto codice di Gaffurio non è del tutto scomparso', *CHM*, i (1953), 25.

SchradCA   Schrade, L.: 'A Secret Chromatic Art', *MD*, i (1946), 159.

SchwarP   Schwartz, R. (ed.): *Ottaviano Petrucci: Frottole Buch I und IV*, Publikationen älterer Musik, 7 (Leipzig, 1935/R 1967).

SeayT   Seay, A. (trans. and ed.): *Johannes Tinctoris Liber De Arte Contrapuncti*, MSD, v (American Institute of Musicology, 1961).

SherrI   Sherr, R.: '*Illibata Dei Virgo Nutrix* and Josquin's Roman Style', *JAMS*, xli (1988), 434-64.

RM   Sherr, R.: 'Notes on Two Roman Manuscripts of the Early Sixteenth Century', *MQ*, lxiii (1977), 48.

VC   Sherr, R.: 'Verdelot in Florence, Coppini in
            Rome, and the Singer "La Fiore"', *JAMS*, xxxvii
            (1984), 402.

SilvaO   Kirsch, W. (ed.): *Andreas de Silva Opera Omnia*,
            CMM 49, i-ii (American Institute of
            Musicology, 1970-).

SlimG   Slim, H. C. (ed.): *A Gift of Madrigals and
            Motets* (Chicago, 1972).

M   Slim, H. C.: 'A Motet for Machiavelli's
            Mistress', *Essays in Honour of Myron P.
            Gilmore* (Florence, 1977), 713.

V   Slim, H. C.: 'An Iconographical Echo of the
            Unwritten Tradition in a Verdelot Madrigal',
            Studi Musicali, xvii (1988), 33-54.

SmijT   Smijers, A., and Merritt, A. T. (eds.): *Treize
            livres de motets parus chez Pierre Attaignant en
            1534 et 1535* (Paris and Monaco, 1944-64).

SnowMM   Snow, R.: 'The Mass-Motet Cycle: A Mid-
            Fifteenth Century Experiment', *Essays in
            Honour of Dragan Plamenac*, ed. G. Reese and
            R. Snow (Pittsburgh, 1969), 301.

SparksCF   Sparks, E.: *Cantus Firmus in Mass and Motet,
            1420- 1520* (Berkeley, 1963).

StäbH   Stäblein, B.: *Hymnen I: Die mittelalterlichen
            Hymnenmelodien des Abendlandes*, Monumenta
            monodica medii aevi, 1 (Kassel and Basel,
            1956).

StaeM — Staehelin, M.: 'Möglichkeiten und praktische Anwendung der Verfasserbestimmung an anonym überlieferten Kompositionen der Josquin-Zeit', *TVNM*, xxiii (1973), 79.

StewV — Stewart, R.: 'Voice Types in Josquin's Music', *TVNM*, xxxv (1985), 97.

StraePB — Sraeten, E. van der: *La musique aux Pays-Bas avant le XIXe siècle* (Brussels, 1867-8/R 1969).

StrohmB — Strohm, R.: *Music in Late Medieval Bruges* (Oxford, 1985).

StrunkMT — Strunk, O.: 'Motet Types in the Sixteenth Century', *PAMS*, (1939), 155.

SR — Strunk, O.: *Source Readings in Music History* (London, 1950).

TinctO — Melin, W. (ed.): *Johanni Tinctoris Opera Omnia*, CMM 18 (American Institute of Musicology, 1976).

ToddR — Todd, R. L.: 'Retrograde, Inversion, Retrograde Inversion and Related Techniques in the Masses of Jacobus Obrecht', *MQ*, lxiv (1978), 50.

TorchiM — Torchi, L.: 'I monumenti dell'antica musica francese a Bologna', *RMI*, xiii (1906), 451-505 and 575-615.

TrowSC — Trowbridge, L.: 'Style Change in the Fifteenth-Century Chanson: A Comparative Study of Compositional Detail', *Journal of Musicology*, iv (1986), 146.

TurrV — Turrini, G.: *Il patrimonio della Biblioteca Capitolare di Verona dal sec. XV al XIX* (Verona, 1952).

VelleO   Vellekoop, K.: 'Zuzammenhänge zwischen Text
                und Zahl in der Kompositionsart Jacob Obrechts.
                Analyse der Motette *Parce Domine*', *TVNM*, xx
                (1966), 97.

VerdO   Bragard, A.-M. (ed.): *Philippe Verdelot Opera
                Omnia*, CMM 28, i-iii (American Institute of
                Musicoogy, 1966-).

WA   *Antiphonaire monastique; XIIIe siècle: Codex
                F.160 de la bibliothèque de la cathedrale de
                Worcester*, Paléographie musicale, XII (Tournai,
                1922).

WardL   Ward, T.: 'The Polyphonic Office Hymn and the
                Liturgy of Fifteenth-Century Italy', *MD*, xxvi
                (1972), 161.

OH   Ward, T.: *The Polyphonic Office Hymn from
                1400-1520. A Descriptive Inventory*, Renaissance
                Manuscript Studies, 3 (American Institute of
                Musicology, 1979).

WegmanB   Wegman, R. C.: 'Busnois' *Anthoni usque limina*
                and the order of Saint-Antoine-en-Barbefosse in
                Hainaut', *Studi Musicali*, xvii (1988), 15-31.

WeidenP   Weidensaul, J.: 'Early Sixteenth-Century
                Manuscripts at Piacenza: A Progress Report',
                Current Musicology, xvi (1973), 41.

WeinLC   Weinberg, B.: *A History of Literary Criticism in
                the Renaissance* (Chicago, 1961).

T   Weinberg, B.: *Trattati di poetica e retorica del
                Cinquecento*, 4 vols. (Bari, 1970-4).

WeissB   Weiss, S.: 'Bologna Q18: Some Reflections on
                Content and Context', *JAMS*, xli (1988), 63.

WillO   Zenck, H., and Gerstenberg, W. (eds.): *Adriani Willaert Opera Omnia*, CMM 3, i- (Rome, 1950-).

WitzB   Witzenmann, W.: 'Bibliografie der Aufsätze zur Musik in aussermusikalischen italienischen Zeitschriften IV-VI', *AnMc*, iv (1967), 207; v (1968), 338; and vii (1969), 248.

WolfI   Wolf, J. (ed.): *Heinrich Isaac: Weltliche Werke*. DTO, xxviii, Jg. xiv/1 (1907/R1959); xxxii, Jg. xvi/1, suppl. (1909/R).

WrightC   Wright, C.: 'Performance Practice at the Cathedral of Cambrai 1475-1550', *MQ*, lxiv (1978), 295.

WyattO   Muir, K., with Thompson, P. (eds.): *Collected Poems of Thomas Wyatt* (Liverpool, 1969).

YatesM   Yates, F.: *The Art of Memory* (London, 1966).

YoungPM   Young, I. (trans. and ed.): *The Practica Musicae of Franchinus Gaffurius* (Madison, Wisc., 1969).

ZarlinC   Zarlino, G.: *The Art of Counterpoint*. Part 3 of *Le istituzioni harmoniche*, trans. and ed. by G. Marco and C. Palisca (New Haven and London, 1968).

INDEX OF NAMES